Church Multiplication Guide
Revised

The Miracle of Church Reproduction

George Patterson
And
Richard Scoggins

William Carey Library
Pasadena, California

Published by
William Carey Library
P.O. Box 40129
Pasadena, CA 91114
(626) 798-0819
www.wclbooks.com

Library of Congress Cataloging-in-Publication Data

Patterson, George, 1932-
    Church multiplication guide: helping churches to reproduce locally and abroad / George Patterson and Richard Scoggins.
       p.   cm.
    ISBN 0-87808-447-9
    1. Church development, New. I. Scoggins, Richard. II. Title.
BV652.24.P36   2001
254'.1--dc20   CIP number available from publisher

Art work by Miguel Dubon and George Patterson, revised by R & D Design Services.

Printed in the United States of America

Church Multiplication Guide

Revised

The Miracle of Church Reproduction

CONTENTS

To use this table of contents as a menu or checklist to monitor progress, check off boxes to the left of items that need no further attention or do not apply to your work. Select items not by their order but according to what you or your coworkers currently need to emphasize.

To locate items by their number:

The number = *chapter*.
The letter   = *section*.

Example: **3-b** = Chapter **3**, Section **b**.

1. INTRODUCTION

103226

PART I
CHURCHES MULTIPLY AS WE OBEY JESUS' COMMANDS

6. Obeying Jesus' Command to **Love**

7. Obeying Jesus' Command to **Break Bread**

8. Obeying Jesus' Command to **Pray**

9. Obeying Jesus' Command to **Give**

PART II
CHURCH REPRODUCTION FROM VARIOUS VIEWPOINTS

10. Church Reproduction from the Viewpoint of the **Seeker** (Pre-Christian)

11. Church Reproduction from the Viewpoint of the **Evangelist**

12. Church Reproduction from the Viewpoint of a Mission Task Group

13. Church Reproduction from the Viewpoint of a Field Supervisor

14. Church Reproduction from the Viewpoint of a Cell or House Church

15. Church Reproduction from the Viewpoint of a Mother Church (Sending Body)

16. Church Reproduction from the Viewpoint of Trainers of Pastors or Church Planters

Contents

17. Church Reproduction from the Viewpoint of a Church Leader

18. Church Reproduction from the Viewpoint of a Mission Career Advisor

APPENDICES

ABOUT THE AUTHORS

George Patterson planted churches for over twenty years in Central America; since then he has coached church planters in different cultures. In Honduras he began by training pastors in a traditional, resident Bible Institute with poor results. With the advice of more experienced missionaries and much trial and error, he later saw churches multiply through the instrumentality of "Theological Education and Evangelism by Extension" (TEEE). This non-formal pastoral training resulted in twenty years in about 100 new churches in northern Honduras. This model is now used with similar results in Asia, Africa and Latin America, as well in the United States, and is distributed as *Train & Multiply* ™. For information see Appendix E *Materials for Training Leaders in a Movement of Church or Cell Multiplication*, second item.

George serves as a mentor for those who seek to multiply churches or cells, and long to see daughter churches, granddaughter churches, etc. by using sound biblical discipling principles. Some of those he mentors are doctoral students in the Division of Intercultural Studies at Western Seminary in Portland, Oregon. His experiences coaching church planters have convinced him that these New Testament principles need wider exposure, which is why he joined Dick Scoggins in writing this guide for church multiplication.

"Our objective," George explains, "is to see churches reproduce churches. We pray that God will strengthen your vision and resolve, to help your church multiply locally and in neglected fields. If your church has home groups, this guide should help them multiply also."

Richard Scoggins founded and coordinated the Fellowship of Church Planters in Rhode Island for many years and now works as a coach for church planting teams working among Muslims, in addition to continuing to plant churches in England. He came to Christ through Quidnessett Baptist Church in Rhode Island, which had the goal to reproduce new churches. He was involved in this first effort, the Cranston Christian Fellowship. This followed a centralized, large group church model and emphasized spiritual healing and personal discipleship focusing on Christ as the model for character development. He says, "During this time I learned by personal experience that God provides leaders from a congregation's midst, as we combine opportunities for service with practical training."

Richard was later sent with a coworker to plant the Warwick Christian Fellowship where, as he recalls,

"I realized the benefits of having several elders, as opposed to what I was still modeling--a one-man pastorate with a supporting board. I asked the church to commission me to start a team of men to do church planting and we formed the *Fellowship of Church Planters*. The new church soon settled in a plateau; we seemed no closer to establishing spontaneously reproducing churches than we had been thirteen years earlier, except that we had the vision.

"About this time, George Patterson became our coach and helped us see that those we discipled had to pass on the torch. He helped us to focus more on the second and third generations of discipleship, as in 2 Timothy 2:2. We started a house church in rural Rhode Island and became aware of the family dynamics of the small house church life, where individuals can give and receive love and healing, and the crippling effects of sin are more easily brought to light. We told each other, 'You can run, but you can't hide. And if you run, we will run after you!'"

Since then Richard has affirmed,

"We have seen God raise up new leaders at an extraordinary rate and house churches reproduce into house church networks. George challenged us to reproduce church planting teams in other metropolitan areas. So we have formed the Fellowship of Church Planting Teams, an alliance of teams and churches committed to reproduce disciples and networks of new churches and church planting teams. It has already produced church planting teams in the Boston and Los Angeles areas, and more recently in Seattle. I moved to the UK in 1995 and have begun a network of church planting teams and house churches."

1. Introduction

1-a Bury the Myth that we Need $$$,$$$ to Multiply Churches

A sneaky surmise lurks in the shadows of many Western churches. You may have heard it whimper…

> To multiply churches we'd need more money than what we've got in our nest egg!
> And specialized education, sophisticated organization, highly experienced leaders and costly buildings that we lack.

> Not where I fly.

Let's refute fear with fact: Churches multiply more readily, in general, where precisely the money and other things men associate with power are lacking!

Churches that reproduce spontaneously with their God-given power do not rely on money, degrees, institutions or rarely gifted leadership. Ordinary people do extraordinary things when they simply obey Jesus' commands in love, enabled by the Spirit of God. So.

1-b Think *Reproduction!*

Another myth we must expose is that churches or cells multiply only in certain cultures or under rare conditions. The two authors, George Patterson and Richard Scoggins, bring examples from opposite ends of the cultural spectrum; your field ought to fall somewhere in between. They have mentored workers in many other cultures with the same results. Patterson saw churches multiply among rural, poor, uneducated Hondurans in a pioneer field; Scoggins saw it among urban, educated, affluent, middle-class Americans in the shadow of the oldest Baptist church in the world and the oldest synagogue in the United States (in Providence and Newport, Rhode Island). Scoggins has also worked more recently coaching teams that work with Muslims in North Africa and Asia.

Examples abound of spontaneous church multiplication among people of all major cultural groups. By God's power it happens wherever we find good soil for real church growth. What is good soil? For real church growth--through conversion--it is *bad people!* Where sin abounds, grace abounds even more, Romans 5:20. Some people groups respond easier than others do, but church multiplication is happening to some degree within every major cultural group. In hostile Muslim fields it goes slower, but it happens.

We emphasize *church* multiplication because the church as a body--the living body of Christ--is what reproduces other churches, not its individual members. An obedient church has an inherent, God-given power to multiply, just as all other living things that God created.

We emphasize *church **multiplication*** because church growth by multiplication is more strategic and biblical than growth by addition *only*. Non-Western churches multiply this way more often than Western ones; some Western traditions hinder multiplication. We will explain these.

Addition We find growth by *addition* in Acts 2:41, where 3,000 converts were added by baptism to the new church in Jerusalem. Throughout Acts, God works 'from the inside out' starting with a nucleus--a convert or his family--then spreading the Good News through their network of relatives and friends.

Growth by *multiplication* appears in Acts 8, 10, 13, 14 and 16 where God multiplies those nuclei around which addition easily takes place. The church, through its apostles, penetrates other social circles, near and far, **Multiplication** to reproduce itself. This leads to exponential increase as daughter and granddaughter churches are born and reproduce like the grain in the planter's parable, thirty, sixty and a hundred times.

1-c Think *Simplicity!*

**"Lord, help us discern
between those things that
are merely *helpful* and
those that are *essential*."**

We could list hundreds of *helpful* items to start churches, but we can count on our fingers and toes those few *essentials* that make the crucial difference between *reproductive* and *sterile* churches. Blessed is the Christian worker who knows the difference!

Our purpose is not to add to the excellent *methods* that others have written about for planting churches, but to help you build your ministry on universal New Testament principles that we see God blessing consistently in different continents. They take on surprisingly novel forms as the Holy Spirit leads workers to apply them in distinct ways to divergent cultures to multiply churches.

Simplicity !

1-d   Plan with Coworkers to Multiply

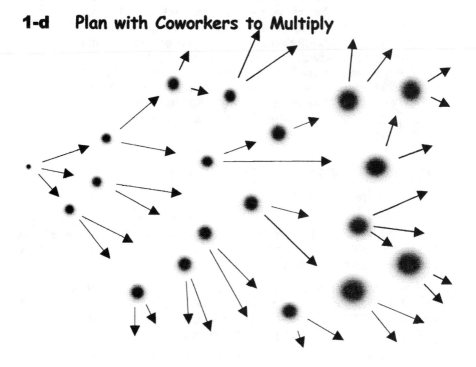

As you read about New Testament principles in this book, share them with your coworkers. Plan together. Consciously prepare your people for multiplication. This guide to develop and multiply churches is for you and your coworkers to apply to your ministries. As you read it, record your plans. To plan effectively, include activities that *your disciples and their churches* will do, not merely what *you* hope to do.

1-e Evaluate your Progress Ruthlessly

Plan for reproduction and chart your progress. Churches reproduce if their leaders make plans that are easy to implement and explain. The enemy of church reproduction is tradition. Often a leader responds to an urgent need by establishing policies or programs that help for a time but continue after the need is met, becoming hollow traditions that absorb resources like a sponge. Objective evaluation detects and eliminates these parasitic growths from the church body.

Scoggins discovered the value of ruthless evaluation:

The first church I helped plant was born and grew through neighborhood evangelistic Bible studies. After about four years, however, no new believers were being added to the church through the Bible studies. They were still well attended--but by church members, not unbelievers! After trying to revive them for a year to fulfill their original intention, we concluded they could not be revived and so we ended them, which caused an uproar by the congregation. The valuable resources (the teachers), we concluded, could be better used in other areas. Make no mistake, if you desire to grow and reproduce, you will have to make some unpopular decisions, based on clear objectives and ruthless evaluations.

1-f If Necessary, Train Workers in a Temporary Training Church

If you use this book as you train a church multiplication task group, you might find it helpful to form a *temporary* training *church*. We acquire church multiplication skills by working with others as a body, not from lectures or books--including this one.

We cannot learn church multiplication skills in a *classroom* where only the gift of teaching is in operation. We acquire them within an obedient congregation. If you hope to be the exception, good luck! You might as well try also to learn high diving in the same classroom.

To form a temporary training church, name temporary *elders* and do the activities described in each chapter. Meet with these elders to plan worship as a small group and celebrate Communion. Make plans for everyone in the group to serve one another in love with their different spiritual gifts. Let the Holy Spirit harmonize their gift-based ministries in a *living church body* in love, as in 1 Corinthians 12 and 13.

The value of church-centered training becomes apparent as you do it. You not only learn the skills for church reproduction but also experience that dynamic church *life* that sustains the cycle of normal reproduction.

Cross-cultural church planters need *stretching*. God stretched Peter in Acts 10 by telling him to eat 'unclean' food. Let the temporary training church stretch you and your trainees! The strain reveals tensions that we face when adapting to other cultures. Make your mistakes now where they won't do permanent damage!

Cross-cultural church planters need to practice the *essential elements of worship*. We distinguish these essential elements from external worship *forms* that evolved in our culture. A *temporary training church* enables us to discern them as we adapt worship to a small group without electronic sound, skilled musicians or a large sanctuary.

Our *flock* is to multiply other *flocks* ??

You've soared too high, birdbrain /

Lack of oxygen left you spaced out /

So clip my wings with your shabby shears of tradition /

We'll multiply as we prepare and send out from the nest those who fly far away by God's apostolic gift /

Those with itchy feet will carry our flock's spiritual DNA to reproduce it elsewhere /

1-g Recognize and Replace Traditions that Stifle Reproduction

A blind spot grew like a cancer during the 20th century that makes it difficult for many Western Evangelical churches to reproduce normally. That is the error of using God's Word only as *content* for messages or Bible study. The irony of the age was that pastors who would have died before denying the truth of its *content* unconsciously dismissed the New Testament as the norm for *procedures* and *organization*. As a result, many clear New Testament operations that are vital for church or cell reproduction have been inadvertently replaced by some spiritual-sounding tradition that stifles it.

Tradition? In *Evangelical* churches?

Yes. We're human, too. A *tradition* normally begins for worthy and godly reasons. But in time the need passes or a good thing is taken to excess. It evolves into a nice, gentle *sacred cow*. Then, history shows, the bovine becomes fertile and breeds a formidable herd with bulls that abandon any pretext of gentleness! the moo becomes a raging bellow. The revered church pet gores God's prophets who dare call His people back to New Testament norms! It tramples guidelines that are vital for normal church body life under adamantine hooves! But when you recognize the brute for what it is, it's rather fun to play the matador!

So, as you read these chapters, if you objectively and prayerfully examine your traditions you may find that some run counter to what Jesus and His apostles clearly require us to do. These may include some of the following church *practices*:

organization *structures*, especially to harmonize gift-based ministries,

evangelistic *technique* and follow-up *procedure*,

Christian education *methods*, especially for dealing with families,

worship *practices*, especially for small groups,

church spending *priorities* and *attitudes* toward wealth,

leadership training *philosophy*,

formation and *activities* of home groups,

missionary placement *programs*,

mission agency *management* as it deals with gifting,

task group *formation*,

inter-church *polity* for mutual cooperation,

disciplinary correction policies,

leadership *styles.*

1-h Define Terms (as Used in *Church Multiplication Guide)*

Apostle: One who is sent to a new area or culture. The New
Testament uses the word *apostle* in two ways:

1) for the *twelve* whom Jesus chose to accompany Him,

2) for any "sent one."

We use the word 'apostle' in the second sense, as Luke did in Acts to
refer to Barnabas and others who were not of the original Twelve.

Cell: a small church, often part of a larger one.

**Church: A group of believers in Christ who are committed to obey
His commands.** Our Lord in his Great Commission commands us
with "all authority in heaven and earth" to disciple all peoples by
teaching them to obey all his commands. These include celebrating
the Lord's Supper and other activities that are done only by a church
body.

Church growth: *Conversion of sinners to Jesus Christ.* We are not
concerned with growing big by attracting believers from other
churches. That is not growth in God's sight.

**Church reproduction or multiplication: a church gives birth to, and
nurtures, daughter churches or cells.** These bodies reproduce
granddaughters, and so on. This multiplication is purposeful, voluntary
and relies on God's power.

Corporate disciple: One who participates in a *relational* body.
God calls believers into a special relationship with others in His
kingdom. Corporate disciples build and strengthen the church body by
cooperating in love with others (Col. 1:24-29).

Elder: a *shepherd*. Elders shepherd God's flock (1 Peter 5:1-4). Normally
several elders serve as co-pastors. They oversee the work by
coordinating the use of different spiritual gifts in the body. In many
churches one elder, the most experienced or one most gifted as a
leader, is called 'the *pastor.*' Scripture reveals no difference between
elders and *pastors.*

**Evangelist: One who witnesses for Jesus in private or public and
brings converts into fellowship with a church body.**

**House church: a small congregation meeting in a home, office, and
etc.** Healthy house churches interact closely with other churches,
including churches that meet in traditional buildings.

Liturgical church: a church that follows the classic liturgy, such as
Lutheran, Anglican, Roman Catholic and Orthodox. All churches
follow some liturgy in a technical sense; there is a Pentecostal liturgy
and a Quaker liturgy, etc. The primary meaning is simply whatever
churches do in divine worship. For those that adhere to the older
forms we use the word *liturgical* with its popular meaning.

Mentor (a Christian mentor): **one who disciples *leaders* as Christ and the apostle Paul did.** He listens to them, shares their burdens, models skills and keeps them focused on edifying the churches or small groups that they or their trainees are leading.

National church: a church made up and led by people who are of the *local culture*.

Nationals: People who are native to the land and embrace the local culture.

Pastor: *a* shepherding elder (not simply a preacher).

People group: the largest number of people among whom the gospel can flow freely, unhindered by barriers of *any* kind.

BARRIERS THAT SET THE OUTER LIMITS OF A PEOPLE GROUP

long standing distrust between otherwise compatible societies,
disparate economic or social levels,
unfamiliar languages,
immigration laws or border guards at national boundaries,
clashing religious backgrounds,
contrary political ideologies,
opposite world views,
incompatible life styles or technology,
different race or caste,
conflicting lore,
opposing cultural norms and values,
mountains, oceans, deserts or jungles,
just plain geographical distance,
whatever stops familiar communication.

Pioneer field: a people group lacking obedient, culturally relevant, *reproductive churches led by their own people.*

Progress Chart: a checklist of ministry activities that mentors and their trainees use to track progress.

Sending church: a church that takes responsibility, or shares it with a mission agency, to train, send and hold accountable missionaries to another area or culture.

Small group (home group or cell): a discipling community that practices pastoral care, evangelism and the other ministries required by the New Testament. A healthy small group is not merely Bible study or fellowship.

Task group: a *temporary* ministry team focused on a specified task.

Part I

Churches Multiply as We Obey Jesus' Commands

2.
Aiming First for Total, Childlike *Obedience*

"If you love me, obey my commands." John 14:15

That word 'obey' sticks in my craw ! !

Don't cage me !

Yeah ?

Disobey God and he'll singe your tail feathers!

You'll end up stuck in the most confining cage of all--one that you make yourself !

Find in Acts 2:36-41 what the 3,000 converts did in obedience to Jesus, in order to be baptized and added to the church:

When the people heard this, they were cut to the heart and said to Peter and the other apostles, "Brothers, what shall we do?" Peter replied, "Repent and be baptized, every one of you, in the name of Jesus Christ for the forgiveness of your sins. And you will receive the gift of the Holy Spirit. The promise is for you and your children and for all who are far off-for all whom the Lord our God will call." with many other words he warned them; and he pleaded with them, "Save yourselves from this corrupt generation." those who accepted his message were baptized, and about three thousand were added to their number that day.

Find in the same account (verse 42-47) what they did in obedience to Jesus immediately after baptism:

They devoted themselves to the apostles' teaching and to the fellowship, to the breaking of bread and to prayer. Everyone was filled with awe, and many wonders and miraculous signs were done by the apostles. All the believers were together and had everything in common. Selling their possessions and goods, they gave to anyone as he had need. Every day they continued to meet together in the temple courts. They broke bread in their homes and ate together with glad and sincere hearts, praising God and enjoying the favor of all the people. And the Lord added to their number daily those who were being saved.

2-a Obey Jesus' Commands Above All Else

The most important thing to multiply churches is to obey our Lord Jesus Christ in childlike faith and love. This is no preachy platitude. Of all the feedback we get from the field, our trainees consistently thank us most heartily for urging them to obey Jesus' commands above and before all else. God blesses our loving obedience and nothing else.

Did you hear a contradicting whisper just now in the back of your mind, "But our organization's policies come first!"?

If so, you have a hard decision to make. It will determine whether or not God can use you to multiply vital discipling groups. Will you put the Lord Jesus Christ and His clear commands before all else? Will you build your plans, activities, and commitments on obedience to His revealed will--the things he taught in many ways that His disciples must do?

Jesus ordered over forty things; we can group them under seven basic commands. In Acts 2 we see the 3,000 converts of the first New Testament church obeying *all* of them in their basic form.

Please memorize these basic commands; they are the foundation upon which we build all other teaching and ministry:

21

Basic Commands of Christ

1. **Repent, believe,** and **receive the Holy Spirit** (conversion), Mark 1:15; John 3:16; 20:22

2. **Be baptized** and live the new life it initiates, leading to all that has to do with ongoing transformation, Matthew 28:18-20

3. **Love** God, neighbor, fellow disciples, the needy--in a practical way--and enemies (forgive), Matthew 22:36-40; John 13:34-35, Luke 10:25-37; Matthew 5:43-48

4. **Break bread** (Communion, related to all that we do to worship), Matthew 26:26-28; John 4:24

5. **Pray** (private and family devotions, intercession and spiritual warfare), John 16:24

6. **Give** (stewardship of our time, treasure and talents), Luke 6:38

7. **Make disciples** (witness for Christ, shepherd, apply the Word, train leaders, send missionaries), Matthew 28:18-20

We also obey Jesus when we observe His apostles' commands. They spoke and wrote with the inspired authority of Christ. The commands in their letters, however, are not *basic*. They are not the foundation or 'basement floor' of the building; they belong to the second story and on up, for leaders and believers already baptized and under a church's care.

George Patterson relates:

We discovered the value of simple, direct, childlike obedience to Jesus' commands amid painful controversy. When churches began to multiply in Honduras, the more traditional leaders saw it as a threat. The work was growing where they could not control it; they criticized vigorously. (If you plan for God to use you as an instrument to multiply churches, be ready to duck!)

I felt insecure. Were we doing God's will? who was to say what was right or wrong? Christian brothers whom we loved opposed us. Some followed whoever shouted the loudest or were higher in the organization. I tried shouting, too. It didn't work. I had no title or authority. I was merely mentoring voluntary, lay pastoral trainees in an informal extension program.

Confused and bruised, we called our discouraged trainees together to pray. We decided, "From now on, we will base everything on the commands of Jesus for his disciples." We memorized the commands of Christ and learned to tell our

critics, "We are obeying Jesus' commands and imitating his apostles. Do you prefer that we obey and imitate you instead?"

God blessed this commitment. Criticism continued but we felt liberated. We were on solid ground--we were obeying Jesus, the divine Head of the church (Col. 1:15-20), so let the critics say what they may!

We obey our Lord because we love Him for what he did and does for us. He said, "If you love me, obey my commands" (John 14:15). Consider Jesus' claim on our obedience. During His incarnation on earth He did so many miracles and good works that people whispered that He was the promised Messiah. A few ventured to say He was the *Son of God*, so the Judean Supreme Court tried Him for blasphemy. The high priest asked Him, "Are you the Son of the Blessed?"

Everything hung on Jesus' answer. He knew it meant death but he spoke the most earth-shaking truth ever uttered by a human on this planet--a clear "I AM" (the first person singular verb form of the most holy NAME *in Hebrew* of the living God).

That ended the trial! the high priest tore his robes in fury. Immediately the council condemned Jesus to death for blasphemy. This made His resurrection doubly significant; it proved that *He is who He said He is.*

Shortly before His ascension to glory, on the basis of His proven deity our risen Lord commanded His followers, "All authority is given to me... Therefore make disciples of all nations. . . teaching them to obey all that I have commanded" (Matthew 28:18-20). Discipling is *obedience training*.

Healthy churches stem from loving obedience to the commands of Him who has "all authority in heaven and earth." The apostles started the first New Testament church in Jerusalem while the master's Great Commission still rang in their ears. **"Disciple all peoples. . . teaching them to obey all my commands."** The Holy Spirit came and gave them the power to begin; they did exactly what Jesus said to do (Acts 2). They started discipling a nation, a *people group,* their Jewish countrymen, by instructing them to obey all of Jesus' commands.

The First New Testament Church

The 3,000 new believers in the first New Testament church started doing all that our Lord Jesus Christ commanded without delay:

They *repented*, *believed* and *received the Holy Spirit*,

They immediately confirmed this with *baptism*,

They celebrated the *Lord's Supper* (in homes),

They *loved* God and one another, with fervent fellowship,

They *prayed*,

They *gave* generously,

They made *disciples* (they devoted themselves to the apostles' teaching and witnessed to others).

The new church, which was a cluster of house churches or what some would call cells, was obeying all of Jesus' commands in their embryonic form. Such obedience did not occur by chance. The apostles taught the converts from the very beginning to obey Jesus' commands.

This provides our model for basic discipling. The activities in Acts as well as the commands in the Epistles built on these basic commands of our risen Lord. This establishes Jesus as the true Head of the church in every way. All ministries required by the New Testament build upon these commands of Christ. For example, Paul's command to Titus to establish elders in Crete (Titus 1:5) grew out of Jesus' command to disciple all nations; the apostle delegated it to his disciple Titus who assigned the new elders. Paul's letter to Titus gives him detailed instructions for these elders. No totally new commands appear in the Epistles; everything the apostles tell us to do stems from Jesus' original commands or applies them to new situations.

There is no other foundation for Christ's church. He is the Rock. Only our loving, faithful obedience to the divine Head of our church lays the true groundwork for normal growth and reproduction of churches or cells.

2-b   Note Plans to Disciple for Loving Obedience

What is your commitment to help believers obey Jesus' commands?

_____

_____

_____

_____

_____

_____

_____

_____

_____

_____

2-c Help Converts to Obey Without Delay

For newly converted, repentant believers, obedience in Scripture started with baptism (Acts 2:36-42, etc.). Baptism has vertical and horizontal dimensions; converts declare their commitment to God and also to fellow believers (Acts 2:41-47). Baptism of an adult should be an effective initiation into *corporate* discipleship. A hermit cannot carry out the commands of Christ.

A heavy emphasis on doctrinal teaching as the initial foundation, without the corresponding application of loving obedience, reflects the crippling rationalism and individualism of the West of the 20th century, not Kingdom theology. *Nothing* takes precedence for a new believer over loving, faithful, childlike obedience to our loving Lord.

Without this orientation to obedience to Jesus Christ, Christian workers follow church traditions, rules, and human scruples that stifle spontaneous church growth and reproduction. Especially in pioneer fields that lack a model for a well-organized church and mature pastors, inexperienced leaders emphasize nonessentials. They seek subsidies and control God's people with *non-biblical* rules for ordination, baptism, marriage, evangelism, church planting and pastoral training.

A church planter who emphasizes knowledge over obedience rarely makes *corporate disciples.* He looks for understanding rather than obedience. Seeing the potential leaders' limited comprehension of the Word, he distrusts their ability to lead and over-controls the new church, stifling the nationals' initiative and creating a crippling form of legalism. We must have patience with new churches and new leaders, and let them take their baby steps.

This means learning the New Testament way:

> **Hear** and **do,** **hear** and **do,** **hear** and **do,**
>
> *Not*
>
> **Hear, hear, hear** and maybe sometime later do.

If you teach converts in a new field to obey Jesus, they will give *love* top priority. This normally enables their church to be healthy enough to reproduce. It will not be easy; you may have to first overcome barriers to love in your own life. But if you lean on and learn from the Lord, He will empower you and your coworkers to start a network of reproducing churches that "infect" their area of world for the Lord Jesus!

Church reproduction in the power of the Spirit of God, then, requires developing churches whose activities rest squarely on the commands of

Jesus. New churches simply and purposefully do what He says. They consciously follow the example of His apostles, who discipled for obedience.

We endanger the spiritual life of a newborn babe in Christ if we force upon him the 'heavy meat' of detailed Bible doctrines *before* he learns basic obedience in love. That invites pride. It's like hitting a baseball and running directly to *2nd* base! the Holy Spirit's power to transform the converts in Acts 2 was evident in their immediate, loving obedience. To make corporate disciples in a truly biblical way, we teach obedience to our Lord Jesus Christ before all else. We obey our divine Head at once without argument or discussion. Baptism, for example, as practiced by the apostles, came immediately after conversion. It was not a graduation ceremony following a long time of indoctrination and probation. Healthy, *normal* church reproduction requires disciples who before all else obey in love the commands of Him who has all authority in heaven and earth.

We do not *vote* to see if we obey one of these commands. That puts the authority of the *majority* above that of Almighty God! His church is not a democracy. It is a monarchy--a kingdom. We obey Jesus' commands simply and directly, like a child would, in *love*. To obey for other motives is legalism, which God condemns (Rom. 13:8-10; 1 Cor. 13:1-3). Jesus summarized the Old Testament law, including the Ten Commandments, in the dual command to love God and our neighbor (Matthew 22:34-40).

As disciples begin to obey the basic commands of our Lord, barriers to obedience appear in their attitudes and feelings. As they honestly face these, confess and repent, their obedience leads to progressively deeper love for God and their neighbors. As we practice corporate discipleship, any lack of love becomes apparent, more evident toward our visible brothers than toward our invisible God, although the two loves go together.

2-d Measure Growth in Christ as He Did--By Loving Obedience

We evaluate spiritual growth of a new church in two ways:

First, we measure progress in obeying the commands of Jesus and His apostles, beginning with baptism of repentant converts (Acts 2:41; Heb. 5:11-6:12). **Do *not* count non-baptized converts**. That is contrary to apostolic practice and makes it impossible to accurately evaluate our evangelism methods.

Second, we measure progress in mobilizing more mature members for gift-based ministries, to edify each other in love (Eph. 4:1-16).

The *amount* of Bible knowledge a believer has accumulated is not a valid measure of growth. Some members of false cults know the Scriptures well. Others attend good churches and know the Word but fail to live it. We find converts who after a few weeks show more maturity in their understanding and conduct than others do who have heard the Word for years.

A healthy church body harmonizes its different spiritual gifts to multiply daughter churches within a responsive people group. Trust God to give your church those to whom He has gifted as apostles, to reproduce it. They will also have other gifts; an effective church planting effort will sooner or later need workers gifted for leadership, evangelism, training pastors, mercy ministry and healing.

2-e Consider Manmade Church Policies as Temporary

Man-made rules for church work, if not recognized as such, can keep your church or cell from reaching its maximum potential for shepherding and reproducing. Three assumptions especially breed stifling policies:

> ***First***, the myth that it is *spiritual* to delay commissioning workers to start new churches or cells ("Don't we need a strong home base first?").

> ***Second***, the temptation to focus all resources on that part of the Lord's work over which we have control ("We lack funds to meet our own needs, let alone those of a new church!").

> ***Third***, the fear that love for Christ and doctrinal purity will gradually diminish in a chain reaction of new churches--daughter church, grand-daughters, great-granddaughters, *etc.* ("Won't false beliefs creep in?").

> This fear of corruption is normal. We want our children to be healthy; we want our new churches to be doctrinally sound. But the real source of sound doctrine is not human control but loyalty to Christ. Failing to see this, we expect any multiplication to extend from our own church like spokes from one hub--no *granddaughter* churches. We must control it all. Our church is somehow superior to all later churches in the chain. God gives the Holy Spirit to other churches in a lesser amount! But Jesus reminds us that a grain of wheat engenders a new plant with the same potential as its parent. The same principle of reproducing after its own kind applies to churches in His kingdom (Mark 4). New churches have the same potential, the same love for Christ and the Word. History shows that normal church multiplication in itself does not lead to doctrinal error, and that *sterile* churches far

27

more often fall prey to it.

The reason for the church's existence, according to Jesus' mandate, is to make (and be) obedient disciples. This takes precedence over all other policies and plans. We need human rules, of course, to maintain order. We agree on temporary policies for orderly organization and operation. A congregation needs to know where to meet and at what time, who will do this or that, and dozens of other routine decisions. We erase these human regulations, however, when conditions change or a need is dealt with. Otherwise they become permanent traditions--sacred cows that stand with horns lowered against simple obedience to Christ and the freedom that stems from it.

2-f Discern New Testament Commands

Find in Matthew 15:1-8 how Jesus dealt with traditions that hinder obedience:

Then some Pharisees and teachers of the law came to Jesus from Jerusalem and asked, "Why do your disciples break the tradition of the elders? They don't wash their hands before they eat!" Jesus replied, "And why do you break the command of God for the sake of your tradition? for God said, 'Honor your father and mother' and 'Anyone who curses his father or mother must be put to death.' But you say that if a man says to his father or mother, 'Whatever help you might otherwise have received from me is a gift devoted to God,' he is not to 'honor his father' with it. Thus you nullify the word of God for the sake of your tradition. You hypocrites! Isaiah was right when he prophesied about you: "These people honor me with their lips, but their hearts are far from me. . ."

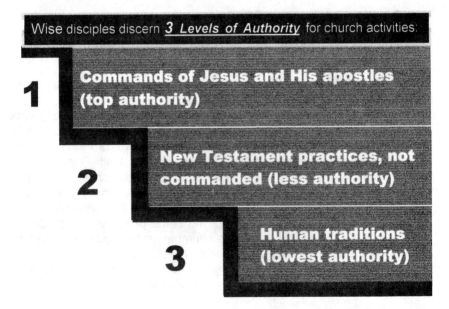

Wise disciples discern *3 Levels of Authority* for church activities:

1 Commands of Jesus and His apostles (top authority)

2 New Testament practices, not commanded (less authority)

3 Human traditions (lowest authority)

To establish authority for discipling, we help our people discern these levels of authority.

3 Levels of Authority for Church Activities

1. **New Testament** *commands* form the basis for discipling and ministry. We must obey them above and before all else.

2. ***New Testament practices*** (not commanded) serve as examples, which we might or might not follow, depending on local circumstances. For example, Paul had Timothy circumcised in Lystra in Acts 16 out of respect for the Jewish culture, but spoke harshly against it to the Galatians because in that gentile culture it led to legalism.

3. ***Human traditions*** not mentioned in the New Testament should be followed with even more caution because they can hinder obedience. Most traditions are good. A church cannot function without established customs. For example, a congregation agrees on when and where to meet; that's a necessary human regulation and therefore a good tradition. The problem comes when we fail to see such traditions as man-made and temporary, or force our own on other churches.

Most church divisions stem from power-hungry people who emphasize a human tradition or an apostolic practice that was not commanded, in order to secure a following. They place it on the level of a command by the force of their personality or the organization's bylaws. Painful divisions and discouragement grow out of a dogmatic attitude toward **non-biblical requirements** for worship, church procedures, membership, baptism, dress, ordination, pastoral training, and a dozen other things. We cancel spontaneous, loving obedience to Jesus when we confuse His authority with man-made rules.

Examples of New Testament practices that were not specifically commanded for everybody:

- Laying on of *hands* to receive the Holy Spirit,
  - Speaking in *tongues* and the exercise of other spiritual gifts,
    - Sharing material goods *in common*,
      - Using *one cup* for the Lord's Supper,
        - Celebrating the Lord's Supper *in homes each Sunday*,
          - Baptizing *immediately*,
            - *Fasting*.

We do not demand that everybody follow these apostolic practices; only Christ has the authority to make such universal laws for His church. On the other hand, since the apostles practiced them, we cannot prohibit them to everybody. People are free to do as the apostles did when it is practical.

Some *evangelical traditions* not found in the New Testament:

These traditions help discipling in some cultures but hinder in others:

- Christian education programs that segregate young people by *age*,
- Pulpits, loudspeakers, pianos, organs, televised worship,
- The public invitation to raise hands or come forward to accept Christ,
- Disciplining in terms of *time periods* of exclusion from communion,
- Specific styles of pulpit lectures,
- Preparing leaders in an academic institution outside of the church ,
- Professional, paid church staffs,
- High profile, institutional mission agencies,
- Ordination prerequisites that go beyond what Scripture requires.
- Defining with a constitution and bylaws how many persons are to serve in certain ministries and for how long.

Human customs should receive lowest priority. One must not demand them as a pagan king would by lording it over his subjects; we agree upon them in love. We follow them if they edify and discard them when they hinder obedience to Jesus. They become dangerous when they become institutionalized, achieve much popular attention, attract a lot of contributions or are supported by civil law or the power of a large organization for its own advancement.

We stifle spontaneous reproduction of churches in pioneer fields when we embrace *non-biblical policies* for:

confirming conversion,

naming and training new pastors or elders,

the Lord's Supper, baptism, and marriage,

organizing new churches,

control from the outside (especially with foreign funds).

2-g Note Plans for Obedience to Christ

Please write your general plans to help your people to obey the commands of our Lord Jesus Christ in childlike faith and love. Do this with your coworkers if possible.

_____

_____

_____

_____

_____

_____

_____

_____

_____

_____

_____

_____

_____

_____

_____

_____

_____

_____

_____

_____

3.

Obeying Jesus' Command to

Repent, Believe and
Receive the Holy Spirit

> Repentance is for the buzzards! Don't make it harder for seekers. A 'decision' is enough!

> Then why doesn't the New Testament mention 'decisions'?

"The time has come," he said. "The kingdom of God is near. Repent and believe the good news!" Mark 1:15

He told them, "This is what is written: the Christ will suffer and rise from the dead on the third day, and repentance and forgiveness of sins will be preached in his name to all nations, beginning at Jerusalem. You are witnesses of these things." Luke 24:46-48

"For God so loved the world that he gave his one and only Son, that whoever believes in him shall not perish but have eternal life." John 3:16

"Receive the Holy Spirit." John 20:22

Find in the Great Commission *in Luke* 24:45-51 (below) two things:

1) What *two central historical facts* are we to proclaim as we evangelize?

2) What *requirement for forgiveness* are we to proclaim to all nations?

> Then He opened their minds so they could understand the Scriptures. He told them, "This is what is written: the Christ will suffer and rise from the dead on the third day, and repentance and forgiveness of sins will be preached in his name to all nations, beginning at Jerusalem. You are witnesses of these things. I am going to send you what my Father has promised; but stay in the city until you have been clothed with power from on high." When He had led them out to the vicinity of Bethany, He lifted up his hands and blessed them. While He was blessing them, He left them and was taken up into heaven. Luke 24-45-54

Jesus' emphasis on His resurrection is an essential of the gospel proclamation, also the need to repent. These vital elements are often omitted from gospel presentations. Jesus pronounced His Great Commission to go and disciple all nations in several ways before He ascended to glory. Please find additional vital elements of our witness for Him in John 20 and Acts 1:

> Again Jesus said, "Peace be with you! as the Father has sent me, I am sending you." and with that He breathed on them and said, "Receive the Holy Spirit. If you forgive anyone his sins, they are forgiven; if you do not forgive them, they are not forgiven." John 20: 21-23

> But you will receive power when the Holy Spirit comes on you; and you will be my witnesses in Jerusalem, and in all Judea and Samaria, and to the ends of the earth." Acts 1:8

3-a   Require what Jesus Said for Salvation-- *Repent and Believe*

Perhaps you've heard a whisper, "All you need to do to be saved is make a *decision*." Is it? if so, you'd think something so eternally important would be mentioned at least once in Scripture. It is not. What Jesus and the apostles emphasized in many ways for converts of "all nations" is that we must *repent* (Luke 24:46-48; Acts 11:18).

Repentance is not simply a *decision* (Western thinking). It means a change of heart, *turning to God* with His help. It begins the eternal process of our transformation by His Holy Spirit.

A particular modern school of theology weakens God's command to repent. It claims that repentance is no longer required for salvation, that this would be salvation by works. We all agree that we are not saved *by* works. But we certainly are saved *for* works (Ephesians 2:8-10). This group claims that where the Bible calls sinners to repent to be saved, it was for Jews in a 'transition age' shifting from the Old Testament to the New. But Jesus, in His Great Commission in Luke 24:46-48 commanded, "Repentance and forgiveness of sins will be proclaimed in His name to all nations." Peter also clarified that gentiles must repent to be saved: Acts 11:18. He still taught this long after any 'transition' time: 2 Peter 3:9. Paul likewise required Gentiles to repent to be saved: Acts 20:21; Acts 26:20. He wrote to gentiles, "Godly sorrow brings repentance that leads to salvation" (2 Cor. 7:10).

On the negative side of repentance, we die with Jesus to sin. On the positive side, we participate in his new, pure resurrection life by faith (Romans 6:1-14). To achieve merely the negative side, even to arrive at complete sinlessness, brings us up only to the level of a neutral object or irrational animal (a rock or toad is sinless!); one still needs positive love and ongoing transformation in the image of Christ.

God revealed to Patterson the error of exporting Western decision-making methods to another culture:

Several times in Central America we participated in evangelistic campaigns with mass meetings and personal evangelism, using methods developed in American culture. We found it easy to get decisions but follow-through was nil. We could not multiply churches with such evangelism methods. We had to rethink what conversion really is. We met with our workers and asked them *not* to report again as converts those who had merely made a decision or raised a hand to 'accept' Jesus. Such decisions were not valid in that culture: less than one in a hundred followed through. We prayed and asked the workers to aim rather for repentance and a living faith in Jesus.

They were doubtful at first; slaying sacred cows is always painful. with Bibles open we thought it through: to be saved from our sins, all are commanded by our Lord to repent, believe, and receive the Holy Spirit (Mark 1:15; John 20:22). We group these three things together because we cannot do one without the other two. To repent and believe means we turn from sin and follow our risen Savior Jesus in childlike faith. This requires the work of the Spirit of God within us. There is no other way to be saved from the consequence of our sin, which is eternal judgment (Acts 4:12; Rev. 20:11-15).

Richard Scoggins found a similar problem with "decisions" in a more educated society:

> We found in Rhode Island that evangelism that seeks only a decision is destructive when measured against the gospel that calls people to join Christ in his Kingdom. Often people made a profession of faith, but their life was left untouched by God's Spirit. They evidenced none of the power of the Spirit, who enables them to love God and their neighbor. In such cases we found them indeed unsaved but they thought they were! Satan is a master of deception; he marks the road to hell with signs, "Heaven--this way." How sad to see so many that profess belief in Christ deny Him by their life! Such persons will awaken to a tragic eternity (Matthew 7:13-27).
>
> We encourage our church planters and leaders not to count someone as in the Kingdom (i.e., as a convert) until he does what the first converts did in Acts 2: repent, be baptized, and be added to the congregation of believers.

Pastors are to mobilize their people to witness for Christ (Acts 1:8). Upon receiving the Holy Spirit at Pentecost, the apostles witnessed with power. They called the people in Jerusalem to repent, believe and confirm it with baptism. Obedient missionaries and their disciples will witness in a way that brings repentance and faith to those who have not yet received the Good News. Converts must appreciate the value of Jesus' death *and resurrection* for them and their families (Luke 24:44-48; John 11:25-26; Acts 16:31).

What are the essential elements of our witness for Christ? What must a gospel message proclaim? What news brought faith and repentance in the power of the Spirit in the apostolic church? the apostle Peter proclaimed, as Jesus commanded in Luke 24:44-48, the following truths when he witnessed for Christ in Acts 2:

- **Who Jesus *is***: a man accredited by God by miracles, Lord and Messiah (Acts 2:22-36),
- **The value of his *death* for us**: forgiveness (Acts 2:23, 38),
- **The value of his *resurrection* for us**: victory, life through God's Holy Spirit, salvation (Acts 2:24-36, 38-40),
- **Our *response***: repentance, faith in Jesus, baptism, being added to a community of believers (Acts 2:38-41).

3-b Note Plans to Call Unbelievers and Nominal Christians to Repentance

Please write your plans to call people to repent, believe and receive the Holy Spirit. Consult with your coworkers if possible.

_____

_____

_____

_____

_____

_____

_____

_____

_____

_____

_____

4.
Obeying Jesus' Command to
Baptize

Then Jesus came to them and said, "All authority in heaven and on earth has been given to me. Therefore go and make disciples of all nations, baptizing them in the name of the Father and of the Son and of the Holy Spirit, and teaching them to obey everything I have commanded you. And surely I am with you always, to the very end of the age." Matthew 28:18-20

"Repent and be baptized, every one of you, in the name of Jesus Christ for the forgiveness of your sins. And you will receive the gift of the Holy Spirit." Acts 2:38

Find in Matthew 3:4-10 and Luke 3:10-14 what kind of people John baptized--those who felt they were *good enough* to deserve it, or *bad enough* to need it?

John's clothes were made of camel's hair, and he had a leather belt around his waist. His food was locusts and wild honey. People went out to him from Jerusalem and all Judea and the whole region of the Jordan. Confessing their sins, they were baptized by him in the Jordan River. But when he saw many of the Pharisees and Sadducees coming to where he was baptizing, he said to them: "You brood of vipers! who warned you to flee from the coming wrath? Produce fruit in keeping with repentance. And do not think you can say to yourselves, 'We have Abraham as our father.' I tell you that out of these stones God can raise up children for Abraham. The axe is already at the root of the trees, and every tree that does not produce good fruit will be cut down and thrown into the fire. Matthew 3:4-10

"What should we do then?" the crowd asked.

John answered, "The man with two tunics should share with him who has none, and the one who has food should do the same."

Tax collectors also came to be baptized. "Teacher," they asked, "what should we do?"

"Don't collect any more than you are required to," he told them.

Then some soldiers asked him, "And what should we do?" He replied, "Don't extort money and don't accuse people falsely-be content with your pay." Luke 3:10-14

Find in Acts 8:26-39 *who* was baptized, *how soon*, and *by whom*:

Now an angel of the Lord said to Philip, "Go south to the road-the desert road-that goes down from Jerusalem to Gaza."

So he started out, and on his way he met an Ethiopian eunuch, an important official in charge of all the treasury of Candace, queen of the Ethiopians. This man had gone to Jerusalem to worship, and on his way home was sitting in his chariot reading the book of Isaiah the prophet. The Spirit told Philip, "Go to that chariot and stay near it."

Then Philip ran up to the chariot and heard the man reading Isaiah the prophet. "Do you understand what you are reading?" Philip asked.

"How can I," he said, "unless someone explains it to me?" So he invited Philip to come up and sit with him. The eunuch was reading this passage of Scripture: "He was led like a sheep to the slaughter, and as a lamb before the shearer is silent, so he did not open his mouth. In his humiliation he was deprived of justice. who can speak of his descendants? for his life was taken from the earth." the eunuch asked Philip, "Tell me, please, who is the prophet talking about, himself or someone else?"

Then Philip began with that very passage of Scripture and told him the good news about Jesus. As they traveled along the road, they came to some water and the eunuch said, "Look, here is water. Why shouldn't I be baptized?"

Philip said, "If you believe with all your heart, you may."

The eunuch answered, "I believe that Jesus Christ is the Son of God." and he gave orders to stop the chariot. Then both Philip and the eunuch went down into the water and Philip baptized him. When they came up out of the water, the Spirit of the Lord suddenly took Philip away, and the eunuch did not see him again, but went on his way rejoicing.

4-a Confirm Salvation with Baptism Without Undue Delay

Inexperienced pastors often delay baptism out of misguided caution. If safety is our concern, let us rather be careful that new believers *obey* Jesus without delay. *Delaying* obedience in order to follow man-made rules sends a totally wrong message. The apostles baptized both Jewish and gentile converts without delay in Acts 2:41; 8:12, 36-38; 10:44-48; 16:14-15, 29-34; 18:8; 22:12-16. They had no other practice.

Scoggins warns from experience with new churches:

New leaders often worry too much that tares will be admitted with the wheat. We teach them from the beginning that Satan is expert at making counterfeits. Our strictest precautions with baptism and addition to the church will not deter his counterfeits. Instead of requiring extended probation, the church needs to learn and practice church discipline (Matthew 18:15-20). God himself did the first act of church discipline (Acts 5:1-11). Jesus taught, and Paul reinforced the idea, that the church itself is to take responsibility for maintaining purity (1 Cor. 5:1-13). We find that "low" barriers to being baptized and added to the church cause no problem as long as the church disciplines its members. But by delaying baptism and therefore neglecting church discipline, we make converts doubly disobedient! These are unpopular decisions for those who develop reproducing churches in a tolerant, rebellious world.

Patterson adds:

In Honduras a sharp conflict arose about baptizing "too soon" according to our older pastors. We missionaries at first

taught them to be *too careful* whom they baptized. They considered it spiritual to delay baptism until all aspects of a convert's life were in order. But when we began discipling the way that Jesus and the apostles did, we set this extreme carefulness aside. Our newer workers became "careless" with the grace of God; they let it slop over on the unworthy!

The results were encouraging. This 'sloppiness' enabled the less careful pastors to bring nearly all of their converts to maturity and obedience. Nearly all of the more "careful" pastors' converts fell back into their former life without Christ. One of these "careful" pastors criticized us vigorously, "Oh, we could fill our churches also if we baptized just anyone like you do, without straightening out their lives first!"

This sort of criticism grew intense; we again felt insecure. Our converts were obviously growing and obeying Jesus to a much greater degree than those in the legalistic churches. But that only prodded our "careful" brothers to seek more and more things to complain about. We found that nothing would satisfy them, short of turning control of our pastoral training program completely over to them! They would have ended our course of obedience. What pained most was that this condemnation came from brothers in Christ whom we loved and respected. They tried to kill what they could not control.

We helped our workers rediscover baptism in the Bible: the apostles from the very beginning helped repentant converts to obey Jesus, starting with baptism. Seeing that the 3,000 converts in Acts 2 were baptized the same day they received Jesus, we knew we had God's permission to do away with our many man-made rules for things to do before baptism. These rules required *good* things; the problem was that they led to legalism by canceling the grace of God. We didn't make an issue of how soon it had to be; we did not baptize as soon as the apostles did, for example. But our converts, like those in ancient Jerusalem, were assured as babes in Christ of their salvation and acceptance in the church body, and started at once to obey Jesus. They received detailed doctrinal study *after* baptism, as in Acts 2:41-42.

Jesus instituted baptism to confirm one's salvation. Especially in new fields, we must not introduce man-made decision rites from our own culture to confirm it. The invitation of the apostles, for example, was not to raise one's hand or to "come forward." They simply told those who trusted in Jesus to show their repentance by being baptized (Acts 2:38; 22:12-16). Any decision-making ritual that man has devised to replace baptism as the instrument to confirm salvation has had a much poorer record for determining who are sincere. The follow through, or conservation of converts, has always been much higher when we confirm their repentance the New Testament way.

The church planting task group that went with Peter to Cesarea baptized the converts as soon as they saw that they really knew Christ. They did not use baptism as a graduation ceremony following a long time of indoctrination. Peter considered it disobedience to God to delay baptism when he and his companions saw that Cornelius and his people had been received the Holy Spirit (Acts 10:44-48).

We must never delay baptism so long that converts become discouraged. In pioneer fields Christian influences are lacking and converts consider baptism both as identification with Christ and the confirmation of their acceptance by His people.

Churches that practice infant baptism do not rebaptize adult believers. They should celebrate a meaningful confirmation, however, to assure them that they have been received by God and His people. We must not let confirmation become mechanical.

4-b Assure Baptized Converts of Jesus' Loving Presence and the Indwelling Holy Spirit

Baptism in the Bible is more than the moment of the ritual with water. It includes the continued new, eternal life in the risen Lord Jesus Christ (Rom. 6:1-11; 1 Cor. 12:13). We should assure converts, when baptized with water, of Jesus, presence in their hearts, and the Holy Spirit's corresponding spiritual baptism, sealing, and sanctifying.

Scoggins discerned the corporate aspect of baptism:

For some churches baptism and being added to the church are synonymous. We have found in America, however, that teaching about baptism sometimes involves only the *vertical* component--that a person has decided to follow Jesus. Baptism also includes the *horizontal* component: being baptized into Jesus' body means a person also has been called into service and the fellowship of His church (1 Cor. 12:12-13). It sometimes takes a while in the radically individualistic West for new disciples to appreciate this horizontal dimension. We find it helpful to baptize them while they are still learning the meaning of the corporate salvation to which they have been called.

Once new disciples realize the nature of their corporate calling, we encourage them to *covenant* with the church. This is usually confirmed symbolically at a meeting where hands are laid on the disciples after they affirm their desire to follow the Lord in the service and fellowship of the church. In Acts baptism was a one-step process with both vertical and horizontal components: confirming repentance and being added to the church at the same time. Some have replaced it with a two-step process, being baptized and later being added to the church. Ideally, these two things will still occur at the same time, but often they do not. We try to get them to occur as closely as possible; both are essential steps of obedience.

Some church planting task groups serve with a mission organization that is not itself a church and therefore do not baptize. They must separate new churches from the parent organization in order for them to baptize and serve as "mother" churches from then on.

4-c Note Plans for New Testament Baptism

Please note your general plans in response to Jesus' command to baptize. Do this with your co-workers if possible.

_____

_____

_____

_____

_____

_____

_____

_____

_____

_____

5.
Obeying Jesus' Command to
Make Disciples

"Therefore go and make disciples of all nations..." Matthew 28:19

Discipling is only for little chicks.

Just help them take off and fly straight.

That's just part of it, featherhead !

Jesus didn't limit His discipling to new believers.

During most of His ministry he discipled top flight eagles, the very apostles of the church !

Find in Matthew 28:18-20 with what *authority* Jesus orders us to make disciples by teaching them to obey Him:

Then Jesus came to them and said, "All authority in heaven and on earth has been given to me. Therefore go and make disciples of all nations, baptizing them in the name of the Father and of the Son and of the Holy Spirit, and teaching them to obey everything I have commanded you. And surely I am with you always, to the very end of the age.

Find in John 14:15 the correct *motive* for our obedience to His commands:

"If you love me, you will obey what I command."

Several pastoral ministries grow out of this general command to make disciples:

evangelism,

nurturing new believers,

cultivating the spiritual life,

teaching the Word and biblical doctrine,

pastoral care and counseling,

foreign mission work,

pastoral training,

children's instruction,

shepherding in general.

5-a Teach New Followers of Christ to Be Doers of the Word

Jesus commands us to hold to his teaching and to disciple others (John 8:31; Matthew 7:24-29; 28:18-20). The new disciples in Jerusalem devoted themselves to the apostles' teaching from the beginning, starting immediately after their baptism (Acts 2:41-42). We teach a new believer that God is bringing him into a family where we get to know each other intimately. Our lives are lived out with fellow believers so that barriers to the spirit-filled life become apparent and repentance and renewal can take place.

Scoggins found healthy new dimensions of disciple making:

We helped new believers to see themselves as highly disciplined pilgrims in search of a better country. The journey is difficult but exhilarating. What a privilege to labor in Jesus' Kingdom! What joy! We were created--and re-created--for this! We help brand new believers to find real joy in serving our King. This joy of serving is not reserved for some elite group in the Kingdom (e.g., full-time clergy).

Every child of God is enlisted in God's army to wage warfare. They are not volunteers in an auxiliary branch of the army who serve when they feel like it, and leave most of the 'real work' to the 'clergy' of the regular army. George Washington found that such an army of temporary reservists could not win the war. When we are conscripted into this army, we find a whole new discipline; our whole life is changed.

As we grow in obedience, change occurs in our actions and attitudes toward others. In a discipling church the motivations for our behavior are exposed and developed in the power of the Holy Spirit. Healing occurs, freeing a corporate disciple for more effective service (Gal. 5:13). We carefully help disciples to become part of the body and its corporate life. For adult converts this normally starts with baptism. We help them to covenant with other believers to obey Jesus Christ and his apostles as a body. They become active in ministry and are voluntarily accountable to a loving discipler (John 13:34; Acts 2:41-37; Heb. 13:17).

5-b Help Converts Still Outside the Church Become *Corporate Disciples*

If one merely "decides" to accept Jesus--a concept foreign to the New Testament--his chances of following through are slim. Jesus told his disciples, "Follow me, and I will make you fishers of men" (Matthew 4:19). Discipling from a biblical perspective normally starts with witnessing to seekers. Those who receive Christ become corporate disciples, being added to the church through repentance, faith, and baptism (Acts 2:38-41). As discipling continues, the new Christian learns to obey the other commands of Christ and to serve in ministry. We build all ministries on loving obedience.

5-c Relate the Word to Life and Ministry as Jesus and His Apostles Did

Biblical truth is intensely practical. We teach to build up the body of Christ, not just to impart knowledge. Good teaching applies God's Word to our people's lives and ministries. 2 Tim. 3:14-17 reveals the purpose of biblical instruction: to equip for service. Teaching has the specific objective of mobilizing church members for ministry (Eph. 4:11-16). God demands in 1 Corinthians 12 that we use the gift of teaching in harmony with the other gifts given to the body.

5-d Disciple on All Levels of Maturity

As churches mature, we disciple on four levels:

1. The **unsaved**: the *nations* (literally, 'pagans') whom we disciple (Matthew 28:19),
    2. **Converts**: those whom we baptize and teach obedience (Matthew 28:19),
        3. **Growing Christians** (John 8:31; John 21:16),
            4. **Leaders**: pastors (elders) or missionaries (Mark 3:13-19).

5-e Teach with *Loving Authority*

We teach, or mentor, with Jesus' authority, not our own. Our authority as leaders and teachers is real, but derives from Christ. We are to command with the Word of our Lord and his inspired apostles (1 Tim. 4:11). Our discipling becomes weak and legalistic if we depend only on the authority of a human organization ("Obey me because I've been named to this position over you!") We teach our people to obey Christ and His apostles because they love Him. He said:

If you love me, obey my commands. John 14:15

You are my friends if you do what I command. John 15:14

Training with proper authority requires a loving, confidential relationship between the disciplers and those they train, especially if the trainees are pastors or elders. Unless it builds on loving relationships, authoritative discipling stifles initiative. A good teacher is a mentor. He listens to his disciples and shares responsibility for their effective ministry. The trainees then eagerly follow the counsel and imitate their mentor's example.

We train leaders more effectively when we look beyond them to focus on those they serve in a church or home group. Truly biblical teachers build up the church body through their students (Eph. 4:11-16).

Our disciples do what we teach them, not because we are above them in the organization (such leadership is condemned by Jesus in Matthew 20:25-26) but because we love them and they have confidence in us. To mobilize new workers, we develop a loving relationship with those corporate disciples who respect our God-given authority under Christ as his under-shepherds (Heb. 13.17).

5-f *Integrate* Church Planting and Pastoral Training

In a pioneer field that lacks culturally relevant, reproductive churches, church reproduction goes hand in hand with pastoral training and evangelism. We mentioned four levels of discipling that a church does: for the unsaved, converts, growing believers and leaders. Jesus spent most of His time discipling leaders (the twelve original apostles).

Discipling leaders, a form of Christian mentoring, almost became a lost art in the twentieth century. Pastors saw themselves as professionally trained generalists who did all aspects of the ministry and were trained to do *everything*. This contradicts 1 Corinthians 12 and other passages about spiritual gifts in God's Word. It cancels out the interactive life of the

46

church body. It undermines the health of any Christian organization. A wise pastor or elder *oversees* ministries even though he delegates full responsibility for them to others. For example, an elder oversees congregational worship by asking others who are more musical than he is to do it. He makes sure they do a good job.

Elders in a healthy church constantly reproduce themselves in all that they do, equipping others to teach, counsel, lead meetings and disciple.

13).

Every pioneer church planting task group needs at least one gifted teacher or mentor with pastoral experience to train new pastors on the job. Patterson's workers integrated church planting with pastoral training:

> **When we started using TEE (Theological Education by Extension) in Honduras, we followed the only model we knew, that of the Presbyterians in Guatemala. We started classes in village churches. This made pastoral training available to those who could not leave their crops, families, jobs or animals to attend a resident Bible Institute. This model had worked in Guatemala because they already had the churches and needed only to train their pastors. But we did not have the churches yet. Ours was a pioneer field with no experienced pastors or well-established churches.**

> **Our method failed. Those we trained by extension were still unable to raise up churches and pastor them. So. . . Another plans meeting! the workers pleaded, "Not more changes!" We faced the fact: we could not multiply churches without shepherds. We could not train shepherds without churches. We decided to do both together. We started modeling on-the-job training for new leaders. We enrolled only *elder* types, not the single young men who had previously come to our resident Bible Institute. We helped them to grow along with their congregations. Churches multiplied.**

> **Again, criticisms! Our national association of churches raised loud objections. We were putting unqualified men into pastoral leadership! in their national assembly they voted our training program out of existence. But we kept on existing anyway. God continued to multiply churches. The leaders of the national association sent a harshly worded petition to our mission board demanding that I be removed from the field. The board sent me a copy and asked me to reply to the accusations. We decided only to pray rather than fight the issue in the arena of church politics, so I wrote no letter in reply. Rather, I penned references to Bible verses that**

supported our practices in the margin of the petition and returned it to the board. They let me stay on the field and the controversy fanned itself into a tornado.

We had more meetings to encourage our workers, now officially disowned by our national leaders. We urged them simply to keep obeying Jesus and close their ears to the criticisms. We told them, "Keep praying, training and mobilizing the elders the way the Word says. Just imitate the apostles. They were criticized, too."

Like Paul, we commissioned as elders the more mature men whom God provided. Paul named fairly new Christians as elders in Acts 14:23 where there were no experienced leaders available. We called these new pastoral leaders `provisional elders.' We explained to them that they were too new to be confirmed permanently in the pastoral role.

The marriage became complete and was fruitful: the Holy Spirit united church planting and pastoral training in one combined program of church reproduction.

5-g   Help Converts to Teach Their Families

Scoggins focuses on the family:

During our Sunday meetings our churches help families prepare for their teaching times. The leaders provide a Bible reading schedule to use in the homes. Heads of families learn from the beginning to take responsibility for shepherding in the home. This is often the first step in discovering and developing leaders, since leaders must be able to care for their families. These reading schedules consist simply of a few assigned verses for each day, with a question to start discussion; stories can be added for the children. The families are encouraged to spend up to five minutes each day reading the assigned passage and discussing the question, usually at mealtime. This forces adults and children out of a passive learning role, so prevalent in churches today. It encourages family heads and potential teachers to apply God's Word first to their family.

This family focus is a powerful tool for training and mobilizing new group leaders and pastors. Some heads of families take turns teaching during Sunday worship, simply leading discussion on the same Bible passages they have been discussing with their families during the past week. We develop as leaders those men who shepherd their families and evangelize their friends. As people are added to the church, those who brought or initially befriended them take responsibility to ground them in the faith. We have developed simple materials to help young believers shepherd the newer ones. Discipleship "chains" come into existence along relational lines. These who bring in new ones learn to shepherd; leadership develops naturally around these discipleship chains. Men shepherd their wife and other men; women shepherd women.

These emerging shepherds lead new believers through repentance, baptism, and preparation for *covenanting* (agreeing formally with the other members of the church to work and worship together with them in loving harmony and in obedience to Christ). Older leaders often phase out as these new ones phase in, and take a coaching role only. This frees up the older leaders to start another church. Of course they can "do it better," but if they do, the newer ones will never learn. The newer ones may surprise you too!

5-h Note Plans for Making Disciples

Please note your plans for making disciples the way Jesus and His apostles said and did. Plan this with your coworkers if possible.

_____

_____

_____

_____

_____

_____

_____

_____

_____

_____

_____

_____

_____

_____

_____

6.
Obeying Jesus' Command to
Love

"A new command I give you: Love one another. As I have loved you, so you must love one another. by this all men will know that you are my disciples, if you love one another." John 13:34-35

Find in Luke 10:25-37 what God counts as true Christian love:

On one occasion an expert in the law stood up to test Jesus. "Teacher," he asked, "what must I do to inherit eternal life?"

"What is written in the Law?" he replied. "How do you read it?"

He answered: "Love the Lord your God with all your heart and with all your soul and with all your strength and with all your mind;" and, "Love your neighbor as yourself."

"You have answered correctly," Jesus replied. "Do this and you will live."

But he wanted to justify himself, so he asked Jesus, "And who is my neighbor?"

In reply Jesus said: "A man was going down from Jerusalem to Jericho, when he fell into the hands of robbers. They stripped him of his clothes, beat him and went away, leaving him half-dead. A priest happened to be going down the same road, and when he saw the man, he passed by on the other side. So too, a Levite, when he came to the place and saw him, passed by on the other side. But a Samaritan, as he traveled, came where the man was; and when he saw him, he took pity on him. He went to him and bandaged his wounds, pouring on oil and wine. Then he put the man on his own donkey, took him to an inn and took care of him. The next day he took out two silver coins and gave them to the innkeeper. `Look after him,' he said, `and when I return, I will reimburse you for any extra expense you may have.' Which of these three do you think was a neighbor to the man who fell into the hands of robbers?"

The expert in the law replied, "The one who had mercy on him."

Jesus told him, "Go and do likewise."

6-a Let New Leaders Develop Ministries Without Fearing Their Superiors

Churches reproduce much more readily in an atmosphere of freedom. Perfectionism and fear of making mistakes paralyzes the Lord's work. He warned us against over-control in Matthew 20:25-28. If you are a leader, please consider your leadership style as you read the following.

How great a need the church has for leaders who humbly encourage ministry by every member of the body! Yes, immature members will make mistakes as we give them opportunities to grow in ministry. New leaders, like new churches or cell groups, must learn first to take their baby steps. Don't dampen their spirit by pointing out every little mistake and putting unnecessary boundaries around them. Remember the failures Jesus allowed his disciples to make, and the ups and downs of our own children as they develop. Failure and experimentation are a natural part of development. We urge you not to fear failure, either on your part or on the part of those you are training. We should rather be concerned that we all learn from our failures.

Scoggins discovered "leadership from within" (*serving within* the flock rather than *lording over* it):

We learned to make an important distinction. Does a man (or woman) serve because he seeks self-promotion, or because he is heeding the call of the Holy Spirit on his life? Motives are central in Christian service (see 1 Cor. 3:10-15, 4:6). We found that *leadership from within* is a better model for leaders in the church. When the pastors take a servant-leadership position within the flock--not over it--they get to know the people, as the shepherds of old did (unlike the 'ranchers' in some churches). They serve as examples of dying to self as they discern what is pleasing to the Lord. They are in a better position to discern the Spirits of the people as they seek the Lord's will for themselves and for the church. Close relationships are necessary in order to help members see the hidden motives of their hearts. God protects them from their selfish motives in "spiritual service." Many a sincere saint has been destroyed by hidden, carnal motives in their service to the king.

We found that leadership from the top down controls and thus limits the avenues through which the Holy Spirit can speak and work. Leadership from *within* the body, however, encourages individual initiative, broadening the avenues through which the Holy Spirit can speak and work in the church. Leaders who stay close to the sheep are also better able to discern the dangers that come through carnal motives. Although we can seldom predict very far into the future the direction the Spirit is leading, leaders who work from within are far more able to detect dangers as they creep up. Such leaders are also far more apt to release others for the spontaneous reproduction of churches.

The New Testament emphasizes servant leadership. Jesus warned us against exercising authority for the purpose of control; human authority exercised from the top down violates this command of Jesus (Matthew 20:25-28). It often stifles church reproduction. Such top-down control assumes that God will lead the church only through those presently in leadership. It leaves the so-called laity behind. They must wait passively until their leader comes down from the mountain with a revelation from God as to what they should do. This kills individual initiative and narrows the avenues through which the Holy Spirit can speak to the church. Servant leaders help others to take responsibility before the Lord and do their part.

Patterson also learned to build organization on loving relationships:

At first, in our work in Honduras, leaders felt they had authority simply because they were above others in the organization. When we began more biblical methods of discipling, including as we mentored leaders, we saw that authority should be exercised through loving relationships. We needed organizational structures for order but taught our people to place the authority growing out of our man-made organizations lower than that of Christ and His apostles' commands. We taught our new leaders to build their authority on loving relationships, as Jesus did. He told His disciples in John 14:15, "If you love me, obey my commands."

I learned that if my students love me and know that I am helping them have a more effective ministry, they will be intensely loyal and do what I suggest even though I have no organizational authority over them.

We taught our people that for the sake of order, authority might be *defined* by the bylaws of our churches and their regional associations, but it was not to be *based* on them. The more traditional pastors kept rewriting their constitutions and bylaws to maintain control. The question of authority came to a head again when we organized regional associations of churches to coordinate inter-church projects for evangelism, fellowship, pastoral training and community development. The more traditional pastor who lived in distant cities and held the highest positions in our national association of churches complained that our regional associations would undermine their power to exert discipline and undermine their authority as national leaders. They visited our area to warn our pastors, "Things will grow out of control; we will have confusion."

Our workers grew weary again of the criticisms, and we held another meeting. We prayerfully examined the Word to find God's guidelines for churches to relate to each other at a local level. We found that in both Jerusalem and in Ephesus that the churches were meeting in homes. Today these churches would be considered clusters of house churches or cells. Those clusters, however, were called 'the church' of that city. The New Testament commands to work lovingly with one another applied to their interaction as small congregations.

So we agreed to do what the apostles taught the New Testament churches. The church in Jerusalem, for example, began at once to practice loving fellowship, caring for one another in a material way (Acts 2:44-45; 6:1-5). Our reorganization on an inter-church level grew out of Jesus' command to love, have fellowship and develop mercy ministries, rather than man-made bylaws. We did write bylaws, however, to define how our servant-leaders could maintain this inter-church cooperation.

The regional organization among churches did not cause confusion as our critics had prophesied. It visibly strengthened fellowship between our new churches and strengthened their ministries. Our regional directors had far more influence and discipline by building their authority on loving relationships as servants, than those at the national level who ruled with clenched fist.

6-b Start from the Beginning to Disciple a New Believer with Loving Care

New believers feel that God accepts them when we (the church) accept them in love. A newborn infant thrives on its mother's love but becomes stunted for life socially if its mother's love is lacking. Likewise, newborn Christians in the church are stunted spiritually, often permanently, if they fail to receive loving discipled following conversion. Scoggins learned this from experience:

For a church to grow and reproduce, it must find ways to integrate newcomers into its life and heart. Our experience with some churches shows that it often takes months, and sometimes even years, for newcomers to sense that they have become insiders in a church. One way to avoid this delay is to teach our people to see each newcomer as a door to a new social circle that God might add to the church. The person who brings a newcomer should immediately begin to shepherd that person in the basics of the faith. If people do not know how, we show them. We also train newcomers to share their faith at once with their social circle to penetrate it for Christ. In some cases a whole network of friends and relatives was thus harvested for the kingdom. We have watched new churches be born because of such a harvest, and others where the entire social circle joined an already existing church with dynamic results. We must avoid extracting a person from his or her social circle into the church before we try to penetrate that circle for the sake of the Kingdom.

Since some newcomers simply show up at the church, we should ask volunteers to be on the lookout for them and begin at once to befriend them and to shepherd them in the basics of the faith. Such a "Barnabas ministry" is essential to the healthy growth and reproduction of the church (Acts 9:26-28).

6-c Encourage New Believers at Once to Care for the Needy

The church in Jerusalem took care of its needy people from the very beginning. As the church grew in numbers they found that they had to name special servants (that's what the word *deacons* meant then) to coordinate and carry out this work. From the very beginning we teach new believers to obey the greatest commandments, to love God with all our heart and our neighbor as ourselves. We are to do good to all men, starting with the family of God (Gal. 6:10; 1 John 3:16-18).

We help new believers to begin at once to show their love for God and their neighbor in a practical way (Luke 10:25-37). We teach them that they have been saved to serve (Gal. 5:13). Each one has something to offer the believing community as well as his or her unconverted *neighbor*.

We avoid a self-centered approach to discipleship that tells new believers that God's main interest is to meet their needs and make them more prosperous and comfortable. Jesus never promised material riches on earth, but a painful cross. Our daily bread, yes, but a yacht and a private airplane, no. The gifts that God promises in this life are explicitly defined as a means to serve *others*. Everyone who has the Holy Spirit has been given something to give others.

Spiritual healing brings a servant's heart. We receive much when we become part of God's living community, but our motive is to give, not to get. Anything we receive should be seen not as what we *deserve* but rather as an undeserved gift of pure grace. Likewise, our responsibility is to give freely. Caring for the physical needs of others is a basic way to show our love for God (Luke 10:25-37; 1 John 3:16-18).

We should provide new believers opportunities to practice simple acts of love and mercy before entrusting them with the more influential ministries of teaching and leading. A church's foundation crumbles when human termites that have not learned to love in a compassionate way worm their way to positions of power. God gives spiritual gifts to cultivate practical love, heal broken relationships and physical sickness, deal with poverty, and develop edifying relationships between workers. These include the gifts of compassion, giving, helps, service, and hospitality.

6-d Where Poverty Reigns, Wed Church Planting to Development Work

Good development requires persons with different spiritual gifts. Depending on the need, they might include:

Compassion. In poverty areas church planting should incorporate mercy ministries or small businesses. We must not confuse mercy with mere pity that gives help in a way that creates dependency. Workers accustomed to do emergency relief need to be retrained to avoid simply giving things away if they are sent to permanent development projects.

Prophecy. Especially among people of limited education or radically different culture, this gift may enable creative, powerful and artistic ways to communicate God's messages. The biblical prophets often used poetry as well as powerful symbolism.

Giving. your task group may need a businessman whose capital maintains a business that provides employment for fellow workers or nationals. The business might also enable workers to reside in areas where the government refuses residence to conventional, full-time missionaries.

Healing or casting out demons. In pioneer fields where Satan has had complete control of the people's minds for centuries and they hold a world view totally incompatible with Christianity, God often confirms the gospel message with healing and signs, as He did under similar circumstances in Acts. Even missionaries from churches that normally do not deal with these gifts report such 'power encounters.'

6-e Let the Holy Spirit Harmonize Gift-Based Ministries in Love

To mobilize church members in ministry, we integrate their ministries in love, in the power of the Holy Spirit. We do not isolate all ministries as separate programs or departments. Scripture urges us to use the spiritual gifts that the Holy Spirit has given us to serve one another in love as a closely knit body (Rom. 12; I Cor. chapters 12-13; Eph. 4:11-16).

During the 20th century Western churches began seriously to compartmentalize their ministries, creating separate programs for evangelism, Christian education, community development, worship and pastoral training. This Western style of organization creates "turf" in which individuals gain influence and power. The church body breaks up into separate departments with little cooperation between them. Often simply maintaining one's position of power within that program becomes the important thing. Attempts to remove such a grasping person or to reduce his budget results in verbal combat. Once a person becomes jealous of his turf and protects it, he resists change regardless of what the Holy Spirit might say. Such fragmented organization hinders the Spirit's work, since "God is opposed to the proud, but gives grace to the humble." Fragmented, program-oriented organization fails to promote humility, forbearance, or cooperation on the part of every member of the body. We need these virtues to edify the body by harmonizing its gift-based ministries in love (Eph. 4:11-16).

The 20th century Western tradition of compartmentalized organization may bring efficiency to a mission agency but fracture the church body. For church reproduction in poor, pioneer fields, the biblical style of organization allows church planting to go hand-in-hand with poverty work and pastoral training as one integrated effort. This interaction between persons of different gifts produces balance and a much healthier church body. Such networking cannot be controlled from the outside without doing violence to the churches' ability to meet needs as they arise. Once again we see the need for leadership from within rather than 'top down' control.

6-f Select 'One Another' Verses that you Should now Give Attention

Galatians 5:13 reveals the reciprocal nature of Christian ministry:

For you, dear friends, have been called to live in freedom, not to satisfy your sinful nature, but to serve one another in love.

There are many such 'one another' verses in the Bible. We practice them not only *within* groups but also *between* them. Persons encourage one other, pray for each other, confess faults to one another, etc. We cannot do this in large meetings; that is why we also organize small group meetings--home groups or cells.

This 'one another' church body life is not confined to one's own group. We practice it between groups, because a group small enough to do it with all of its own members is too small to have a complete gift balance (God gives so many spiritual gifts!). For example, if our group is weak on evangelism, don't go looking around for another method to witness. Look rather for who can help you, someone in another group or church that is willing to help you, as you in turn help them in some other way. Almost nothing is more powerful to build ministries than this voluntary, loving interaction between groups and churches. We organize it in our own way by building on relationships, so it happens easily and joyfully.

A List of New Testament 'One Anothers'

(For building loving fellowship one with another in and between groups)

Let a group decide which ones they need currently to study and apply:

To build edifying relationships

Love:
- ☐ Love one another: John 13:34-35; 5:12, 17; Rom. 12: 10; 1 Thess. 4:9; 1 John 3:11,14, 23; 4:7, 11, 12; 2 John 1:5; 1 Peter 1:22
- ☐ Love one another to fulfill the law: Rom. 13:8
- ☐ Increase our love one for another: 2 Thess. 1:3
- ☐ Abound in love for another: 1 Thess. 3:12
- ☐ Love each other deeply, to cover a multitude of sins: 1 Peter 4:8

Interact with care:
- ☐ Have fellowship one with another: 1 John 1:7
- ☐ Forgive one another: Eph. 3:13; 4:32; Col. 3:13
- ☐Greet one another with a holy kiss (an embrace in some cultures): Rom. 16:16; 1 Cor. 16:20; 2 Cor. 13:12; 1 Peter 5:14
- ☐ Wait for one another to break bread: 1 Cor. 11:33
- ☐ Bear one another's sufferings: 1 Cor. 12:260

For serving one another (in and among groups)

Serve:
- ☐ Serve one another with the gifts each person has received: 1 Peter 4:10
- ☐ Serve one another in love: Gal. 5:13
- ☐ Be kind to each other: 1 Thess. 5:15
- ☐ Care for one another: 1 Cor. 12:25
- ☐ Bear the burdens one for another: Gal. 6:2
- ☐ Wash one another's feet as a sign of a humble servant's heart: John 13:14
- ☐ Work with one another: 1 Cor. 3:9; 2Cor. 6:1

Teach :
- ☐ Teach one another: Col. 3:16
- ☐ Instruct one another: Rom. 5:14

Encourage:
- ☐ Encourage one another: Col. 3:16; Heb. 10:25
- ☐ Exhort one another: Heb. 3:13
- ☐ Speak the truth to one another: Eph. 4:25
- ☐ Lay down our lives one for another: 1 John 3:16
- ☐ Spur one another to love and good deeds: Heb. 10:24

Edify:
- ☐ Edify (strengthen, build up) one another: 1 Thess. 4:18 & 5:1, 11
- ☐ Edify one another gathering together each one with a hymn, a word of instruction, a revelation, a tongue or its interpretation: 1 Cor. 14:26

Give spiritual care:
- ☐ Confess our sins one to another: James 5:16
- ☐ Pray for one another: James 5:16

For cultivating unity one with another

Act with humility:
- ☐ Honor one another: Rom. 12:10
- ☐ Be of one mind one with another: 2 Cor. 13:11; Rom. 12:16; 15:5
- ☐ Do not criticize one another: Rom. 14:13
- ☐ Do not speak bad one of another: James 4:11; 5:9
- ☐ Submit to one another: Eph. 5:21
- ☐ Be clothed with humility toward one another: 1 Peter 5:5

Live in harmony:
- ☐ Have patience one with another: Eph. 4:2
- ☐ Live in peace one with another: Matthew 9:50
- ☐ Receive one another with hospitality: Rom. 15:7; 1 Peter. 4:9
- ☐ Glorify God together: Rom. 15:6

6-g To Detect and Develop Spiritual Gifts *Release* Potential Leaders to Work with New Churches or Holistic Small Groups

Find in Exodus 18:14-24 a reason to establish small groups and prepare their leaders:

When his father-in-law saw all that Moses was doing for the people, he said, "What is this you are doing for the people? Why do you alone sit as judge, while all these people stand around you from morning till evening?"

Moses answered him, "Because the people come to me to seek God's will. Whenever they have a dispute, it is brought to me, and I decide between the parties and inform them of God's decrees and laws."

Moses' father-in-law replied, "What you are doing is not good. You and these people who come to you will only wear yourselves out. The work is too heavy for you; you cannot handle it alone. Listen now to me and I will give you some advice, and may God be with you. You must be the people's representative before God and bring their disputes to Him. Teach them the decrees and laws, and show them the way to live and the duties they are to perform. But select capable men from all the people-men who fear God, trustworthy men who hate dishonest gain-and appoint them as officials over thousands, hundreds, fifties and tens. Have them serve as judges for the people at all times, but have them bring every difficult case to you; the simple cases they can decide themselves. That will make your load lighter, because they will share it with you. If you do this and God so commands, you will be able to stand the strain, and all these people will go home satisfied."

Moses listened to his father-in-law and did everything he said.

The 'love chapter,' 1 Corinthians 13, should be read together with chapter 12 to appreciate its true significance. It is part of Paul's exhortation to use different spiritual gifts in loving harmony. Gifts used without love possess no value for God. We can put most of a church's members to work if we help them discover their gifts in small group ministry where loving relationships are easier to form.

We help members to detect and use their gifts in a small body in several ways:

- **Join ministry or evangelistic groups** to use their spiritual gifts to minister to the unsaved community and to each other. Seekers are easier to bring to faith and follow through with small groups.

- **Start new home groups or churches**.

- **Help existing groups to add ministries.** Deal with felt needs and opportunities for witnessing or serving others. Shepherding groups minister to communities or families with different needs and bring together different gifts, as in Romans 12:3-8.

- **Develop children's ministries** and show them how to serve their parents and each other. Help older children to disciple the younger.

- **Name persons with a loving, helping disposition to disciple newer Christians on a personal or family basis.** This discipling is easier in small groups, especially *new* small groups. The apostolic churches did it in homes (see Acts 2:46; 5:42; 20:20; Rom. 16:3-5; Philemon 2).

- **Awaken and practice the most edifying gifts.** What is most edifying depends upon current needs and circumstances.

We seek people with the following gifts to help a group build its organization on loving relationships (rather than on abstract policies and positions):

Leadership.
Healthy groups need a leader who inspires the people with the vision, who knows what God wants His people to do and can coordinate their gift-based ministries.

60

Evangelist.

Healthy groups "do the work of an evangelist" (2 Tim. 4:5) and need a person with this gift to stimulate and furnish a model for the others.

Pastor (shepherding elder).

Healthy groups need at least one shepherd. This person isn't always a teacher; he isn't always the leader. He has a shepherd's heart and watches over the flock, read to give loving care to any member who needs it.

Teacher or mentor.

Healthy groups need mentors that help each person to apply the Word of God to his or her life.

The gift of teaching, as Scripture demonstrates it', is sometimes absent in traditional church classrooms. We may see someone standing in front of a group, merely downloading information. That is a form of teaching but is not what God reveals that teaching should be when He speaks of it in the Bible. The Christian teacher's task is to mobilize the others for their different ministries (Eph. 4:11-16) and "for every good work" (2 Tim. 3:16-17). This requires mentoring. A traditional teacher who does not mentor must name helpers who do. In some traditional groups a teacher takes the title of leader but does not really lead; he just teaches.

Scoggins discovered the value of teaching in the home:

> **Our experience shows that as a head of a family carries out his God-given responsibility to teach, his giftedness becomes apparent. Even if he is not gifted as a teacher, he is still required to teach his family, for which God will give him grace. Because of this, we train our members who are heads of families in the basics of teaching, at least for family devotions.**

One person might have more than one of these gifts but almost no one has all of them. Even if they did, they would not have time to exercise them, and if they tried they would only hinder others in the group from developing their gifts.

In addition to the gifts of *leadership, evangelist, pastor* or *elder*, and *teacher*, other gifts yield more specialized ministries. Some groups specialize in marriage or family counseling. But they must not neglect the other areas. Others deal quite successfully with drug or alcohol abuse recovery, and they, too, must deal with the other gift-based ministries as well. Other groups offer recovery from grief; they must not focus exclusively on this ministry, however, or they will rob their members of a balanced Christian life. As we have pointed out in other contexts, a struggling group's greatest weakness is invariably its greatest strength taken to excess. Some groups focus on the needs of singles or the elderly; these groups also need persons with gifts of *exhortation, discernment, compassion, or helps*, etc.

Many groups pray for the unsaved, the sick, and the hurting. Those who take the lead in this may be people with the gifts of *faith, healing, or freeing those who are oppressed by demons.*

Groups doing community development need persons with the gifts of *discernment, giving*, and *compassion*. But, to maintain balance, they also need persons with the other most common gifts of teaching, shepherding and evangelism.

For groups meeting in homes, someone needs the gift of *hospitality*.

Groups ministering cross-culturally need persons gifted as *apostles* (sent ones, or missionaries), along with the other common gifts. In pioneer mission fields task groups must train pastors and need at least one instructor with the gift of *teaching*.

If you are a leader, please fix in your mind the Bible passages that instruct us how to harmonize spiritual gifts in love: **Romans 12, 1 Corinthians chapters 12-14** and **Ephesians 4:11-16**.

Hey, this is important !

Groups small enough to enable the 'one-another' ministries are *too small* to have a complete balance of all useful spiritual gifts.

So we arrange for them to practice 'one-another' interaction *between* groups. When elders or group leaders meet to coordinate this group interaction, they often need to correct trends or errors. For this the gifts of *wisdom, prophecy, discernment* and *leadership* are useful. So is *experience*.

6-h Review Spiritual Gifts Mentioned in the New Testament

We help everyone to know and use their gifts to serve one another in love. To help people remember and understand the different gifts, you might relate the biblical *examples* for gifts that need clarification. These are mentioned beside each gift, below. Some passages may be too long to read during a meeting; you can recount by memory the relevant parts. Bear in mind that the church ministries found in the New Testament require the use of several gifts working together. An evangelist, for example, works closely with other teachers and leaders to follow up converts.

Mark the box ☐ by gifts that need to be developed in your group. You may need to arrange for help from *other* groups (and give help to them in areas in which your group is strong):

Spiritual gifts listed in Romans 12:4-8:
☐ **Serve**: Samuel, 1 Sam. 1:20-28; 3:1-21; Deacons, Acts 6:1-7; Dorcas, Acts 9:36-41

☐ **Prophesy**--messages from God for strength, consolation and encouragement; 1 Cor. 14:3

☐ **Give**--Abigail, 1 Sam. 25; guidelines: 2 Cor. 9

☐ **Teach**--Ezra: Neh. 8; purpose, Eph. 4:11-16

☐ **Encourage**--exhort: Paul with the Ephesian elders, Acts 20:17-38

☐ **Lead**--servant leader who helps others to minister: Moses, Ex. 18:13-26

☐ **Show mercy**--The sheep and goats, Matt25:31-46; Good Samaritan, Lk10:30-35; David with Saul, 1 Sam. 24

Additional gifts listed in 1 Corinthians 12:7-11, 27-30:
☐ Counsel with **wisdom**--Solomon, 1 Kings 3:5-28

☐ Base decisions on **knowledge** (facts)--Bereans' searching the Word, Acts 17:10-12

☐ **Help**--Aquila and Priscilla, Acts18:1-5, 24-28

☐ Go, as an **Apostle** (sent one, with itchy feet, a spiritual entrepreneur)--Rom. 5:20-21; Paul and Barnabas, Acts chapters 13-14

☐ **Discern**--Nathan, 2 Sam. Chapters 11-12; Paul, Gal. 2:6-21

☐ **Heal**--Jesus and the paralytic, Mark 2:1-12; Peter and John heal the crippled man, Acts chapters 3-4

☐ **Administrate**--Nehemiah: Neh chapters 2-3

☐ Do **miracles**--Elijah: 1 Kings 18:16-46; Elisha: 2 Kings chapters 2-5

☐ Speak in **tongues**--Cornelius' household, Acts 10:44-48. Use this gift with the following:

☐ **Interpret** tongues--see cautions in 1 Cor.14

☐ Use **faith** (all need it but some stir it in others)--the leper and the centurion, Matthew 8:1-13; Old Testament faithful, Heb. 11

Practice additional gifts listed in Ephesians 4:11:

☐ Announce the Good News (**evangelist**)--Philip; Acts 8:26-40

☐ **Pastor** (shepherd) -- Acts 20:28-34; 1 Peter 5:1-4 (see *Vital Pastoral Duties*, below)

6-i Note Plans to Harmonize Spiritual Gifts

Note plans to harmonize gift-based ministries in love and in the power of the Holy Spirit, both within and between churches or home groups, so that most members have an effective ministry. Consult with your coworkers if possible.

_____

_____

_____

_____

_____

_____

_____

_____

_____

_____

_____

6-j Detect and Deal with Personal or Family Needs in Small Groups

Cell groups or house churches should take advantage of their small size to deal with personal and family needs and ministry opportunities as they arise (Ex. 18:24-26). Home groups enable elders to listen to everyone in their group to know their personal needs, pray for each one and help all to participate. They enable all members of the group to have a ministry of caring. We mobilize as group leaders only persons who will take the time to give loving care; sometimes they are men who are already quite busy.

Scoggins relates how house churches enable listening and caring:

> In our experience with house churches men who will take
> time to listen and care will come to the surface when given a
> chance to do so. Some will come of their own volition; many of
> these surprise us. with proper discipleship and care, many
> who are at first reluctant to lead make radical changes in their
> lives to become effective elders. Some require a challenge to
> consider if God has indeed called them to be a shepherd. We
> do this with great care and prayer, realizing that the call is
> from God. The individual weighs the cost and the call before
> the Lord, to determine if he is able and willing to follow. This
> response often begins in the home; we detect potential leaders
> by seeing how men shepherd their families. A call to shepherd
> normally shows itself first with one's own family.

6-k Keep the *Three Dimensions of Discipling* in Balance

Some teachers with an academic orientation to ministry focus only on
the content of their teaching, rather than the task and the people. We help
them correct this imbalance by working closely with others who apply the
teaching to the people's lives, families and ministries.

Think about how the Persons of the Trinity relate to each other; one
does not exist or work without the others. Similarly, the three primary
dimensions of discipling harmonize with each other to form what we call
balanced discipleship. These three dimensions correspond somewhat to
the roles of the three Persons of the Trinity. These roles are 1) *loving
father authority*, 2) the *Word made alive in our lives through Christ's
presence in us,* and 3) *Spirit-empowered ministry*. Let's examine these
three elements of discipling that we must keep in balance.

1) **Loving father authority** leads to proper **relationships** and our
   submission to proper authority. Love emanates from **God the
   Father**--"God *is* love." We receive His love and pass it on as we
   submit to His father authority.

2) **The eternal Word becomes incarnate in our lives** as we abide
   in Christ. **God the Son** is the eternal, living Word, the very image
   of the Invisible God. He transforms us to conform to the image of
   Christ. The *written* Word, the Bible, likewise takes on flesh as we
   apply it to our lives and ministry in the power of the Holy Spirit:

3) **Spirit-empowered ministry** focuses on the **task**. **God the Holy
   Spirit** empowers us for our work.

The three Persons of the Trinity are *One*, never separate, always
working in harmony. Likewise the three dimensions of balanced discipling
should always harmonize in perfect equilibrium. Building on **loving**

relationships, disciplers teach **the Word** for a **task empowered by the Holy Spirit**. Just as Jesus the eternal Word took on flesh to make the invisible God known to us, the written Word the Bible also takes on flesh as the Holy Spirit enables us to apply it in our lives and churches.

Discipling with this balance greatly enhances our pastoral ministry. Here are some areas in which many of us can improve the balance:

Some teachers emphasize the *Word* so exclusively that, unlike Paul, they pay little attention to a student's present pastoral work. They make little effort to adapt their teaching to the current needs of his flock and share no responsibility for his effectiveness in ministry. Their ministry is greatly enhanced when they listen to the students to know their needs, interests and ministry opportunities. It also helps to communicate with the churches in which their students work, to coordinate their teaching with the student's ministry.

Some churches emphasize *loving relationships* so exclusively that they neglect the Word and other pastoral work, becoming ingrown and sterile. Their ministry is easily improved by focusing on the tasks that the New Testament requires for a church, and cooperating closely with other churches whose gifts and ministries complement theirs.

Some mission agencies put unbalanced emphasis on the *task*. Their workers neglect their families, bruise one another in their drive to achieve and often burn out. Their ministries are strengthened significantly by making a prayerful effort at keeping the balance by developing relationships, teaching the Biblical basis for all they do and cooperating more closely with churches that provide strength in the areas they lack.

Blessed is the discipler who understands why discipling begins with baptism in the name of the *Father*, and of the *Son*, and of the *Holy Spirit*. Balanced discipling, starting with baptism, brings one into a proper relationship with each person of the Trinity. This lays the groundwork for the integration of the three essential dimensions. We do not simply *add* equal portions of all three. They *produce* one another.

Balanced **Discipling** begins with baptism in the name of each Person of the Trinity (Matthew 28:18-20) and our relationship with each.

Good *relationships based on loving authority* leads to powerful teaching of the Word and effective task-oriented ministry.

Teaching the Word kept in balance with the other dimensions of discipling mobilizes our disciples for the task and builds relationships based on loving submission to God's authority.

Task-oriented ministry empowered by the Holy Spirit leads both to good relationships and doing the Word.

Conscientious disciplers and mentors recognize the area in which they are weak and work closely with others who are strong in it, to keep the balance. No one, working alone, can keep this balance.

6-1   Plan to Implement Practical Love

Note plans for your people to serve one another and other churches or groups in love, strengthen loving family life, forgive and seek reconciliation with enemies, and do balanced discipling through loving relationships and normal church body life:

_____

_____

_____

_____

_____

_____

_____

_____

_____

_____

_____

_____

_____

_____

7.
Obeying Jesus' Command to
Break Bread

While they were eating, Jesus took bread, gave thanks and broke it, and gave it to his disciples, saying, "Take and eat; this is my body."

Then he took the cup, gave thanks and offered it to them, saying, "Drink from it, all of you. This is my blood of the covenant, which is poured out for many for the forgiveness of sins." Matthew 26:26-28

Hey, those believers are too new to break bread! They'll assume it's magic or something !

I'm more concerned that they obey Jesus than have perfect understanding at this time.

They don't need to be wise old owls to see that God's work isn't superstitious magic! You keep warning them against overemphasizing the mystery. Do you want them to take a purely rationalistic view that throws God out altogether? That's far worse !

Find the importance Jesus attached to our participation in His body and blood in John 6:51-63:

I am the living bread that came down from heaven. If anyone eats of this bread, he will live forever. This bread is my flesh, which I will give for the life of the world."

Then the Jews began to argue sharply among themselves, "How can this man give us his flesh to eat?"

Jesus said to them, "I tell you the truth, unless you eat the flesh of the Son of Man and drink his blood, you have no life in you. Whoever eats my flesh and drinks my blood has eternal life, and I will raise him up at the last day. For my flesh is real food and my blood is real drink. Whoever eats my flesh and drinks my blood remains in me, and I in him. Just as the living Father sent me and I live because of the Father, so the one who feeds on me will live because of me. This is the bread that came down from heaven. your forefathers ate manna and died, but he who feeds on this bread will live forever."

He said this while teaching in the synagogue in Capernaum. On hearing it, many of his disciples said, "This is a hard teaching. who can accept it?" Aware that his disciples were grumbling about this, Jesus said to them, "Does this offend you? What if you see the Son of Man ascend to where he was before! the Spirit gives life; the flesh counts for nothing. The words I have spoken to you are Spirit and they are life.

Is not the cup of thanksgiving for which we give thanks a participation in the blood of Christ? and is not the bread that we break a participation in the body of Christ? Because there is one loaf, we, who are many, are one body, for we all partake of the one loaf. 1 Corinthians 10:16-17

Find in Acts 2:41-46 *where* the converts in the first New Testament church broke bread:

They devoted themselves to the apostles' teaching and to the fellowship, to the breaking of bread and to prayer. Everyone was filled with awe, and many wonders and miraculous signs were done by the apostles. All the believers were together and had everything in common. Selling their possessions and goods, they gave to anyone as he had need. Every day they continued to meet together in the temple courts. They broke bread in their homes and ate together with glad and sincere hearts.

Find in 1 Corinthians 11:27-34 why God punished the Corinthians who failed to discern and respect the mystical presence of the body of Christ:

Therefore, whoever eats the bread or drinks the cup of the Lord in an unworthy manner will be guilty of sinning against the body and blood of the Lord. A man ought to examine himself before he eats of the bread and drinks of the cup. For anyone who eats and drinks without recognizing the body of the Lord eats and drinks judgment on himself. That is why many among you are weak and sick, and a number of you have fallen asleep. But if we judged ourselves, we would not come under judgment. When we are judged by the Lord, we are being disciplined so that we will not be condemned with the world.

Find in Acts 20:6-7 *how often* the new churches broke bread:

But we sailed from Philippi after the Feast of Unleavened Bread, and five days later joined the others at Troas, where we stayed seven days. On the first day of the week we came together to break bread. Paul spoke to the people and, because he intended to leave the next day, kept on talking until midnight.

7-a Glorify Jesus by Remembering His Sacrificial Death as He Said to Do

Regular, obedient celebration of the Lord's Supper helps keep a church body healthy and disciplined. In new fields where inexperienced workers lead tiny churches in homes, the regular celebration of the Lord's Supper brings seriousness and authenticity to the worship.

Scoggins discovered of the value of the Lord's Supper for new churches:

We found in Rhode Island that the celebration of the Lord's Table is very valuable for new churches. We encourage them to make the celebration meaningful. Too often we fall into ruts that obscure the meaning of the celebration. Often we celebrate it as part of an event of importance for the church community. Such an event is when new members are being "covenanted" into the church. Another is when we send members off to start a new congregation, or when two or more of our churches meet together. We may celebrate it during a Sunday meeting or at a midweek meeting when we do not expect many unbelieving visitors.

We often have the Lord's Table around a fellowship meal. Sometimes we do it at the beginning of the meal, other times at the end. Still other times we have the bread at the beginning and the cup at the end, symbolizing our communion with the Lord throughout the meal.

The church may authorize any man who is a covenanted member to officiate the Lord's Table. Obviously, if the man has had no previous experience, he will review the procedure first with someone more experienced. We consciously avoid a single pattern, preferring a "menu" approach; the one who leads the ceremony prayerfully considers suitable *options* for activities that make the experience more meaningful.

Patterson also struggled to enable new churches to benefit from the Lord's Supper:

At first, our new churches in Honduras seldom celebrated the Lord's Supper—only when a missionary or ordained pastor was present. They missed God's fullest blessing because they had to disregard Jesus' command to break bread. Conscious of this shortcoming, they did not take their church and its worship very seriously; they felt that they were second rate. So we adapted ordination requirements to the culture, authorizing elders in our pastoral training program to officiate the Lord's Supper, under the authority of experienced pastors. We asked only that they meet *biblical* requirements for a pastor, nothing more.

Some of the leaders of our national association rushed to our area for an emergency session. They voted not to recognize the lay pastor's licenses that we gave to biblically qualified elders. They prohibited these men to serve the Lord's Supper. One lay pastor stood to defend his pastoral role but tears filled his eyes; he could not speak. He took his lay pastor's license from his pocket, tore it up and threw it on the floor, then walked out of the meeting, crushed.

I determined that it would never happen again. We met again with our workers and affirmed in prayer that we would obey Jesus and break bread in spite of the ruling of our national association of churches. Our churches continued to obey Jesus' command to "do this in remembrance of me." Some used a free and spontaneous style; others kept parts of the classic liturgy. But all took it seriously. I rejoiced to see them discover profound communion with God and the presence of Christ in the Eucharist.

7-b Avoid a Purely Rationalistic View of Communion

Some Evangelicals, in their zeal to avoid any association with the Roman Catholic dogma of transubstantiation (that the bread and wine become the literal physical body and blood of Christ) disallow any supernatural work. They leave God out entirely; they permit no mystery of any kind.

The mystery is the invisible work of the Holy Spirit. The miracle is His transforming work in *us*, the church *Body* (there is no benefit in transforming inert pieces of bread!). He strengthens our unity with Christ and his Body as we partake worthily of the consecrated bread and wine. Out of respect for Christ's body we examine ourselves as Paul directed, and confess our sins.

Some churches in new fields neglect the Eucharist. For whatever reason the missionaries fear to let new Christians obey Jesus by "breaking bread." Contrary to Scripture they start a 'preaching point' and provide a long time of doctrinal preparation before converts are allowed to obey Jesus. This fear--whether we fear too much sacramental emphasis or too little--breeds human rules, limitations and rationalistic definitions that weaken the celebration. Other churches fail to obey Christ because they lack clergy approved to lead the ceremony. Others with roots in rationalistic cultures neglect it because, having denied any supernatural work by the Holy Spirit in the Eucharist, they see little value in it, and fear that their people will take the medieval magical view still held by traditional Catholics.

Satan uses these fears of both extremes. Some Evangelicals defend the mystical view of the real presence of Christ; they will say without hesitation, "This *is* the body of Christ." Others defend the rationalistic view that the Eucharist is only a symbol serving as a visual aid to memory and nothing more. They are more comfortable saying, "This *represents* the body of Christ."

Some missionaries, fearing they will offend somebody, simply avoid the sacrament!

Fear is contagious. Can we trust the Holy Spirit to illuminate the minds of our people as they prayerfully examine what God says about the Eucharist in John 6:26-69; 1 Corinthians 10:16-17, 16-17; 11:23-34? or must we give them reactionary formulas that often appeal to philosophical explanations of symbol and sacrament, rather than to these inspired passages?

7-c Let God Work Powerfully in the Eucharist

We learn to keep still and let the consecrated bread and wine speak for themselves through the power of the Holy Spirit. Let's not turn this most sacred ceremony into merely another teaching time! if we seldom see tears of repentance or joy, we are not letting God make his intended impact. Jesus ordained it for us to remember His sacrifice and our oneness with Him, and to encounter his presence in a stirring, edifying way. He enables us through our physical senses to recall our sins and his blood that was shed to forgive them.

Patterson found that he had to escape from prejudices against "liturgy:"

I winced when a poorly educated village pastor handed a rather large, full glass to each person for Communion, with a whole tortilla, without the usual admonitions and explanations. "I'll have to straighten him out," I thought. The people slowly took small bites of the tortilla and sips from the glass. They lingered, holding the glass as though it contained priceless diamonds, eyes closed in meditation. I squirmed, fearing that it would take forever. These poor, illiterate *peasants!* Then I noticed the tears. I had never seen such a united, contrite spirit around the Lord's Table! Everyone was in rapt communion with Christ--except me. What had I missed?

I returned home humbled and prayed as I looked again at what the apostles taught. Like many whose churches avoid the word "sacrament," I felt uneasy when someone expressed anything mystical; I feared that superstition would distort the ceremony instituted by Christ. But wait! with my rationalistic background, was not the greater danger to *resist* the supernatural element?

I compared churches in Honduras that enjoyed the mystery of the Eucharist with those that neglected it or resisted anything supernatural. Our churches were definitely healthier when they celebrated its drama and embraced its mystery. I recalled some friends in America that had left churches that avoided any sort of historical liturgy for churches that, as they said, allowed God to work in us as we broke bread.

Having heard many warnings of excessive mysticism in the Eucharist, I read again the apostles' warning in 1 Corinthians 11. Oh, oh. He warns against *failing* to recognize the mystery! Had I *over-reacted* against one extreme to err in the other? Was I basing my theology on fear rather than the Word of God? Was I keeping my students from "discerning the body" as 1 Corinthians 11:29-32 requires? Do we celebrate the 'real presence' of the King, or his real absence?

I wondered, "Discern *which* body?" The church body? The bread that, when eaten, is a participation in Christ's body? They physical body of Jesus that hung on the cross? What's the connection? Can bread be His body?

Wrong questions, all of them! Let God worry about how it all works. Define the mystery in human terms and you kill it.

I read what Paul wrote, "And is not the bread that we break a participation in the body of Christ? Because there is one loaf, we, who are many, are one body, for we all partake of the one loaf" (1 Cor. 10:16-17). There it was again--the inescapable mystery. I had taught with no qualms about God's supernatural work in uniting a couple in marriage as one flesh and its mysterious connection with the union between Christ and his church (Eph. 5:25-32). But I had failed to see--feared to see--that Christ and his apostles taught the same mystical union with the body of Christ in the Eucharist!

I turned to my church history books. Until the last two centuries, virtually all churches held the Eucharist to be the core of their worship, whether Protestant, Catholic, or Orthodox. Long after the Protestant Reformation even non-liturgical churches kept the table for the Lord's Supper, or a kneeling rail to serve it, in the central position in the front of the sanctuary; the pulpit was off to one side. During the last two centuries, however, with the rise in education and the growing need to correct false doctrine, many churches gave the central position to the pulpit. The altar shifted to a lower position, with flowers on it three out of four Sundays. Now contemporary churches use no pulpit at all; the worship team is the center of focus during the praise time.

I learned to teach new leaders what the Bible says about the Eucharist without prejudicing them with my inherited fears. They acquire a balanced view free of fear and either crippling extreme.

Scoggins adds:

> I also observed stronger discipline in churches that emphasized regular Communion. Their exclusion of unruly members from Communion was a powerful aid to restoration. Other churches, however, disciplined with an Old Testament mentality of legalistic enforcement of rules. They failed to discipline altogether except for gross sexual immorality.
>
> After much reflection I encouraged our churches to follow the apostles' model for the Lord's Supper as they found it in Scripture, avoiding human biases one way or the other. No church got carried away or lapsed into the superstition of transubstantiation, as some critics had predicted. It was a blessing, as when an ailing body finds a vitamin it had been missing.
>
> How often should a church celebrate the Lord's Supper? Liturgical churches normally celebrate it the first day of the week, as mentioned in Acts 20:7. Many Evangelical churches, fearing that Communion might become mechanical, celebrate it only once a month. Weekly celebration was typical of Catholic, Orthodox and virtually all Protestant churches for at least three centuries after the Reformation. Evangelical churches in pioneer fields without experienced preachers and worship leaders would do well to celebrate it weekly to assure that the people experience serious, edifying worship and encounter God as a body.

7-d Practice All Vital Elements of Worship

A new church in a pioneer field must set apart a definite, regular time for serious worship, especially if it meets in a home with only a handful of members. Patterson discovered the importance of countering the informality of a private home:

> When meeting in a home that lacked the worship atmosphere of a chapel, we needed to do something to convert a private room into a temporary sanctuary. It helped to have a definite beginning and end for the worship. Often we started with a call to worship during which we stood while someone invoked the Lord's presence and blessing. Sometimes we stood in a circle while the hostess brought the bread and wine of the Lord's Supper and placed them in the center. It helps to arrange the chairs in a circle. Sometimes we started in a home with only three or four converts for several weeks before inviting the public, to make sure that the new leader could direct things with confidence first. On occasion

only one or two converts and I were present when a church in embryo first met to celebrate the Lord's Supper.

Missionaries to new fields must understand *small group worship*. For this they need to discern the **Essential Elements of Group Worship**:

Prayer

Praise

Teaching the Word of God

Confession of sins and assurance of forgiveness

Communion (Lord's Supper)

Giving

Fellowship

House churches or serious cells might add another guideline, although it's not found in Scripture: to have a **definite beginning and end** for the worship time. Let the people know the moment when the living room in a private home becomes a sacred and public sanctuary, and also when it becomes an ordinary, private room again.

These elements of worship take on different external forms. Praise, for example, may be sung, read from Psalms or a liturgical manual, chanted, prayed, dramatized, shouted or meditated in silence, standing or lying on one's face. God doesn't care *how* we do it as long as it comes from the heart.

These acts of worship also may be combined. For example, we might combine three of them by reading the *Word* as a *prayer* to *praise* the Lord. Some Psalms lend themselves beautifully for this.

7-e Celebrate Sacred Seasons and Holidays

Liturgical churches follow a church calendar that provides for a variety of teaching, celebration and use of symbols. Non-liturgical churches sometimes rob their children of a great blessing and powerful teaching tool by neglecting the sacred seasons. Often adults also receive Christ more readily or make serious commitments during Advent and Christmas or Lent and Easter. Other national holidays may also offer an occasion for special celebrations. We should keep an eye on the church year with its seasons, as well as national holidays, for special emphases.

Both the Old and New Testaments affirm seasonal celebrations. In an effort to avoid over-emphasizing saints' days we must not over-react by emptying our faith unnecessarily of valuable seasonal celebrations.

Some *separatist* churches prefer to avoid happy celebrations. They hold expressions of joy in suspicion. Most people are repulsed by such unnatural asceticism. Our Lord took the Jewish festivals seriously and enjoyed happy celebrations. The legalists sneered at Him for being a partygoer and for drinking wine. Mature faith has reverent and sober moments, but there is also a time for joyful celebration on earth as in heaven.

Scoggins learned how to celebrate:

We try to mark special occasions with feasts. These include when a new church begins and when a new member is covenanted in (he or she is the guest of honor, of course). Weddings and anniversaries of key dates in the life of the churches or their members also offer occasions for feasting and celebration.

7-f Note Plans for Worship

Note your plans for meaningful worship, including the Lord's Supper in new, small churches or cell groups. Plan with your coworkers if possible.

_____

_____

_____

_____

_____

_____

_____

_____

_____

_____

_____

_____

_____

_____

8.
Obeying Jesus' Command to
Pray

Prayer has great psychological benefits.

It lets you soar.
A spiritual high !

Is that the only reason you pray ?

To get high ?

You clip your spiritual wings !

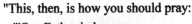

"This, then, is how you should pray:
"'Our Father in heaven,
hallowed be your name,
your kingdom come,
your will be done on earth as it is in heaven.
Give us today our daily bread.
Forgive us our debts,
as we also have forgiven our debtors.
And lead us not into temptation,
but deliver us from the evil one.'" Matthew 6:9-13

"So I say to you: Ask and it will be given to you; seek and you will find; knock and the door will be opened to you." Luke 11:9

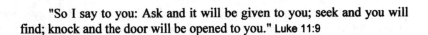

Genesis 18:16-33 recounts what Abraham did to move God to save his relatives. His prayer of intercession was much like an argument. He asked God if he would spare the city of Sodom if there were 50 righteous people in it.

...The LORD said, "If I find fifty righteous people in the city of Sodom, I will spare the whole place for their sake."

Then Abraham spoke up again: "Now that I have been so bold as to speak to the Lord, though I am nothing but dust and ashes, what if the number of the righteous is five less than fifty? Will you destroy the whole city because of five people?" "

If I find forty-five there," he said, "I will not destroy it."

Once again he spoke to him, "What if only forty are found there?"

He said, "For the sake of forty, I will not do it."

Then he said, "May the Lord not be angry, but let me speak. What if only thirty can be found there?"

He answered, "I will not do it if I find thirty there."

Abraham said, "Now that I have been so bold as to speak to the Lord, what if only twenty can be found there?"

He said, "For the sake of twenty, I will not destroy it."

Then he said, "May the Lord not be angry, but let me speak just once more. What if only ten can be found there?"

He answered, "For the sake of ten, I will not destroy it."

Find in Matthew 26:36-46 our greatest example of submission to God:

Then Jesus went with his disciples to a place called Gethsemane, and he said to them, "Sit here while I go over there and pray."

He took Peter and the two sons of Zebedee along with him, and he began to be sorrowful and troubled. Then he said to them, "My soul is overwhelmed with sorrow to the point of death. Stay here and keep watch with me."

Going a little farther, he fell with his face to the ground and prayed, "My Father, if it is possible, may this cup be taken from me. Yet not as I will, but as you will."

Then he returned to his disciples and found them sleeping. "Could you men not keep watch with me for one hour?" he asked Peter. "Watch and pray so that you will not fall into temptation. The spirit is willing, but the body is weak."

He went away a second time and prayed, "My Father, if it is not possible for this cup to be taken away unless I drink it, may your will be done."

When he came back, he again found them sleeping, because their eyes were heavy. So he left them and went away once more and prayed the third time, saying the same thing.

Then he returned to the disciples and said to them, "Are you still sleeping and resting? Look, the hour is near, and the Son of Man is betrayed into the hands of sinners. Rise, let us go! Here comes my betrayer!"

A strengthening, life-giving discipline stems from Jesus' command to pray (John 16:24); we develop regular prayer by the church as a body and daily personal and family prayer.

Scoggins waged spiritual warfare as churches began to multiply:

Our experience shows that prayer partnerships that last from several months to years are powerful to overcome Satan's strongholds. Second Corinthians 10:4 reveals that the weapons of our warfare are divinely powerful for pulling down evil strongholds. These include strongholds in people's lives that cripple them spiritually and keep them from loving one another. The newest believer needs to be trained to use the powerful weapon of intercessory prayer. Older believers need to keep this weapon honed for battle by praying continually for others. Prayers of intercession, praise, repentance, healing, and petition sustain the health of our churches. We wield this weapon of prayer both in public worship and in the quietness of two or three gathered together.

I remember how, in the early days of my walk with God, I met weekly for prayer with two other men. We met one evening

along than I was, and I learned much about prayer from them. We would confess our struggles and our sins to one another, then have lengthy sessions of prayer. When we began new ministries, we bathed them in much prayer. We covenanted to pray for each other every day of the week. We met this way for over two years. It was probably the most significant thing that brought me out of my hermit's shell. I learned to pray for others as well as to be vulnerable, asking others to pray for my weaknesses.

8-a   Seek the Holy Spirit's Ongoing Renewal

God multiplies churches in what men call "people movements," "revivals," "restorations," or "outpourings of the Holy Spirit" when His people pray and let Him *renew us day by day. The* renewal that 2 Corinthians 4:16 promises is not a *temporary experience* but a *daily refreshing*. When the Holy Spirit is working powerfully in a church, He enables its members to do their different gift-based ministries. Humans often try to center renewal around one or two spirituals gift--usually healing, evangelism, prophecy, tongues or teaching. In true renewal, however, the Holy Spirit integrates many gifts in loving harmony in the body.

The Holy Spirit renews apostate, stagnant or sterile churches (that fail to reproduce) when they pray and repent, and glorify Jesus by simply *doing what He says*. We limit this renewal, however, by applying it only to one area of the Christian life or ministry. True freedom in the Holy Spirit releases people to use *all* the gifts that He has given to a church body. He leads a church to separate those with the *apostolic* ('sent one') gift to multiply the church, as in Acts 13:1-3. Those with other gift-based ministries also cooperate to prepare and send them. We do this out of love for Jesus and each other, not out of guilt, ambition, or a desire to achieve goals as we chase our own vision.

Unfortunately, many with the apostolic gift must go outside of their church body to find appreciation for their calling, to prepare, and learn church multiplication. This fractures the body of Christ. Teachers and leaders in such fractured bodies seldom use their gifts to mobilize those with the missionary gift. Their churches fail to reproduce consciously and purposefully as a body through their gifted apostles. We must pray for God's power to keep reproducing as a church.

Church planting task groups in areas where Satan has held total control over the people's minds for centuries, need people with the gifts of faith and healing, who encourage others also to pray.

Patterson found the place of prayer in his early Honduran ministry:

> **Like many new missionaries, I wanted the church growth and multiplication to be seen as the result of *my* ministry. God, however, had a different idea. It would be the result of *His* work. So He let me fail. And fail. I wanted control and recognition. God gave me failures. I finally prayed—and meant it—"Lord, I'm tired of failing. I don't care any more about my own ministry. Just let me help my pastoral trainees to have a good ministry."**
>
> **He answered that prayer. When my pastoral students saw that I was no longer using them to build my own empire but tried to help them have an effective ministry, they took my training seriously. I discovered a power and influence that I had lacked before; I found it only when I did not seek it.**
>
> **Problems still came. I recalled with bittersweet relief how Paul associated the pains of starting new churches with those of childbirth. Many times I prayed for God's help to escape from the worries caused by new churches. I had to keep giving the new churches back to God. I was a slow learner when it came to seeing how church growth and reproduction came not from our strategies for reproduction, our discipling, our**

teaching, or other efforts of ours. God waited for us to ask Him for it! Paul planted, Apollos watered, but God gave the growth. He does not bless methods, only loving obedience supported by prayer.

8-b Practice Personal and Family Prayers and Intercession

The prayers of Jesus and His apostles always had purpose. We are to pray without ceasing; we teach our people to do the same (1 Thess. 5:17). New believers should see family devotions modeled. We may need to name someone in a church or small group to show new believers and families how to have personal and family devotions.

8-c Pray Constantly for the Lost and for Spiritual Growth and Reproduction

The all-powerful God limits what He does on earth to our faith and our requests. If we want sinners to be converted, we ask Him to transform them. We should pray with our coworkers and students for the church to use its God-given power to reach the lost and reproduce.

Jesus illustrated this potential for spontaneous growth and reproduction in his parables about sowing, the mysterious spontaneous growth, and the mustard seed in Mark 4. To disciple a large population or people group, we sow and cultivate the gospel seed so that churches, like plants, reproduce spontaneously in daughter and granddaughter churches.

Look at a grain of corn or rice; consider its miracle. We cannot make it grow; we can only cultivate it, water it, and protect it so that it germinates and reaches its God-given potential. Calculate what will happen if we sow a single grain of rice, corn or wheat in "good soil" and it reproduces to its potential as Christ said, up to a hundred times. Then we sow these 100 seeds for the next harvest, multiplying the amount by 100 and so forth for several harvests. In a very few years we could feed the entire human race with the grain reproduced from that one first seed! Jesus assured us that this is the way His church would grow and reproduce.

Like all living things that God has created, an obedient church has within itself its seed to reproduce after its own kind. Rice reproduces rice; birds reproduce birds; churches reproduce churches. A healthy church is a vigorous, reproducing organism. It is Christ's living body on earth. by faith we tap a church's God-given power to reproduce in daughter and granddaughter churches.

We help our people to trust in God's power given to the church, to reproduce, to be a "mother church" and send workers who carry the seed to plant daughter churches.

Abraham, our model for saving faith, believed God's promise that his descendants would be as numerous as the stars (Gen. 15:6; Gal. 3:6). We join our faith to his, believing in the miraculous reproduction of God's people.

8-d   Plan Prayerfully for Reproduction

Church reproduction is *supernatural*, so prayer is always part of it; God enables churches to multiply in response to our requests. by faith we plan with our coworkers to let our churches and cell groups multiply. A pastor who trains newer pastors or elders within his congregation taps God's power to reproduce by releasing them to start and pastor new churches. In a pioneer field the first tiny congregation will grow and reproduce if the people learn from the missionaries loving, prayerful, faithful obedience. Plan for it! Pray for it! Practice it!

Forces beyond our control can limit church growth and reproduction. Factors that determine a church's potential to multiply include:

God's election,

> **people's responsiveness,**
> > **population trends,**
> > > **materialism,**
> > > > **laws,**
> > > > > **persecution,**
> > > > > **mission policies,**
> > > > > > **gifting,**
> > > > > > **health,**
> > > > > > > **family responsibilities,**
> > > > > > > **weather,**
> > > > > > > > **wars,**
> > > > > > > > > **difficulty in traveling**

plus many others.

Most of these factors lie outside of our control. That's why we must pray. God enables us to deal with forces we cannot control. Without prayer we struggle futilely against them. God sometimes answers our prayer when we are willing to change our approach. If a new congregation prays for help because it has outgrown the home it meets in and cannot afford to rent or construct a building, they must be willing to let God answer in His way; he may, for example, simply help them multiply tiny house churches or cell groups.

Growth is easier when seekers can join very *small* groups. Effective church planters in pioneer fields pray for God to multiply small nuclei-- churches in embryo.

"Good soil" for starting and multiplying churches is *bad people*. Romans 5.20 reveals, "Where sin abounds, grace does much more abound". Missionaries often justify a poor response by claiming that the people are *hard,* so the soil is *poor*. In reality they usually need simply to be more flexible. We pray for wisdom to see how to multiply the kind of small nuclei around which normal growth can easily take place.

Does this multiplication seem like an impossible leap for you? Good! Then you know you must pray and ask your people to pray, so that God will reproduce the new churches or home groups. Some churches need to cooperate with other churches in order to multiply. This, too, needs prayer.

Multiplying churches is almost synonymous with multiplying leaders. This means praying for workers and preparing those that God sends in response to our prayers. Jesus said in Matthew 9:37-38, "The harvest is plentiful, but the workers are few. Ask the Lord of the harvest, therefore, to send out workers into his harvest field." This is our prayer.

8-e Note Plans for Productive Prayer

Note your plans for effective prayer, and for enabling a mother church to use God's power to multiply daughter churches. Do this with your coworkers if possible.

_____

_____

_____

_____

_____

_____

_____

_____

_____

_____

9.

Obeying Jesus' Command to
GIVE

"Give, and it will be given to you. A good measure, pressed down, shaken together and running over, will be poured into your lap. For with the measure you use, it will be measured to you." Luke 6:38

Find in 1 Corinthians 9:3-15 an important *purpose* for giving:

This is my defense to those who sit in judgment on me. Don't we have the right to food and drink? Don't we have the right to take a believing wife along with us, as do the other apostles and the Lord's brothers and Cephas? or is it only I and Barnabas who must work for a living? who serves as a soldier at his own expense? who plants a vineyard and does not eat of its grapes? who tends a flock and does not drink of the milk? Do I say this merely from a human point of view? Doesn't the Law say the same thing? for it is written in the Law of Moses: "Do not muzzle an ox while it is treading out the grain." Is it about oxen that God is concerned? Surely he says this for us, doesn't he? Yes, this was written for us, because when the plowman plows and the thresher threshes, they ought to do so in the hope of sharing in the harvest. If we have sown spiritual seed among you, is it too much if we reap a material harvest from you? if others have this right of support from you, shouldn't we have it all the more? But we did not use this right. On the contrary, we put up with anything rather than hinder the gospel of Christ. Don't you know that those who work in the temple get their food from the temple, and those who serve at the altar share in what is offered on the altar? in the same way, the Lord has commanded that those who preach the gospel should receive their living from the gospel. But I have not used any of these rights. And I am not writing this in the hope that you will do such things for me. I would rather die than have anyone deprive me of this boast.

Find in 2 Corinthians 8:1 -5 what God expects the *poor* to give:

And now, brothers, we want you to know about the grace that God has given the Macedonian churches. Out of the most severe trial, their overflowing joy and their extreme poverty welled up in rich generosity. For I testify that they gave as much as they were able, and even beyond their ability. Entirely on their own, they urgently pleaded with us for the privilege of sharing in this service to the saints. And they did not do as we expected, but they gave themselves first to the Lord and then to us in keeping with God's will.

Find in Corinthians 9:5-12 guidelines to determine the *amount* to give:

So I thought it necessary to urge the brothers to visit you in advance and finish the arrangements for the generous gift you had promised. Then it will be ready as a generous gift, not as one grudgingly given. Remember this: Whoever sows sparingly will also reap sparingly, and whoever sows generously will also reap generously. Each man should give what he has decided in his heart to give, not reluctantly or under compulsion, for God loves a cheerful giver. And God is able to make all grace abound to you, so that in all things at all times, having all that you need, you will abound in every good work. As it is written: "He has scattered abroad his gifts to the poor; his righteousness endures forever." Now he who supplies seed to the sower and bread for food will also supply and increase your store of seed and will enlarge the harvest of your righteousness. You will be made rich in every way so that you can be generous on every occasion, and through us your generosity will result in thanksgiving to God. This service that you perform is not only supplying the needs of God's people but is also overflowing in many expressions of thanks to God.

Find in 2 Thessalonians 3:5-10 Paul's reason to serve *without* pay:

In the name of the Lord Jesus Christ, we command you, brothers, to keep away from every brother who is idle and does not live according to the teaching you received from us. For you yourselves know how you ought to follow our example. We were not idle when we were with you, nor did we eat anyone's food without paying for it. On the contrary, we worked night and day, laboring and toiling so that we would not be a burden to any of you. We did this, not because we do not have the right to such help, but in order to make ourselves a model for you to follow. For even when we were with you, we gave you this rule: "If a man will not work, he shall not eat."

The first converts in Jerusalem started giving generously from the very beginning, as Jesus commanded (Acts 2:45). This did not just happen. Like believers today, they needed instruction. The apostles taught them to give. The ministry of *stewardship* grows out of Jesus' command to his disciples to give generously.

Scoggins learned how to introduce Christian stewardship in new churches:

We constantly challenge new believers who have worshiped at the altar of materialism to repent and consider that God may have a lower view of money than they do. We see men change their highest priority from making money to making disciples. The result is usually a *decline* in their standard of living (and therefore their giving to the church).

We point out to them some basic principles; Galatians 5:13, for example, defines the Spirit-filled walk as an enslavement to one another motivated by love. New believers need to be taught that they have been saved to serve; the norm is for them to look for ways to give rather than receive (2 Cor. 9:7). Indeed, the norm in the early church was to give what one had (Acts 2:42-47; 4:32-37).

Giving can be of time, effort or money. In the West we tend to define giving only in terms of money. To extend God's kingdom this may be the least important thing we give. Ephesians 4:11-16 emphasizes giving one's self (see also 2 Cor. 8:5).

We also point out that the Lord dealt severely with those who gave for selfish motives (Acts 5:1-11). If giving wrongly was dealt with so severely, how much more will the Lord judge those who infiltrate the church with selfish motives, looking to

receive rather than give? Church discipline is necessary in such cases, in order to protect the spirit of generosity (2 Thess. 3:6-15). This is another reason why it is important to define clearly who are the members of the church and what is expected of them (one purpose of covenanting when one joins the church).

9-a Escape Poverty by Practicing Stewardship

Patterson struggled with Christian stewardship among the very poor:

Like most American missionaries, I started out being way too generous with the dollars. Even though the amounts were small, it brought about misery and resentment within the ranks of our closest workers. We did not pay pastors but we subsidized extension teachers (mentors) and other projects with funds from America. One of our most skilled workers came to demand help not for him but for very poor village pastors that he was training by extension. His demands became too forceful and he gave the churches the idea that they could get money from us, weakening their stewardship.

A showdown came when he demanded money for a pastor to help him train others in our extension program. I refused. He became furious, pointed at me and shouted, "If those new churches fall, it will be your fault! I know you can get the money from the churches in the States. It will be your fault before God!"

I had to do something before his attitude spread to other workers. Being poor did not excuse them from obeying God's command to give. We had seen over the years that those who gave sacrificially in love in spite of their painful poverty, escaped from it. But those who gave little because of their poverty remained in it. I replied, "If the churches' life depends on American money and not the Holy Spirit, then let them fall! the sooner the better! if our work is built on American dollars, then we are deceiving ourselves." Soon after, the worker abandoned his very effective ministry to seek more lucrative employment.

It became evident in painfully poor areas that those who gave sacrificially in their poverty after a few years were able to buy shoes for their children, educate them and live healthily, although not in luxury as God did not want to corrupt them. But others who did not give to God's work because of their poverty remained in it. On the other hand in time even the poorest believers who gave sacrificially or tithed met their basic financial needs and escaped from their extreme poverty.

> **We helped these churches develop a realistic budget and emphasized that the treasurer could pay out *only* what was authorized in the budget.**

We rob the poor of a blessing if we do not encourage them to give what they can. If they lack money they can give products of the field or labor.

9-b To Avoid Dependency and Resentment, Fund Work in Poverty Areas with Extreme Care

Nothing stifles the reproduction of churches in another culture worse than outside funding. It carries a subtle form of control. Persons who receive it feel morally obligated to do what the outsiders who furnish the funds want them to do. Paying a pastor with *inside* funds can also stifle church multiplication, if he is not a good steward. Such paid pastors often discourage starting new churches nearby, even in affluent societies. Patterson recalls:

> **Seeing the stifling effect of foreign funding, a perceptive Honduran pastor warned me about helping too much with building programs or workers' expenses, "A demon rides in on every dollar that comes from the United States!"**

> **Subsidizing new churches in any way from the outside in a culture can stifle giving by the local people. If the pastors are poor, they will soon want more. Satan whispers to them, "Why plant more churches? You do not receive enough help now as it is." Church multiplication has dwindled and become almost paralyzed in poorer countries precisely where Americans and Europeans have been most generous with outside funds.**

> **Working as a "tentmaker" as well as "full-time" *both* have the blessing of Scripture in Acts 18:1-5. We must discern where both apply. For church reproduction among very poor people, we use non-funded, *low budget* or *no budget* approaches--do what local participants can provide. Let pastors start out being bivocational. Let poor churches name several unpaid elders as co-pastors who share shepherding responsibilities. Avoid institutional programs for churches and pastoral training. Steer clear of budget-oriented planning, high administration costs, dependency on buildings and paid staff. Encourage volunteers.**

Scoggins advises church planting teams in a poor North African field:

> **Poverty in third world fields creates painful tension for Western missionaries much greater income than local believers have. If they begin sharing it with the church, where will it end? The church becomes dependent on missionary money and attracts "rice Christians." They come not to give**

but to receive, thus undermining the cross-bearing discipleship mentality of the church.

We found a similar problem in the United States. Since we start house churches with unsaved people, normally with two or three families, it usually takes some time for the wallets to get sanctified. If the church planters give to the infant church at that time, it gets a false sense of the financial resources available to it, and the church becomes dependent on outsiders. We encourage the missionary always to take a long-range view of what is best for the church.

Missionaries working in the third world often feel guilt for having so much in comparison with their brothers in Christ. Certainly some may be moved by the Spirit to identify more closely with their target group by forsaking a higher standard of living. We have found it better with house churches not to support the elders financially. We encourage the support, however, of itinerant workers who serve with a network of house churches. This requires faith on the part of the worker and does not strap any one church.

Giving for God's work is an act of worship. To avoid the awkward situation of asking believers to give when visitors are present, some churches provide an offering box, usually placed by the door.

9-c Note Plans to Develop Stewardship

Please note plans for the churches to practice Christian stewardship. Plan this with your coworkers if possible:

_____

_____

_____

_____

_____

_____

_____

_____

_____

_____

_____

_____

Part II
Church Reproduction from Various Viewpoints

10.
Church Reproduction from the Viewpoint of the
Seeker (Pre-Christian)

Let us consider it first from the viewpoint of one who has the most to gain. or lose--the *Seeker* or Pre-Christian.

Soteriologically speaking your reprobationary position is of adamic derivation. In the Greek that's αμαρτια ...

?? ? ?

I wish he'd shut his preachy beak /

We don't understand a peep of what he's chirping about. Let us take our baby chick's steps first!

Find in John 4:25-42 a clue as to the type of people that are most likely to respond to the gospel:

The (Samaritan) woman said, "I know that Messiah is coming. When He comes, He will explain everything to us."

Then Jesus declared, "I who speak to you am He."

Just then his disciples returned and were surprised to find Him talking with a woman. But no one asked, "What do you want?" or "Why are you talking with her?"

Then, leaving her water jar, the woman went back to the town and said to the people, "Come, see a man who told me everything I ever did. Could this be the Messiah?"

They came out of the town and made their way toward Him. Meanwhile his disciples urged Him, "Rabbi, eat something."

But He said to them, "I have food to eat that you know nothing about."

Then his disciples said to each other, "Could someone have brought Him food?"

"My food," said Jesus, "is to do the will of Him who sent me and to finish his work. Do you not say, `Four months more and then the harvest'? I tell you, open your eyes and look at the fields! They are ripe for harvest..."

Many of the Samaritans from that town believed in Him because of the woman's testimony, "He told me everything I ever did." So when the Samaritans came to Him, they urged Him to stay with them, and He stayed two days. And because of his words many more became believers. They said to the woman, "We no longer believe just because of what you said; now we have heard for ourselves, and we know that this man really is the Savior of the world."

The religious Jews despised the Samaritans who had less economic and political power. But Jesus found them, like the poor people in Galilee, to be more responsive than the rich and powerful of Jerusalem.

Find in Luke 10:3-7 a clue as to the type of person to seek first when we penetrate a new community:

Go! I am sending you out like lambs among wolves. Do not take a purse or bag or sandals; and do not greet anyone on the road. When you enter a house, first say, `Peace to this house.' if a man of peace is there, your peace will rest on him; if not, it will return to you. Stay in that house, eating and drinking whatever they give you, for the worker deserves his wages. Do not move around from house to house.

Let us look at church reproduction from the viewpoint of the person who has the most to gain--or lose--from it: the *seeker*.

From the outset, a movement for Christ among a neglected people needs evangelism that is culturally relevant. A good missionary is sensitive to anything that needlessly offends the people, in the way we worship or witness. Patterson learned this by observation:

> We found it hard to get Honduran men, especially heads of households, to attend church, let alone receive Christ. The macho peasant men would come and observe the worship through a window. This showed a hunger for spiritual things. But seeing only women and children, they would shrug their shoulders and walk away. How could we get these mature heads of families excited about the gospel? How could we get them to talk about it to each other and their families? We met to discuss it. The Hondurans furnished the answer.

> What we had to do brought criticism from the old guard. We asked our wives and other women not to take highly visible positions of leadership. Immediately the men started attending services.

> This made us face another problem; most of the men could not read well and were unaccustomed to dealing with abstract truth. So we circulated doctrinal studies in the form of comic books which the men found easier to read. This brought renewed complaints. We switched to a more readable, modern version of the Bible. More complaints!

> Dealing with the men enabled us to take the most important step of all—to aim at *families*. We began with heads of households, as Peter did with Cornelius, and Paul with the Philippian jailer (Acts 10 and 16). Even before the men knew Christ, we asked them to repeat the Bible stories we had told them, to their families and friends. If we related stories in their peasant style, they did not hesitate to repeat them. Soon our churches had more men than women, something new for Honduras.

10-a Plan for a Movement of the People

Good gossip. Churches reproduce spontaneously when we develop a *popular* interest in the gospel of Jesus Christ. by 'popular' we do not mean that the people necessarily like it, but that it is *of the people*. They are interested in it, talk about it and even argue. The common people (not just religious types and clergy) are concerned about the good news of salvation in Jesus Christ. Some may reject it but they are nevertheless concerned.

The fact that Jesus is knocking at our door becomes confidential news and travels along the same lines as *gossip*, between family members and close friends. One way to popularize the gospel in this sense is to use creative, artistic methods of communication among pre-Christians. Find Christians who are artists, story tellers, writers, jokesters, dramatists, poets, interpretive dancers, painters or journalists who can put the good news into a medium that will flow among the people.

Patterson recalls,

When we put biblical doctrine into simple, affordable comic books, it reached the *people*. That does not work for every culture and no longer is as useful in our Honduran field as it once was; but for the initial penetration of the gospel, it got us past our first barriers, to the *people*.

10-b   Do Incarnational Evangelism that Identifies with the People and Culture

Incarnational evangelism imitates Jesus in His incarnation. He emptied Himself of His divine glory and power to become a man, see things from our viewpoint, identify with a culture (Jewish) and draw near to "tax collectors and sinners." Similarly, we empty ourselves of our own cultural prejudice and draw near to those of other cultures. We work within existing webs of relationships, within families and the circle of friends of a convert or seeker.

God does not see a seeker or a convert as an *isolated individual*. He sees him as part of a wider circle of friends and relatives. Except for schizophrenic hermits who isolate themselves from the world, every person has such a 'circle.'

An enemy of incarnational evangelism is our desire to control the process; we evangelize on our turf, where we are secure and can do everything our way. We invite seekers and converts to our house, a place that we rent or a restaurant where we plan to pick up the tab, leaving us in total control. We are at ease but the seeker feels insecure. We extract them from their circle of friends and family and bring them into a new circle of our making.

Such evangelism by extraction was neither Jesus' way, nor that of His apostles'. They evangelized where they were not in control. Peter evangelized a seeker's circle under Cornelius' roof. Cornelius was Italian; Peter and his Jewish coworkers ate non-kosher pepperoni on their pizza! Jewish Christians scolded Peter for that, God had to give him a disturbing vision to prepare him for it.

If you are an evangelist or train them, you must master this essential, apostolic skill of incarnational evangelism. Fundamental and universally applicable, we use it before trying other traditional Western or institutional approaches.

We imitate Jesus in His incarnation when we step outside our church buildings and mission circles to work with the people, rather than developing ever-bigger programs on our own turf to attract people to us. We work within family and social structures, rather than bringing converts into our own organization to find Jesus. We spend time with them in their homes, listening to them and giving them a model for evangelizing that they can imitate at once and pass on to their people.

Relatively few people come to Christ or form basic beliefs through the written page or from pulpit sermons. In most cases the Spirit of God uses friends or relatives. Patterson developed this community approach:

> **When we penetrated a town for the first time with the gospel, we found it unwise to rent a room for meetings and invite the people to a meeting where we controlled everything, where we felt secure but they didn't. On Christmas Eve, for example, instead of inviting them to a celebration in a rented hall, we visited them in their homes and joined in their festivities. Well, not in *all* of them! We made ourselves vulnerable,. We took them cookies or some other small token of friendship, rather than inviting them to an "outsider" meeting without their friends and family, where they felt uncomfortable.**

10-c Help Believers to Recount the Redemptive Events of Scripture

All religions of the world except Christianity (and ancient Judaism) start with a philosophical view of God. Confucius, Buddha, the Hindu holy men who, after years of meditation, wrote the sacred Sanskrit texts, Joseph Smith and Mohammed all contemplated the cosmos and life, then came up with a new ethical or metaphysical system. In time these systems evolved into full-blown religions. Christianity's origins, however, are quite the opposite. Not one major doctrine grew out of some mystic's mind. All basic truths of Scripture have grown out of historical events, such as

Creation
 The fall
  The flood
  Babel
   The pact with Abraham
    The miraculous escape from Egypt
     The giving of the law
      The breaking of the law
        The promise to David that an heir would sit on an eternal throne
         The division of the kingdom
          The exile and protection through Esther's diplomacy
           The return from exile
            Jerusalem and the temple rebuilt
             The expulsion of idolaters and reform under Ezra
              Jesus' birth and childhood,
                Jesus' baptism, temptation and calling His disciples
                 Jesus' miracles, teaching and transfiguration
                  Jesus' arrest, trial and death
                   Jesus' resurrection and ascension
                     The coming of the Holy Spirit at Pentecost
                      The new church in Jerusalem and its witness
                       The Jewish persecution and birth of Jewish churches
                        The conversion of gentiles
                          Churches multiply throughout the Roman Empire
                           Paul imprisoned, writes letters to new churches
                            John, exiled, writes the apocalyptic Revelation

As we relate these historical events, the Holy Spirit uses them to bring men to repentance and transform them. The prophets' and apostles' inspired comments about them form the basis of our theology. So first we tell the stories; later we add the doctrinal commentary built on the historical facts, as in the Psalms, Prophets and Epistles.

The more distant a culture is from the Christian world-view, the more we need to tell Old Testament stories to prepare the people to understand redemption. Old Testament stories enable potential converts to grasp the truths of one holy and all-powerful God who punishes sin. They also lay a foundation for understanding God's election of His people, covenants between God and men, faith, sacrifice for sin, servant leadership, prayer and intercession. They also help us see how God deals with people in blocs (he sees people in solidarity, united as one in marriage, extended families, nations, and the whole human race in Adam). We relate a story from the Old Testament to introduce a concept in its earthly form (such as the need for a sacrifice for sin, as in the account of Cain and Abel in Gen. 4). Later we add the corresponding story from the New Testament, for the spiritual application.

Church planters should develop a repertoire of Bible stories that furnish the biblical foundation for every major Christian truth and duty.

If a people group already have a worldview with one all-powerful and perfectly just creator, we start with the *basic stories of redemption*. We relate the Bible stories about the gospel. Such oral communication of the gospel, including stories of conversions and healing, is normally the cutting edge of people movements for Christ.

Where the people have a pagan worldview, they need a more basic foundation. We begin with Old Testament stories that reveal the holiness of the supremely powerful God. We relate the events of Scripture that the people can begin at once repeating to their family and friends. In most cultures, heads of households and "persons of peace" will repeat these stories, provided we tell them in a way they can imitate. Do not start with a philosophical or theological explanation of the gospels--that comes later.

Stories that are easy for new converts to repeat as they witness include key historical events of Jesus' life include:

> *Jesus raising Lazarus*, John 11
> *Jesus' death*, Matthew 27
> *Jesus' resurrection appearances*, John 20-21

Other stories that edify new Christians are:

> *Jesus' baptism*, Matthew 3
> *Jesus' temptation*, Matthew 4
> *Jesus' miracles*, Mark chapters 1-10; John chapters 2; 6; 9; 11
> *Jesus' parables*, Matthew 13; 25; Luke 10; 15

Stories that reveal the historical foundations for the holiness of God include the flood in Genesis 6-9, the plagues and escape from Egypt in Exodus 11-15, and Elijah's contest with the prophets of Baal in 1 Kings 18.

The flood. Genesis chapters 6-9 emphasize God's holiness as seen in the flood. The ark is a picture of Jesus' salvation. by faith we enter into glory by being *in* the risen Christ the same way that Noah's family and the animals entered into the ark in order to be saved from God's punishment (1 Peter 3:18-22). We allow the Holy Spirit to use the Word of God to convince people of the danger of their sin before God, and the power of Jesus' death and resurrection to save them.

Elijah and the false prophets of Baal. 1 Kings 18 emphasizes the unity of the one true God and His wrath against idolaters. We point out aspects of modern idolatry (greed, lust, etc.) that correspond to that of the prophets of Baal.

The Escape from slavery in Egypt. Exodus chapters 11-15 emphasize the Holy One's desire to separate his people from the godless world around them. It recounts His great power demonstrated in the miraculous crossing of the Red Sea.

If people believe in Jesus the same way Buddhists or Muslims believe in their faith--for cultural reasons only--they lack the Spirit of God. The best evangelists (i.e., the ones most often used by the Holy Spirit to bring about conversion) are normally *new* believers. We show them how to explain to their family and friends that Jesus, God's Son, died and rose again to save us.

They do not need to *understand* at this time the details about how Jesus' death and resurrection save them and their friends; they need only to trust in Him. For assurance, they need to know that they have been born into a new, loving community. Having been forgiven, they enter into a whole New Kingdom. "For you once were not a people, but now you are the people [*ethne*] of God." as citizens of this Kingdom, we have responsibilities to its other citizens. We proclaim this relational aspect of salvation as an essential part of evangelism. The message of salvation includes the purpose God has for us in salvation, to strengthen and extend His Kingdom.

We witness with power when the Holy Spirit uses our words to convince people of their danger. The infinitely holy God cannot look upon sin. We do not teach holiness as simply another item in a list of God's attributes. This appreciation of His absolute holiness awakens the fear of God. He is so good, and we so evil by comparison, that He must punish our sins. Normally seekers see this if we relate Old Testament stories in which God punished men's sin.

10-d Help Converts Pass on the Good News at Once

The light baton. Witnessing so that the gospel flows from friend to friend and family member to family member requires several things:

1. **Communicate the *basic proclamation*** of the gospel
    message: the sacrificial death of the Son of God, His life-
    giving resurrection, forgiveness and life for those who repent
    and believe (Luke 24:46-48).

2. **Pray** regularly and fervently for those we witness to.

3. **Befriend and win the confidence of respected heads of
    households** and help them evangelize their family and
    friends.

Younger church planters tend to reach the youth first. Sometimes that
is all they can do. But other times they fail to reach entire families
because they don't even try. We start with heads of households, as the
apostles did, when possible.

We teach heads of households from the beginning to take responsibility
for reaching their family and social circle. We help them to continue
drawing near to the lost in love and faith, as Jesus did, to widen that
circle. Scoggins explains:

> One way we found to "infect" an entire family is to provide
> the head of the family with weekly reading schedules to read
> to the family. These schedules are quite simple; for each day a
> section of Scripture is indicated, along with a question for
> discussion. We usually print a four-weeks' schedule on a half-
> sheet of paper (two weeks on each side) so that if fits easily in
> the Bible. We encourage the man to read this during mealtime,
> before the plates are removed. He simply opens his Bible to
> the Scripture portion indicated and reads it. He then asks the
> question printed or another suitable discussion question that
> may come to him. A discussion can follow. He then closes in
> prayer. The whole thing takes only three to five minutes, but
> reinforces several healthy principles. The husband takes the
> spiritual lead in the home, evangelizing the wife and children.
> He learns to bring up his children in the discipline and
> instruction of the Lord. He gains the skill of teaching and
> shepherding in a family environment, which enables the
> church leaders to discern how he might minister to the larger
> church body.

4. **Use a method of witnessing that converts can easily
    imitate and pass on** as they witness for Jesus. We help
    them simply to relate the good news, of their conversion
    and relevant Bible accounts. Story telling is a popular
    medium in all cultures; almost anyone can do it.

Scoggins discovered how to let the gospel flow freely among friends and relatives:

> **I finally saw what *missiologists* meant when they talked about focusing on a particular people group and subculture. We were getting far better results when we kept new converts in a loving relationship with their unsaved, pagan friends, and when we took Christ to them (instead of them coming to us) and started a new group or church within their social circle. We no longer jerked each new convert out of his circle and transplanted him into a church made up of the church planting task group members, or of others perceived as outsiders by the convert. We helped them to tell Bible stories about salvation and to witness to their unsaved family members and friends about what Jesus had done for them.**

10-e In New Communities Seek a 'Person of Peace'

> "When you enter a house, first say, `Peace to this house.' if a man of peace is there, your peace will rest on him; if not, it will return to you. Stay in that house, eating and drinking whatever they give you, for the worker deserves his wages. Do not move around from house to house."
> Luke 10:5-7

A 'man of peace' is a person whom God has already prepared, respected in the community. God channels His good news through this contact, as Cornelius in Acts 10 or Lydia and the jailer in Acts 16. We help such persons of peace to pass the gospel on immediately, even before they are saved in some cases, to their family and friends. Do not separate converts from their friends or relatives, except in the case of drug addicts or alcoholics, from fellow addicts. We do not alienate them from their unbelieving friends in order to identify with a church made up of outsiders from our task group.

10-g Form a New Church or Cell Inside One's Circle of Friends and Kin

Keep the number of outsiders, including the task group members, to a minority at meetings during the birth phase of the new church. Scoggins explains:

> **If the husband is able to talk openly with his wife and children, we encourage him to begin a weekly Bible study at his house, where the reading schedule can be used and they can discuss God's Word at greater length. If he has friends or relatives who might come, we encourage him to include them in this "gathering meeting." the missionary or a member of the church planting task group might attend also, but often it is**

better not to. Let the man do as much as he is able. Older believers should not be encouraged to come to these first "gathering meetings" unless they are bringing unbelieving friends or relatives. Once two or three have come to Christ, the group can be encouraged to start meeting as a community on Sundays. These "community meetings" will be where the life of the body is practiced, centered around the Lord's Supper; later other activities are added as needed.

10-g Where Large Meetings Are Illegal Form Tiny Groups

Two or three persons, to begin with, can meet for worship and Communion (Matthew 18:20; Acts 2:46-47). Such tiny groups normally can grow easily.

The size to which we let groups grow depends on the degree of security needed. In many societies the government stipulates a maximum number for an unregistered meeting. Often a great many come to Christ through such tiny gatherings; the growth continues by multiplying more and more such small groups.

10-h Give Ample Time for the Holy Spirit to Convince an Entire Family

Present the gospel in a meaningful way several times before asking for a commitment. Most converts need to hear about Jesus from five to seven times, often weeks apart, before the Holy Spirit enables them to receive Him in their hearts. Scoggins found the need for perseverance:

In the case of Muslims, it is not unusual for conversion to take years. This requires perseverance as well as persistence. One prays for wisdom, as to how to continue to pursue a contact that is open. We usually avoid "shaking the dust off our feet" until the seeker shows evidence of rejecting the message. As long as progress is evident, we persevere. Even if there is rejection, we explain the way back by means of repentance. We encourage those engaged in this evangelism to pray to discern the spirit of the person they are witnessing to. They must acknowledge that we as Christians are the sweet odor of life to those who are saved, but the stench of death to the lost (2 Cor.2:14-16).

10-i Help Seekers to Affirm Verbally the Essential Gospel Truths

We help seekers to grasp and repeat the facts of the gospel. This applies especially to the head of a family, whom we help to communicate the value of the gospel for his wife and children.

Essential Gospel Truths

- the value of Christ's death: *forgiveness*,
- the value of Christ's resurrection: *new, pure, eternal life*
- our response: *faith and repentance*

When a seeker believes, we try to reach and baptize the entire family. Scoggins' churches evangelize through the head of the household:

A husband normally precedes his wife and children in salvation and baptism; in this case he might be authorized by the elders to baptize his own family.

10-j Avoid Manipulating People into Making Crisis Decisions

Western evangelists sometimes manipulate individuals into making a logical, emotion-laden, 'personal' decision. Few such converts show evidence afterwards that the Holy Spirit brought them to repentance. Such an individualistic decision-making ritual, although it has had limited effectiveness in some democratic, educated cultures, is foreign to Scripture. It causes missionaries to waste much time. A harvesting method that produces 95% weed seed yields too few true converts to sustain church multiplication. True conversion is not the result of a mere decision but of repentance; it means moving from one kingdom to another; from the kingdom of darkness to light. The consequences of such radical emigration normally are too important to do all alone. The family needs to weigh and discuss them at length.

Patterson experienced irrelevant Western evangelism in Honduras:

We began witnessing with the usual Western emphasis, without lasting results. Several evangelists who were effective in the United States held campaigns during our first years of work in Honduras, and we helped them set up their meetings. But their methods proved ineffective in Honduras, in terms of converts followed through. This forced us to look again in Scripture at what the gospel was and how the apostles presented it. We did not find the Western emphasis on individual, crisis decisions. We found a greater emphasis than

what we were used to on the *resurrection, repentance,* and *entire families* coming as units to the Lord.

10-k Count Converts as the Apostles Did, After Being Added to a Church by Baptism

We count converts when they do what Jesus and the apostles require: repent and be baptized into Christ and His body the church (Acts 2:38-41; Luke 24:46-48).

Much mischief occurs when evangelists count hands prematurely and report such as conversions to raise funds. Patterson reports:

> **After showing a film about Jesus in several Mexican villages, a mission agency claimed 5,000 conversions and eleven new churches in their fund-raising bulletin. I was visiting the area and tried to help follow up the converts but there were none. There were no churches; they had only held meetings to give away cassettes with gospel music, promised to individuals who made a 'decision.' When I heard their exaggerated report to raise funds I was heartsick. When confronted with the facts, the organization's officials refused to discuss it. Too often the rewards go to the wily. Such dishonest use of statistics by Evangelicals reinforces bad evangelism methods. I wish this were the only case I knew of!**

> **We taught our Hondurans to be leery of counting heads of new 'Kingdom people' before they do the three things taken for granted by the apostles in Acts 2:37-41: repent of their sins, be baptized, and be added to a local community of the people of God. Peter commanded this in answer to the question that faith begs, "Brothers, what shall we do?" These three activities in themselves do not save people but ratify by concrete actions the faith by which God saves us in Christ.**

10-l Follow Up Conversion with Baptism as Soon as Is Practical

The apostles gave extensive instruction *after* baptism. An evangelist's job is done only when a convert is baptized and obeying the commands of Jesus. As seen in Peter's actions in Acts 2 and throughout the book of Acts, an evangelist's duty is not only to witness about Jesus Christ. Peter did not consider his work done until the converts had repented, that is, turned from unrighteousness to new life in Christ, confirmed it with baptism, and were added to a church body. "Belief" that merely acknowledges the facts is a poor criterion to distinguish those in the Kingdom from others outside. Heartfelt belief in Christ and Scripture is always accompanied by works because it includes the regenerating work of the Holy Spirit, as demonstrated in Acts 2:37-47. Some churches require a doctrinal course for baptism that excludes illiterates; baptism becomes a graduation ceremony, something foreign to Scripture.

New converts should also begin celebrating the Lord's Supper as soon as possible. Do this even though you have only one, two, or three converts in a new church in a pioneer field. Saving faith results in good works--at least an attempt at obedience. Make sure converts do not confuse the cause and the result. A convert obeys because he has been saved; salvation does not stem from his obedience but leads to it. We can expect growth--not perfection--in obedience from the beginning. A true convert obeys joyfully out of love for Jesus, not out of a legalistic sense of duty (John 14:15).

10-m Assure Converts of our Loving Acceptance at Once

Converts find it easy to obey Jesus when they know He loves them; and they believe this when His body (the church) shows love for them. We also assure them immediately of the Holy Spirit's regeneration, sealing, and presence in their life. We do not mean a course of systematic doctrine about the Holy Spirit at this time. Physically embracing the convert immediately after baptism will be more assuring at this stage, with simple words to the effect, "You are risen with Jesus for all eternity, by the power of God's Spirit in you!" Some pastors lay hands on new converts when they baptize them, as the apostles did in Samaria, as a physical sign and assurance of having received the Holy Spirit (Acts 8:14-17).

We must deny *formal* acceptance into the church body as an adult member until the convert has repented and been baptized. This protects the assembly from "rice Christians," who are like ticks on a dog--parasites on the body of Christ. Left unprotected, both ticks and dog die, which is good for neither. True believers, however, need to be included as soon as possible, lest they die like abandoned babies in a hostile world. Both Scoggins' as well as Patterson's experience shows that people can be added in a matter of days when properly evangelized and discipled.

10-n   Note Plans for Dealing with Seekers

Please note your plans for seekers. Plan with coworkers if possible:

_____

_____

_____

_____

_____

_____

_____

_____

_____

_____

_____

_____

_____

_____

_____

11.
Church Reproduction
from the Viewpoint of the
Evangelist

If we're saved by faith, a simple *'decision'* is enough !

Wrong!
We repent and trust Jesus to forgive and change us.
We're *hatched again.*
Merely *deciding* to accept Jesus because of social pressure is a *'cultural faith'*--like a Buddhist's.

Find in Acts 9:10-27 things that were done after Paul's conversion, to bring him into fellowship:

In Damascus there was a disciple named Ananias. The Lord called to him in a vision, "Ananias!"

"Yes, Lord," he answered.

The Lord told him, "Go to the house of Judas on Straight Street and ask for a man from Tarsus named Saul, for he is praying. In a vision he has seen a man named Ananias come and place his hands on him to restore his sight."

"Lord," Ananias answered, "I have heard many reports about this man and all the harm he has done to your saints in Jerusalem. And he has come here with authority from the chief priests to arrest all who call on your name."

But the Lord said to Ananias, "Go! This man is my chosen instrument to carry my name before the Gentiles and their kings and before the people of Israel. I will show him how much he must suffer for my name."

Then Ananias went to the house and entered it. Placing his hands on Saul, he said, "Brother Saul, the Lord-Jesus, who appeared to you on the road as you were coming here-has sent me so that you may see again and be filled with the Holy Spirit."

Immediately, something like scales fell from Saul's eyes, and he could see again. He got up and was baptized, and after taking some food, he regained his strength. Saul spent several days with the disciples in Damascus. At once he began to preach in the synagogues that Jesus is the Son of God. All those who heard him were astonished and asked, "Isn't he the man who raised havoc in Jerusalem among those who call on this name? and hasn't he come here to take them as prisoners to the chief priests?" Yet Saul grew more and more powerful and baffled the Jews living in Damascus by proving that Jesus is the Christ.

After many days had gone by, the Jews conspired to kill him, but Saul learned of their plan. Day and night they kept close watch on the city gates in order to kill him. But his followers took him by night and lowered him in a basket through an opening in the wall.

When he came to Jerusalem, he tried to join the disciples, but they were all afraid of him, not believing that he really was a disciple. But Barnabas took him and brought him to the apostles. He told them how Saul on his journey had seen the Lord and that the Lord had spoken to him, and how in Damascus he had preached fearlessly in the name of Jesus.

Scoggins learned a way to prepare evangelists:

We use John 9 to explain the power and cost of a personal witness. We try to encourage people to write out their testimony in such a way that they can share it in a minute or

two. I remember shortly after I came to Christ how I was encouraged to do this. It was pointed out to me that Paul shared all or part of his testimony many times in his letters. After I did so, I shared it probably 100 times in the next year. And this from a recluse who insisted he would never share his faith!

11-a Aim at More than Mere *Decisions*

Evangelism is not complete until converts repent from a life of sin, are baptized and added to an assembly where they learn the new life in the Spirit who dwells in them. At least one worker on a church planting task group or in a small group must use the spiritual gift of evangelism. The gift of evangelism is evidenced only when people do in fact turn from their sin to follow Jesus. Also, the gift of evangelism, like all other spiritual gifts, is to be used in harmony with the use of the other gifts given to the body of Christ (Eph. 4:11-16).

Evangelists working independently from the churches contribute little to church planting and may cause damaging confusion in a pioneer field. They often push people to make decisions, then leave them without pastoral care. They are like a farmer who scatters wheat seed recklessly on a mountainside, then returns years later looking in vain for a harvest. For church reproduction, such irresponsible evangelism adds nothing. It caters to the self-centered; it is not God-centered. Such evangelists present Jesus merely as a ticket to heaven or a cheap answer to all of a persons' problems. In either case, it places Jesus at our disposal and for our use. He becomes a servant of man, rather than a servant of God.

This evangelism that offers cheap grace inoculates a people group against the kind of dynamic discipling that Jesus commands and that results in a Spirit-led movement for Christ. In contrast, the evangelistic messages in the book of Acts proclaimed Jesus as both Lord (master and king) and Christ (Savior or deliverer). Evangelism was God's command to leave the things of this world and follow Him in His Kingdom. Today, God-centered evangelism in a self-centered Western world calls people to change loyalties, from serving themselves to serving the living God (see 2 Cor. 5:14; Gal. 5:13).

Repentance is not "salvation by works." a few popular theologians have claimed that salvation does not require repentance, only faith. They argue that repentance is works and that works does not save us. They may be well intentioned but lack experience in pioneer church planting. If we overlook repentance when we call people to Christ, we do not reproduce healthy churches (I tried it at first—G.P). Jesus commands His followers to repent, in order to enter His Kingdom (Matthew 3:2; 4:17; Mark 1:15; 2:17; Luke 13:3,5; 24:46-48). He expressed repentance in various ways: to be born all over again, to die as a grain of wheat to bring forth new life,

110

to receive His Holy Spirit, to enter God's kingdom as a little child, to turn to God, etc.

These who say salvation requires no repentance relegate Jesus' command to a *transition* age, when Jewish Christians were still under the Old Testament law. by this line of reasoning *no command* of Jesus applies today; He gave *all* His commands to Jews who still followed the Old Testament. Jesus made plain that repentance as part of saving faith applied not only to Jews but also to *all nations*. In His Great Commission in Luke 24:46-48 He states that repentance is for *all nations*. The apostle Peter likewise said in Acts 11:18 that God grants life-giving repentance to the *gentiles*. Paul also told non-Jewish Athenians that God commands men everywhere to repent (Acts 17:30; compare 20:21).

negative side we turn from--or die to--sin, as Romans 6 reveals. There is no merit worthy of salvation in being sinless, or inanimate objects would be virtuous; a worm is sinless; so is a cancer. So we can hardly claim that we save ourselves by stopping our sinning! 1 John 1 reveals that no one is without sin; even mature Christians must continue to confess it. So on the negative side, biblical repentance can hardly be construed as an attempt to justify ourselves by our own good works.

On the positive side, repentance means turning to God. This includes receiving His Spirit who produces in us *His fruit* of love, joy, peace, patience, goodness and so forth. This is not our doing. We bear fruit only because God's Holy Spirit enters our hearts and begins the eternal transformation process; it's His fruit in us. So the positive side of biblical repentance is totally God's work, not ours, except in the sense that we let Him do it. So repentance in its positive sense also cannot be construed as saving ourselves by our good works.

11-b Help a New Cross-Cultural Task Group to Focus on Neglected Fields

The apostle Paul sought to evangelize where Jesus had not been preached, where he would not build on another man's foundation (Rom. 15:20-22). Jesus requires that some of His apostles (missionaries) seek fields that are still neglected; we are to go to all nations (Matthew 28:19; John 4:35; 2 Cor. 10:15-16).

The word "nations" in Matthew 28:19 means specific people groups. We need to help our churches to look at people groups--not just nations in the political sense. China, for example, is a cluster of hundreds of people groups, or nations in the biblical sense.

11-c Use the 'Keys' Promised to All Disciples

Read Acts 3:1 - 4:13 to find how the apostles witnessed with power.

What act of power did they do in Jesus' name?

What, besides Jesus' death, did they emphasize in their message to the people who gathered?

Whom did their teaching disturb and what did they do?

Before whom did they stand trial the next day?

Why were those who sat in judgment over the apostles surprised at their defense?

Effective cross-cultural evangelism by Westerners normally requires that we rework our gospel presentation. The essential gospel message is the death and resurrection of the Son of God, the eternal forgiveness of sins for whoever repents and believes in Him, and our entrance into the New Kingdom (a new, eternal, loving society of believers filled with the Spirit of God). We must not export our Western individualistic approach to witnessing. The apostles also emphasized the resurrection more than most modern Western preachers do. Throughout the book of Acts it was the "punch line" of their witness. Jesus died for our sins but was risen to give us life. The same emphasis appears in the Epistles. The historical fact that God raised Jesus from the dead and promises to raise us in Him is today also the powerful, triumphant event, the supremely good news, which the Holy Spirit uses to convert those who are convicted of their sin.

Westerners, armed with a neat and logical "plan of salvation," often emphasize almost exclusively the legal value of Jesus' death to forgiven sin. They neglect His resurrection. We are risen in Him the same way that we die in Him. His resurrection is the vehicle of our salvation. Our participation in it is the only means of receiving eternal life (John 11:21-26; 1 Cor. 15:12-26, 45-49). We receive this life together with, and united with, others; Ephesians chapters 2 and 3 vividly explain this corporate dimension of our salvation.

A Westerner's witness often emphasizes Anselm's theory of the atonement and neglects other vital aspects of the gospel. This ancient definition of the atonement focuses on the substitution of a sacrificial victim for the sinner, in Jesus' death; He died in our place. As usually explained, however, it overlooks Jesus' resurrection as an essential part of His redemptive work. His resurrection is just as 'vicarious' as His death, because all that are saved participate in it. Scripture shows that we are mortal (Gen. 2:17; 3:4; 1 Cor. 15:53-54; 1 Tim. 6:16); we take on Christ's immortality by being risen in Him (1 Cor. 15:12-28, 42-57; John 5:24-29; 11:23-26; 1 Peter 3:21; Rom. 8:11; Eph. 1:18-2:7; and others).

Many Westerners dwell on Christ's death and the consequent forgiveness of the sinner, which are precious truths but not the whole truth. They teach our justification by faith through Jesus' death, as found in Romans up to chapter 5, but stop there. That does not prepare a convert for the new, Spirit-filled he will live in the power of Jesus' resurrection, as explained in chapters 6-8. These chapters reveal the new life we have by participating in Christ's resurrection. Salvation should result in spiritual and emotional healing. Some might debate whether the total healing promised as part of Jesus' redemption takes place *before* our resurrection (if so, few would ever die and go to heaven). But there is no debate over the fact that Jesus was raised to give us new life, which starts by faith at conversion. The evangelist that proclaims only that by Jesus' death sinners are justified, leaves them impotent in terms of practicing righteousness, heirs of a half-way salvation that is irrelevant for a practical Christian life. Balanced evangelism includes regeneration as well as justification, leading into Kingdom living and continual spiritual healing. For this and other reasons related to culture, the typical Western style of witnessing often fails to bring people to repentance and therefore impedes church multiplication.

We use the "keys" for anointed witnessing. We tap the power of the Holy Spirit who anoints us to witness for Christ (Acts 1:8). This power to witness includes authority to bind or loose. Jesus symbolized it with the "keys to the kingdom." He promised this power first to Peter and later to all His disciples (Matthew 16:16-19; 18:18; John 20:23). The "binding and loosing" mentioned in these passages refer to Christ's forgiveness and to building His church through His witnesses, an *invasion* of Satan's kingdom. In Matthew 16 the power to bind and loose is to invade the kingdom of this world and the "gates of hell" will not resist it. In Matthew 18 it involves correction of sinners, to keep the kingdom of this world from invading the Kingdom of heaven, the church (see also 1 Cor. 5). In both cases God authorizes His church to act on earth in Jesus' all-powerful name, in the power and with the guidance of the Holy Spirit.

Some theologians assign this power of the keys only to the twelve Apostles; others include the bishops who succeeded them. Most Evangelicals agree that any true believer can--must--use these keys--the power to bind or loose sins as he witnesses to an unsaved person or corrects a disorderly Christian through the power of the Holy Spirit in the all-powerful name of Jesus.

What is the power of the Holy Spirit to witness? Is it our courage or our shouting? Hardly! It is the anointing by God's Spirit on our testimony, and on us, as we declare a person's forgiveness in Jesus. We trust God to convince a sinner by His Spirit to repent and believe through our faithful testimony. The Holy Spirit glorifies Jesus in the heart of new believers, not only by convincing them subjectively of sin and the need for salvation, but also by loosing (forgiving) their sin before the Most Holy One. God's conversion of a sinner often depends as much on the faith of the one who witnesses as on that of the convert. The paralytic lowered through the roof to be healed by Jesus was first saved from his sins because of the faith *of his friends* (Mark 2:1-12; compare Acts 16:31).

Highly educated people often find it harder to witness with this kind of confidence, to believe for people who are still unable to believe for themselves. They see their witness as a process only of transmitting *information*. Third world Christians, spared this Western bias, generally witness more fervently than Americans because they are more aware of the Spirit's anointing as they announce the news of forgiveness with supernatural power. Westerners tend to rely more on the logic and accuracy of their witness, rather than on God's power to convey Jesus' actual forgiveness and life.

Using the keys is mentioned in connection with building the church in Matthew 16:15-19. An independent Christian doing his or her own thing, with no accountability to God's leaders in the church, has a rather shaky claim to this authority to bind or loose.

11-d Help Newly Converted Family Heads to Lead "Gathering Meetings"

In some cultures you can ask an adult male convert to invite friends-- non-Christians--to a 'gathering group.' Missionaries might lead such a meeting with the man and his family first in a way that he can imitate it, then let him lead similar meetings for friends, coaching him from behind the scenes.

11-e Where Society Is Hostile, Let Converts Decide how to Testify

Let the converts decide if they want to be baptized publicly or in private (as the Ethiopian eunuch and the Philippian jailer were in Acts 8 and 16). It is their life and jobs that are in jeopardy, not ours, so we let them make the decision. In hostile areas they may decide to meet underground, forming clusters of tiny house churches or cells rather than a typical Western style congregation. They may decide to continue going to a Mosque to pray, as Paul continued to go to Jewish synagogues. This should be their decision; we allow the Holy Spirit to speak to them the same way that He leads us.

11-f   Note Plans for Evangelism

Please note your plans to do the work of an evangelist. Do this with your coworkers if possible.

_____

_____

_____

_____

_____

_____

_____

_____

_____

_____

_____

_____

12.
Church Reproduction
from the Viewpoint of a
Mission Task Group

Why task groups ? A high flyer like me needs freedom to soar alone on high.

I see things from a different perspective !

Jesus and His apostles never worked alone.

Find in Mark 3:13-14 what Jesus did before naming his disciples, and what he appointed them to do:

Jesus went up on a mountainside and called to him those he wanted, and they came to him. He appointed twelve--designating them apostles--that they might be with him and that he might send them out to preach and to have authority to drive out demons.

Find in Acts 10:23-24 who formed Peter's task-group for the new church in Cesarea:

Then Peter invited the men into the house to be his guests. The next day Peter started out with them, and some of the brothers from Joppa went along. The following day he arrived in Cesarea. Cornelius was expecting them and had called together his relatives and close friends.

Find in Acts 13:2-3 how the church in Antioch formed a task group for distant fields:

While they were worshiping the Lord and fasting, the Holy Spirit said, "Set apart for me Barnabas and Saul for the work to which I have called them." So after they had fasted and prayed, they placed their hands on them and sent them off.

Jesus and His apostles never traveled alone; they always worked as a group, a *temporary* team. Patterson discovered the value of working as a small task group:

When we launched our missionary work I was entrenched in typical Western individualism. I did not think in terms of ministry teams. I had come to Jesus through an individual decision. I served with a mission agency that dealt with its missionaries on an individual basis. I stumbled in my individual way for several years before I learned from the Hondurans how easy it was to penetrate a neighborhood with the gospel if we worked as a team. It came natural for the Hondurans--their culture is not so individualistic. I learned from them to work with others with gifts that balance mine. I came to see that it is simply foolish and dangerous to try to do God's work properly as a loner.

I have since learned the importance of sending church based task groups as in Acts 13:1-3. This does not bypass the mission agency, but places the responsibility of sending missionaries on the church rather than the agency. It gets local sending churches more involved, makes it easier to raise support, provides better accountability, assures a more balanced distribution of spiritual gifts on the task group and avoids many problems that lead to missionary "burnout."

For cross-cultural church multiplication, we imitate the apostles, especially Paul:

- God sent Paul to disciple the nations (people groups) and churches were established or strengthened wherever he worked,
  - he worked with temporary task groups,
    - they started clusters of small congregations that multiplied,
      - he willingly worked in dangerous fields with hostile authorities,
        - he worked with his hands and kept close to the people,
          - he often prayed fervently for those that he had discipled, as well as for the sick.

117

12-a Launch a Task Group for a Distant Field with a Serious Separation Ceremony

The church in Antioch separated Paul, Barnabas, and Mark to disciple the nations with prayer and fasting in Acts 13:1-3. We likewise separate and send workers through the power of the Holy Spirit. This assures them of the church's prayerful support and better accountability to the church. It also encourages workers on the field during hard times. We separate them for church planting in another field not only physically but also emotionally, from their home church, family, mission base, or friends. Often teary relatives and friends need this separation ceremony almost as much as the sent ones, to help them release loved ones and coworkers for the job God calls them to.

Some organizations frequently lay on hands for blessing and power for ministry. The separation ceremony may not be very meaningful if all we do is lay on hands again. We make it special, so that all see that the apostles (*sent ones*) have truly been sent by the body through the power of God's Spirit. That is why the church in Antioch fasted first.

12-b Prepare a *Progress* Chart for a New Church

New leaders find it helpful if we give them a checklist for their **church** or **group** to follow. Appendix B *Example of a Progress Chart for a New Church* is an example of a new church's *Progress Chart.* Such a chart should list activities that would include Jesus' commands and other ministries required by the New Testament. These are explained in chapter 17 on the *Church Leader.* Add activities as you see the need.

You might provide another *Progress Chart* for the **task group** itself. Key activities for a church multiplication task group are listed in *Appendix C, An Example of a Progress Chart for Field Workers.* Again, add activities as you see the need.

You might also provide a *Progress Chart* for an individual task group member, as seen in Appendix A, *Example of a Personal Progress Chart*

Patterson observed teams working in Africa and Asia:

> **Some teams fail because they become ingrown. They knew what their task group should do, but they had not listed the activities their converts or new churches would do. They could not *lead* the potential national leaders, because they had no clear vision of where they were going--so they only *taught* them.**

> **Some teams made the fatal mistake of pulling potential leaders out of the new churches to serve on the church planting *task group* along with the foreigners. They forgot that**

the foreign team or task group is merely scaffolding. The scaffolding grew bigger and bigger. In some cases when foreigners or nationals wanted to work on the building itself (the church), they pulled them away to work on the scaffolding--sometimes in the name of *team spirit!*

All this could have been avoided had they begun with a simple checklist or *Progress Chart* listing the things the disciples and new churches would do. It would have helped them focus on the people and what they would do, rather than on themselves. Church planters that bond with the people and their culture find it easier to plant culturally relevant churches.

12-c Plant Churches the Way the Apostolic Task Groups Did

Please read Acts 10 and 11:1-18 to find several guidelines for church planting. Notice things that God, Cornelius, Peter, or Peter's task group did to give birth to the new church.

Did you find the following? (Mark those that you found.)

☐ What first prompted God to move? What were both Cornelius and Peter doing at first?

☐ What did workers from the mother church in Joppa do? How was a *church-based* task group involved?

☐ How did God cure Peter's cultural prejudice?

☐ Who was invited to the *exclusive* meeting in Cesarea, apart from Peter and his companions?

☐ What reputation did Cornelius have with relatives and friends?

☐ What was the content of the witnesses' message?

☐ How did they confirm the converts' salvation?

☐ How much time did they spend with the new church?

☐ How did Peter deal with the Jewish Christians' objections to his cross-cultural approach?

Note that Peter took other brothers in Christ from Joppa when they planted the new church in Cornelius' house in Cesarea (Acts 10:23). As always, they related the *essentials of the gospel* (Acts 10:36-43):

- *Who Jesus is*: Lord of all, anointed by God to do good and heal (10:36-38),
  - *His death for forgiveness of sins* (10:39),
    - *His resurrection from the dead* (10:40-42),
      - Our response: *faith* (10:43)

12-d Deploy Church-Based Task Groups

We eliminate a major cause of missionary failure and burnout by deploying church-based task groups (temporary task groups). Jesus and His apostles did not work alone; they formed temporary task groups (Mark 3:13-15; Acts 10:23-24; 13:1-3). The apostolic bands that accompanied Peter and Paul, like spiritual midwives, enabled churches to reproduce daughter churches—a function of the body of Christ, not of individuals.

Church planters work better together, combining their spiritual gifts. For example, the Holy Spirit normally works far more powerfully though a task group of four than through four persons working alone. The church is repeatedly represented in Scripture as an active army or united body--not a school or a group of individuals.

By forming a church-based task group, we do not mean joining an existing 'task group' already put together on a field by a *mission agency* for administrative convenience. The missionaries' home church forms the task group as an extension of its own church body. They see the missionaries' work as a branch of their ministry. Usually churches form such task groups in cooperation with sister churches and send them through a mission agency. When a congregation really loves its missionaries, they more readily see the need for a church-based task group as opposed to the tradition of sending their people to the mission field as individuals or family units.

Churches that form apostolic task groups, even though they work through a mission agency, take responsibility for their support and hold them accountable to reproduce new churches. In the New Testament living bodies (churches) reproduced themselves in living bodies (daughter churches) through the instrumentality of temporary church planting task groups made up of members from different churches.

12-e Help Married Church Planters to Agree on the Wife's Role in Ministry

A married couple should agree on what the wife does in ministry, to avoid tension in the home. Stress grows out of misunderstandings about what the wife should do. Wise couples discuss this frankly. A husband and wife may have quite different roles, which vary as family circumstances change. If a couple has no child both may give much time to evangelism and discipling. When children arrive the mother becomes more of a homemaker as described in Titus 2:5 and gives up some ministry activities.

This dedication to the home and family can become a problem, however, if a wife feels that her calling is less important before God than her husband's is, or if she and her husband perceive her role differently. This can create impossible tension in the home, especially when neither partner understands the source of the tension.

Missionary couples, especially from West societies that minimize the differences between the sexes, frequently fail with disastrous results to respect the God-given roles of husband and wife. Often the culprit is a mission agency field supervisor who expects a woman to consider her God-given role as mother and wife as secondary and inferior. As in William Carey's and many others of his type felt it was spiritual to neglect their wives in order to serve God. They violated Ephesians 5:25-29 that tells husbands to love their wives as Christ loves the church and treat them as they would their own bodies. Women missionaries, both single and married, often need encouragement to live out God's calling for their lives, rather than the expectations of their college professors, friends, or a misguided spouse.

Those that would deny women missionaries any significant role as leaders, should note that Priscilla, helped disciple Apollos on the leadership level, presumably under her husband's or Paul's authority (Acts 18:1-4). Also, Philip's daughters prophesied (Acts 21:8-9). Thus we see that scriptural admonitions against women's teaching men or exercising leadership in the church are not absolute prohibitions. God enabled women to lead under male authority. Protestant work around the world would be in sad shape indeed if God wiped out all that has been built on foundations laid by women missionaries!

On the other hand, those that would place women on a par with men in every way, denying any significant differences in their respective God-given roles, should note that extremely few cultures in pioneer fields (with no churches) do well with women in high profile positions of leadership. They will often respect a foreigner because of her education and professional poise, but not their own women. In Honduras Patterson had to establish strong male leadership in order for churches to multiply healthily in that macho culture.

12-f Form Temporary Task Groups to Multiply Churches

A task group made up of outsiders normally phases out as local 'inside' or 'national' leaders take on responsibility. Do not let your church planting task group become an end in itself. Remember its midwife role. It is temporary scaffolding, to enable mother church to reproduce. If no 'mother' churches exist yet in a new field, raise them up as soon as possible. At first a new church in a pioneer field might have as few as two or three converts. During this formative phase, task group members from outside the culture must not outnumber converts in meetings, or the new church fails to take its identity with the local community. Some task group members may need to make themselves absent during key services until the newborn church senses its identify within the culture, and the community sees it as a part of its own society. Otherwise, converts feel they are joining a group of outsiders and the church takes on a distinctively foreign quality that fails to reproduce within the culture.

12-g Before Joining a Task Group, Decide Carefully with whom you Should Work

Except for short-term service, seek a task group leader who wholeheartedly encourages you to minister in a way for which you are gifted and to which God has called you. Serve a task group that puts loving obedience to Christ ahead of all other policies, including its own. Join an existing task group only if its leader assures you that your gifts and ministry are needed, wanted, and apt to be productive. Make sure you won't be shunted into a ministry for which God has not gifted you. This happens very often in mission organizations. Avoid leaders who, for the sake of control, force you to follow human policies, especially if they mislabel this enforced conformity as 'team spirit' or 'unity.' Power hungry leaders have only contempt for New Testament, Spirit-empowered unity in

Christ which despises legalistic conformity, brings out our differences and frees us in love for distinct ministries in the united body (1 Corinthians 12).

12-h Appreciate Variety in Cultures

God loves the distinctive features of different races and cultures. He created the nations; every tribe, tongue, and people group is recognizable in glory with their wonderful differences (Revelations 7:9). We violate God's plan when we force cultures to integrate in the name of Christian unity. When we force two cultures to mix in one church, they never *integrate*: the stronger one with more money and political power cancels out the weaker, even though it has fewer people. True unity in Christ retains cultural differences in loving harmony with each other. Sister churches with different customs love one another and cooperate in God's work. Trying to integrate two cultures never unifies them; it brings about the death of one of them. It destroys something that God loves. How incredibly ironic and tragically sad that some missionaries in the name of Christian unity lead cultures into extinction!

12-i Investigate Carefully a New Field and how to Penetrate It

Before planning in detail how to reach a culturally distant people group, we discern its main culture and subcultures. Then we recruit persons who can witness for Christ from the same class of people or a very similar society, matching church planters with people of similar background and culture. Except for tribal work, if we violate this rule we can expect a delay of a generation, for new churches to overcome the stigma of being foreign and to break loose to multiply indigenously.

The first question to ask about a *neg*lected people group might well be **who can more easily reach them?**

Normally the most effective witness comes through people who are culturally close. It is often wiser to mobilize church planters from churches of the third world than for Americans or Europeans to do it alone. This does not rule out totally the participation of a foreigner in evangelism, as Patterson discovered:

> **We found it effective for me to accompany a Honduran to evangelize a new community. My being a 'gringo' attracted the people; the Honduran, however, did the witnessing for Christ. This worked well to get things started; from then on it was imperative that converts witness to their friends and relatives, for the gospel to flow freely.**

12-j Focus on a Specific People Group and Subculture

For church reproduction we work *within* a people group. by a people group we mean the largest number of people among whom the gospel can spread without being hindered by barriers of any kind, including class or cultural differences. Missionaries seldom plant a national church that reproduces spontaneously in a pioneer field without focusing on a specific class of people. When workers of another economic level, social class or subculture converts outnumber the converts in the meetings, the local people fail to see the church as *their* church.

In a pioneer field the most responsive people are normally of the working class, but not necessarily the poorest. For example, the apostle Paul at times worked with people of a disenfranchised middle class--an economic group of hard-working folk who had been successful economically but who would never rise to a commensurate social status. These included freed slaves such as Onesimus, merchants of non-aristocratic birth such as Lydia or exiled Jewish merchants such as Aquila and Priscilla. The most responsive people in a pioneer field are those who not only are open to change but desperately seek it.

12-k Arrange On-the-Job Training if Needed, for Task Group Members

We need workers who are of the same or a very compatible culture as the people group we are evangelizing. Workers from another country or race who join your task group nearly always need help to gear their methods of communication to the other community, even though they come from a culturally close people. There are always some significant differences in customs that they must respect, and they are often ignorant of incarnational evangelism methods. If you mobilize workers from another country for a task group who are culturally closer to the people you focus on, they will need some training. The first thing you must explain is that they will not be doing the preaching in the churches. They will train the local nationals to serve as pastors and preach. (You may be surprised at how many volunteers suddenly forget their 'call' when they hear this!) National workers on your task group might need vocational training for skills needed for self-employment or small business, especially for fields of restricted access. Remember, we do not expect *outsiders*, even if they are culturally closer than we are, to reproduce churches. The impulse for spontaneous multiplication comes from the Holy Spirit to the local people. Outsiders must mentor leaders from *behind the scenes*.

12-l Find the Responsive Segment of the Population

Jesus sent His apostles to people who responded to the gospel. He warned them to 'shake the dust off their feet' as a sign of God's judgment against those that did not heed it (Luke 10:4-16). He also told us to open our eyes and see the fields that are ripe for harvest (John 4:35). This means *research* for most new fields. Faith faces the facts. Non-faith leans on wishful thinking and wispy dreams. Unfortunately some missionaries waste years on people whom God has not chosen for salvation, neglecting others close by whom God has prepared. This often becomes strikingly evident when missionaries shift their attention to another people group and see more fruit in a few weeks than they saw in years previously.

12-m Help New Leaders Take Pastoral Responsibility as Soon as Possible

As soon as you start training a pastor or elder, start giving him more and more responsibility. A church seldom reproduces if it depends on outside control or subsidy. For the Holy Spirit to move local leaders to multiply daughter churches, they must take the initiative in freedom. New pastors *in a pioneer* field should be trained on the job to assure church multiplication. National leaders in pioneer fields who are trained in traditional, classroom-only institutions almost never think in terms of church growth by reproduction (this weakness does not apply so universally to fields with mature churches and elders).

12-n Avoid Burnout by Turning Problems over to New Elders

As churches start to multiply, the original task group leader feels more and more pressure to deal with stressful situations. All effective church planters experience this stress. Paul agonized over the problems in the infant churches in Galatia: "My dear children, for whom I am again in the pains of childbirth. . ." (Galatians 4:19). After listing many perils and painful adventures experienced in his church planting work, he added, "Besides everything else, I face daily the pressure of my concern for all the churches. who is weak, and I do not feel weak? who is led into sin, and I do not inwardly burn?" (2 Corinthians 11:28-29).

When churches begin to multiply, we do what Jethro advised Moses to do, and what Paul did with Titus. We turn over pastoral care to others with the pastoral gift. When pressures accumulate we put distance between the people and ourselves. This forces new elders to do more problem solving. We who are more experienced deal only with the tougher problems, the chronic ones that keep cropping up. We let the new leaders make their mistakes. They will make many, perhaps even as many as we make. We become less available. We hand over responsibility to those whom Paul called the 'presbytery' (1 Timothy 4:14); this group of elders oversees as a body the work of the churches. Some churches don't like the biblical word 'presbytery' and call it an association, alliance or synod. I doubt if God is very concerned with our preferences in terminology. The crucial point is not to ask an elder to tackle a stressful problem alone; arrange for him to handle it with other elders.

Patterson learned to deal with stressful situations:

When a new church lacked mature elders to handle a painful situation, we created a temporary committee of elders. We brought together as many as possible from nearby churches to deal with the problem. In cases of a breach of pastoral ethics, we also invited pastors from other churches not of our fellowship. They studied the case, interviewed the persons involved, and then gave to the suffering church their recommendation. In every case the church heeded it. As an outsider, I made it a point not to be present at these meetings although I helped arrange them.

Even so, workers continued to come to me with many serious problems. To protect my health and my family, I put physical distance between the new churches and myself. We moved to a new area and began new churches far from the first ones. I also started taking more short vacations with my family. This lessened the strain considerably. The pastors and elders saw me less often and took on more responsibility. You could see them grow!

Also, to avoid stress I disciplined myself to keep turning over all the churches with their problems to God in prayer. I had to become more willing to trust Him, against all human odds, to bring the church through their birth and adolescent pains. Often I prayed, for the sake of my own mental health as well as for the churches, "Lord, they're your churches, not mine. If they depend on me, then let them fail! If you want them to keep growing and reproducing, only you can do the work of grace needed to overcome their problems. I am willing to let them fail. I disown any claim to ownership. They are yours. Simply use me as an instrument to do your will." Many times I had to rededicate myself to simply obey God's New Testament commands and leave the rest to Him, trusting Him to help the new elders, inexperienced as they were, to deal with the problems.

I also asked my wife to schedule all my appointments and ration the time I spent with stressful problems. That forced me

to delegate and pray more. Had I not done this, I'm such a 'workaholic' I'd probably have died of stress years ago!

Yes, some churches—a very few —did fail when I gave their problems less attention. These were the habitual complainers, churches that lived in chronic crisis, enjoying the attention that their endless problems drew. Analyzing them with our Bibles open, God soon gave us the assurance that a church that remains dependent on outsiders' help deserves to fail. It is a parasite on the body of Christ—a sponge that absorbs pastoral care and seldom develops outgoing pastoral work or spiritual effort of its own. A person with the pastoral gift may want to continue shepherding such churches, but an apostle called to be a cross-cultural church planter should shake the dust off his feet as soon as he detects this abnormal lack of spiritual vitality.

God created *time;* He knows how much we have. He knows better than anyone that a church planter lacks time to worry about all the problems that new churches create. That is why Paul told Titus to establish elders in all the churches so that he could turn over the pastoral work to them. Things that you lack time to do unless you neglect your family, or that burn you out physically, emotionally, mentally or spiritually, are simply *not God's will* for you! Delegate or simply drop them! Don't 'dance with the devil' by running to put out every fire that hell's arsonist lights!

12-o Recruit Workers who Commit to See the Job Through

Effective church planters commit simply to do what Jesus says: to disciple a people group, no matter how long it takes or what sacrifice God requires. If your church has 'adopted' a *negl*ected people group and is praying for it, God will raise up people with the apostolic gift that your church can send. If your church is small, it can cooperate with sister churches to put together an apostolic task group. For cross-cultural church reproduction, especially in difficult pioneer fields, a *'do what Jesus says'* commitment is essential for church multiplication. For a person who knows that God has given him the apostolic ('sent one' or 'missionary') gifting and calling to a particular people group, a short-term commitment is totally incompatible—except to gain experience as an apprentice or investigate a field or potential task group. One's gifting defines what he *is.* For the 'sent one' calling, God honors commitment not to stay a certain number of years but to go and do just as He says: *disciple the people.* Short-term commitments to serve in distant fields are valid to gain exposure, discern one's gifts and call from God, and gain experience that will enrich the home church. Short-term work in another culture does not produce church reproduction.

12-p Filter out Non-Essentials

Discern and lay aside all nontransferable methods, attitudes, and equipment--including the way we teach or preach and a distinctly Western style of worship. Do nothing in another culture that is not easy to imitate and be passed on at once.

Patterson brought this filtering process to church planting task groups in Asia:

> **I asked the Asians to define what kind of churches would take root and reproduce among their people in their setting, rural or urban. They started to define a church theologically, describing the ideal church in abstract terms. Not helpful.**
>
> **I asked them if these churches would start with the people sitting on benches as we were doing. They said no, that most churches would start in very poor homes and they would sit on the floor. So we moved the benches back and sat on the floor for worship. Again I raise the question as to what a culturally relevant church would look like and they caught on. We took off our shoes. The women sat to one side. They took a few minutes to compose a praise song from a line in the Psalms and sing it in their musical style (the cook, a neighbor and a friend rushed into the room, happily surprised to hear praises sung in their music form!).**

In most remaining unevangelized fields, only *criminals* can plant churches (according to the laws of such countries). In these fields of restricted access we work underground. Our methods are radically different. We are far stricter in filtering out Western traditions. What we must screen out becomes obvious if we use the New Testament as our filter. We confuse the filtering process if our criteria for filtering come only from anthropological studies. The greater the cultural difference and the more hostile the authorities, the more careful we are to filter out what the New Testament does not explicitly require.

12-q Select Coworkers who Qualify for your Field and Ministry

Look for persons who:
* are like-minded and work well together (Satan cannot sidetrack them into endless disputes about philosophical issues),
* are willing to work bivocationally when necessary (especially if working in very poor fields or in fields of restricted access),
* are heartily recommended by those who know them well and

who pray continually for them in their home church (good ministry grows out of good relationships),

❖ are called by God to serve as career church planters (not those who use church planting only to launch *other* ministries),

❖ readily bond in love with the people of a new culture,

❖ submit willingly to the task group leader(s),

❖ agree on objectives and general methods,

❖ agree on basic doctrinal and church practices,

❖ share similar social, economic, and educational backgrounds,

❖ receive ongoing training and evaluation,

❖ can mentor and delegate responsibility to new local leaders,

❖ pray and resist Satan (the ultimate battle is not against culture, Islam, or other religions, but against the devil and his demons, who only use culture: Ephesians 6:11-13).

❖ have a cross-bearing disciple's commitment (are willing to give their life, if necessary, to extend the Kingdom of God among the people: Luke 9:23-24).

12-r   Discern and List Key Activities for a Church Multiplication Task Group

Ask the Lord to help you see what your churches will be doing in the future. If you lead a church planting task group, you will find your job easier if you use a *Progress Chart* as a checklist. It should includes these activities for task group members:

☐ Prayerfully select and focus on the specific people you plan to disciple, preferable people who are culturally similar to you or some of your task group members.

☐ Bond with the people.

☐ Maintain constant, fervent prayer for the unsaved and for converts.

☐ Seek good contacts (persons of peace).

☐ Witness for Jesus in a way that converts immediately imitate and pass on.

☐ Baptize without undue delay. When possible, baptize entire families as the apostles did.

☐ Break bread. Celebrate our participation in Christ's body.

☐ Teach in a way that new leaders immediately imitate and pass on to other leaders.

☐ Organize by building on *relationships*, not *rules*.

☐ Workers agree with their wives on her ministry.

☐ Keep doing evangelism in the community. Don't stop after public worship services begin!

☐ Let worship be an edifying, inspiring celebration.

☐ Give responsibility to the local leaders and avoid over-control, which usually comes with subsidy from outsiders.

☐ Arrange for clear, regular accountability for everybody.

Appendix C, An Example of a Progress Chart for Field Workers, includes activities for:

- Starting a new church.
- Organizing for church multiplication.
- Managing one's time for church multiplication.
- A separation ceremony for the task group.
- Different categories of people to mobilize on the field (listed in section **13-f**).
- And, add plans to your *Progress Charts* to mobilize church planting task groups.

12-s   Note Plans to Agree on Guidelines for the Mission Task Group

If applicable, please note plans to mobilize a church planting task group. Plan together with coworkers if possible:

_____

_____

_____

_____

_____

_____

_____

_____

_____

_____

13.
Church Reproduction from the Viewpoint of a
Field Supervisor

Find in Matthew 20:20-28 a leader does in God's Kingdom:

Then the mother of Zebedee's sons came to Jesus with her sons and, kneeling down, asked a favor of him. "What is it you want?" he asked. She said, "Grant that one of these two sons of mine may sit at your right and the other at your left in your kingdom."

"You don't know what you are asking," Jesus said to them. "Can you drink the cup I am going to drink?" "We can," they answered.

Jesus said to them, "You will indeed drink from my cup, but to sit at my right or left is not for me to grant. These places belong to those for whom they have been prepared by my Father."

When the ten heard about this, they were indignant with the two brothers. Jesus called them together and said, "You know that the rulers of the Gentiles lord it over them, and their high officials exercise authority over them. Not so with you. Instead, whoever wants to become great among you must be your servant, and whoever wants to be first must be your slave-just as the Son of Man did not come to be served, but to serve, and to give his life as a ransom for many."

Find 1 Peter 5 what leaders in the church are to do:

To the elders among you, I appeal as a fellow elder, a witness of Christ's sufferings and one who also will share in the glory to be revealed: Be shepherds of God's flock that is under your care, serving as overseers-not because you must, but because you are willing, as God wants you to be; not greedy for money, but eager to serve; not lording it over those entrusted to you, but being examples to the flock. And when the Chief Shepherd appears, you will receive the crown of glory that will never fade away. Peter 5:1-4

Patterson enjoyed having a good field supervisor as a mentor:

During my first term on the field we served under Virgil Gerber, a rarely gifted and flexible field supervisor who knew what discipling is. He was the first person I heard use the word 'disciple' as a verb. And he applied it to training pastors! Today's society might understood better if we call it Christian *mentoring*.

Virgil made me set goals and plan the small steps to reach them. He told us to stop training pastors in our traditional way, when it didn't produce results. At first I felt a bit hostile toward him but God used Virgil to start me thinking as a discipler and mentor. I came to appreciate a tough but caring field supervisor.

13-a Help "Apostles" to Select Their Field Wisely

A pioneer cross-cultural church planting task group needs workers with the apostolic gift and calling to work where the gospel has not yet entered (Romans 15:20-22). We help them to find the receptive people within a field and to trust God to lead them to those whom He has prepared, who have been chosen from before the foundation of the world (Ephesians 1:4).

The most receptive social networks are often those most hidden. Most fields and all growing cities have a variety of people groups or subcultures. Common workers and the oppressed are the most receptive but also the least conspicuous to a Western missionary. Jesus made a point of the fact that He came to proclaim the gospel to the *poor*. He began His public ministry among the working class in Galilee. Had He begun in Jerusalem or another influential city with the rich and powerful, they would have crucified Him prematurely.

The satisfied middle classes that wield power resist change and seldom respond during the first generation of discipling. They will occasionally convert as individuals, especially students, but in a pioneer field they rarely join together for a grass-roots people movement for Christ.

When they first penetrate a new field, American missionaries often form friendships with people of the middle class because of similar education and economic backgrounds. Do not assume that you can reach a *neglect*ed people group in a pioneer field from the top down, unless it is a small, closely-knit tribe. The middle class does become receptive as a class, however, with second- or third-generation Christians. We see this happening now in Latin America, Africa south of the Sahara, the Philippines, South Korea, and Southern India. When we first enter a new field, we seek to detect a responsive subculture within a people group. Economic differences will define this subculture as much as racial.

Missionaries sometimes describe a people as hard when in fact the people would be receptive to Christ if He were presented in a culturally relevant way. Church planters sometimes needlessly provoke a negative response by overreacting to, or prematurely attacking, idolatrous practices and other sins of the society. Let us exercise at least as much patience as we expect others to have with the obvious shortcomings of our own evangelical subculture.

13-b Evangelize Victims of Brutal Class Discrimination in Resistant Fields

For the initial penetration of restricted areas as in North Africa and much of Southern Asia, seek to live and work where you have access to people who want change. Also, try to work where authorities do not watch closely. You will find people who are painfully oppressed by political, racial or social discrimination. They are generally more receptive. But also take care not to engage in messy foreign politics.

13-c Help Workers to Bond with the People and Their Culture

Church planters must feel God's call to a people and dedicate themselves to disciple them as Jesus commands, not simply to do a project among them. They need to live among them and appreciate their distinct ways. No matter how corrupt a culture may be, God has planted beautiful things in it. Ruth is an example of bonding with another culture. Her loving relationship with her mother-in-law Naomi and later with Boaz enabled her to bond thoroughly with the Israelites and their culture. This is the better way. Our deepest social needs should be met by the people we bond with, except, of course, our immediate family.

13-d Help the Task Group to Make Disciples the Way Jesus Commanded and Modeled

Jesus told His disciples to:

Fish for men (Matthew 4:19).
We witness to people who are lost (e.g., Jesus and Nicodemus, the Samaritan woman, the 'nations' of Matthew 28:19).

Teach obedience to His commands (Matthew 28:19-20).
We go to neglected peoples and form obedient congregations. New believers need this orientation to obey in order to become the loving, active disciples that Jesus seeks.

In case you do not remember, let us review Jesus' commands:

- **Repent, believe, and be filled with the Spirit** (turn from sin and serve God),
- **Be baptized** (and continue in the new, holy life that it initiates),
- **Celebrate Communion** in union with Christ and His Body the

church,

- **Love God and men** in practical ways, forgiving, showing mercy,
- **Pray**,
- **Give**,
- **Make disciples** witnessing, shepherding, training, and bearing the cross.

Jesus told His disciples to bear their cross. *Total* commitment. Live sacrificially; accept death to carry out His commission (Luke 9:23). Concerning such dedication Patterson confesses:

In seminary I privately suspected that such sacrificial discipleship was fanatical. I did not really want to practice or preach it. I sought security and position with an established church or mission agency.

After my first convert in northern Honduras was hacked to death by machete following his baptism, God forced me to rethink my life's commitment. I saw that my security-minded attitude would only stifle church reproduction. A *measured* commitment is contagious; other workers will soon begin to vie for comfortable positions. With my change of attitude the leaders I mentored also became more sober. A new group of dedicated workers emerged that left the semi-committed ones far behind.   God used them to multiply churches.

13-e   Train New Leaders The Way Jesus and His Apostles Did

Jesus and His apostles showed us how to disciple on a *pastoral* level. This is *Christian mentoring.* We train pastors and missionaries the way Jesus trained the twelve apostles, which was essentially the way Paul trained Timothy and Titus, and Aquila and Priscilla trained Apollos. They personally mentored them, modeling skills and sharing their burdens.

In foreign fields we aim to mobilize local nationals for ministry. Healthy churches need local elders—soon. In the beginning we can use their home as a classroom. Their flock is their wife and children, who usually do a good job exposing their flaws! They practice shepherding skills, including teaching and discipline with their families. Normally other friends and relatives are added to the flock very soon. The home is an ideal place to learn basic shepherding skills. Many a leader has been undone by failure in his home.

We use the congregation as the main learning arena. Outsiders on the task group help local leaders immediately to begin shepherding and mentoring other leaders. They mentor new leaders in a way that they can imitate. In most of the remaining neglected fields we avoid 'classroom only' teaching in which professors take little personal responsibility for the present, effective ministry of their students. In restricted fields, where growth comes from multiplying clusters of tiny home churches, God's 'sheep' need very many more shepherds than traditional churches would provide. New pastors of tiny house churches should begin training 'Timothies' for daughter churches as soon as possible.

Let us examine some of the things a Christian mentor does:

- **Maintain a caring, personal relationship** with our apprentices, spending time together and giving each one attention. We listen to each trainee to know the needs of his flock. For a beginner this 'flock' may be his family, which will soon become a cell or church. We share the responsibility for the discipline and effective ministry of each trainee.

  Clarification: Personal discipling on the pastoral level is *not* one-on-one tutoring. It may be with one person, but tutoring is not its main purpose. Jesus discipled twelve leaders; sometimes he dealt with only three; on rare occasions he worked with only one. Paul always had a small apostolic band.

- **Model** ministry skills. New Testament mentoring requires accompanying leaders in their fieldwork. Planting churches by making forays out of a mission station or base is ineffective. We live among the people, bond with them, and work closely with the new leaders.

- **Share responsibility for the effectiveness of each trainee's current ministry**. Your trainee serves under your guidance. He meets regularly with you to report progress, plan activities, discuss the Word and pray.

- **Relate the Word** directly to each trainee's fieldwork. We recommend the '**menu**' approach:

  LISTEN to each trainee report what his *flock* is doing:
  Like a waiter in a restaurant, we first listen to hear what a trainee's group or church is 'hungry' for.

  PLAN:
  We help each trainee plan what his group will do for the next week or two. Write down these plans and

hold him accountable for them.

LOCATE the corresponding studies on the menu:

The menu is a checklist or *Progress Chart* listing ministries required by the New Testament, key doctrines, Bible passages and commands of Jesus. Give (sell) the studies that support what your trainee has planned.

13-f   Plan Strategically to Mobilize People

If you help plan field strategy, you must envision the various categories of *persons or groups* at work. Wise mission planners, like military strategists, begin the process of planning by stating the long-range objectives so clearly that preparatory steps are obvious, almost self-evident. To plan strategically for a specific people group, we envision the results God will produce 20 years from now. What will the churches look like? How many? What size? Led by whom? How will they reproduce?

We keep these objectives for pioneer mission work in view along with important facts about the people such as their limited resources or freedom, then reason *backwards* through the intermediate steps, to foresee what must happen to reach the objectives. We envision preparatory steps that require only those resources that the national converts and leaders have, to avoid programs too expensive or too electronic for them.

The fourteen mobilization categories listed below appear in **backward order**. The count down from 14 to 1 helps us think strategically. We reason from the farthest future objectives back to the present. We envision the final objective by faith with God's help, then reason carefully step by step, asking what has to happen *prior* to each step. If you're going to see churches multiplying in a chain reaction, for example, what has to happen first to prepare leaders to coordinate such a movement for Christ?

When we focus on an objective in the list below, and the realities of the field that bear on it, we consider what must happen *first*, the prior step, then plan the still earlier steps leading to it.

For example, before defining in detail what the task group will do, we determine what the *nationals* will do. Then, what the task group does for the most part comes naturally. Before we try to define how to prepare the task group, we need first to have a fairly clear picture of what they will help the *nationals* do.

After we know what kind of task group we need and how to prepare it, we are ready define the methods of those who work at home to prepare and send the task group.

Take a moment now for *backward* planning. Examine the 'backward' list of steps for mobilizing categories of people who may need to participate. As you work through the backward list, you will start with your final objective, then reasoning back to the present. You will define for each step what must happen prior to it. Mark items that need special attention.

Strategic Objectives for a Pioneer Field
(starting with final objectives and working back)

! sdrawkcab knihT

☐ *14* **Churches organize on a national or large regional level to continue cooperative reproduction.**

This widespread conquest requires that in the future many national, indigenous churches serve and reproduce among a currently neglected people.

Ask yourself and your coworkers:

> How will this reproductive organization happen?
>
> Who will take the responsibility for it?
>
> What must happen first?

Reasoning backwards, strategic planners see what must happen prior to such widespread church multiplication:

☐ *13* **National workers prepare to serve on a national or regional level as humble servant leaders to coordinate inter-church cooperation.**

Such leadership on the regional or synod level requires that national servant leaders mobilize and humbly, lovingly

138

oversee newer pastors or elders. They acquire this skill from 'apostles' who take personal, caring responsibility for their fruitful ministry, as the Apostle Paul did for new workers. Otherwise, the first national leaders, lacking maturity for work at this level, easily become grasping and demanding.

Ask: How will pastors learn to become regional servant leaders?

Who will model servant leadership for them?

How? Where?

Strategic planners envision what must happen first, to prepare such regional level servant leaders as pastors of pastors:

□ *12* Local churches mature and bring transformation to surrounding communities.

New churches grow in Christ and practice all vital New Testament ministries, led by caring servant leaders. These new pastors not only shepherd their flocks with loving care but also mobilize other newer pastors for ministry. They acquire this skill on the job, not in classrooms. In pioneer fields missionaries demonstrate it for the first new leaders.

Ask: How do we assure that churches practice all essential New Testament ministries?

How do we make sure that their shepherds learn servant leadership?

Who will model it for them and how?

To prepare shepherding servant leaders, strategic planners envision first the kind of pastoral training that assures it:

□ *11* Training is made available for many national leaders— as many as needed to perpetuate church reproduction—with guidance during their years of inexperience and formation, to shepherd their people with loving care and not just preach and enforce rules.

Educators do not simply pass information on to pastoral students but train them to *edify* and *equip* the local body of Christ for ministry (Ephesians 4:11-16). For this, trainers with the gift of teaching must work in harmony with others who have different spiritual gifts, as 1 Corinthians 12-13 requires. Good leadership training requires *balanced* discipling that relates the Word to the work through loving relationships, in the power of the Holy Spirit. Educators in a pioneer field, where new shepherding elders cannot leave their flocks, avoid impractical formal institutional training. Otherwise, economically motivated youths will respond but, lacking adequate preparatory education or experience in well established churches, they fail to assimilate the intensive teaching. They also have not yet had models for effective shepherding and cannot realistically relate what they learn to their ministry.

Ask: How do we prepare the people and their future pastors to appreciate and understand loving servant leadership?

What kind of discipling will lay a foundation for it?

Strategic planners, reasoning backwards, see that we must model loving discipling first on a beginning level:

□ *10* New Christians learn through caring discipling to exalt Jesus by obeying His commands in love.

Disciplers teach new believers to obey Jesus' commands before and above all else. Jesus requires us to believe, repent, be baptized and receive the Holy Spirit, love, break bread, pray, give, and disciple others. We avoid long indoctrination *before* obedience training; it stifles loving discipleship and makes it harder to mobilize passive hearers later on for active ministry. Building on this foundation, the new believers practice New Testament church body life, serving one another with their God-given gifts in the power of the Holy Spirit. They observe their disciplers forming the loving relationships needed for this type of obedience. They see their disciplers make disciple in a way they can imitate at once with their family and friends.

Ask: Who will disciple new believers this way during the initial stages of evangelism when there are no national leaders yet?

What kind of churches will provide the right environment for it?

How will the disciplers learn to do it?

Strategic planners recognize that such relational discipling and loving obedience requires spending time with people, especially right after they first come to Christ. This requires a much more relational form of evangelism than what tradition offers:

□ **9** **Seekers take their first steps of faith with the help of a caring church body.**

When seekers repent and discover the new holy and eternal life in Christ, their conversion is confirmed by being added to a loving church body by baptism. We help seekers see the crucified and risen Christ living in us (2 Corinthians 5:15). We model the sacrificial pilgrim life in a hostile world.

Ask: How will we assure that such a caring church body will exist that early in the church planting project?

Who will lead such embryonic churches?

What will they do to lay a foundation for loving disciple making?

Reasoning backwards, strategic planners see that loving, need-oriented evangelism requires that we first form a church planting task group skilled in incarnational evangelism and relational discipling:

Strategic Objectives for 'Outside' Workers

□ **8** **Workers penetrating a new community or field identify with its social life and culture.**

Workers from the outside bond with the people and culture, and learn the language if it is different from theirs. They discern and use methods of evangelism and teaching that the people can afford, imitate and use without delay with others. They focus on a specific people group and ways to penetrate it. They use different spiritual gifts to deal with the diverse needs of the people group. They ruthlessly screen out technology, equipment, and methods that are beyond the reach of the people. They recruit coworkers from among the people or from a very similar culture who can readily identify with the culture.

Ask: Who will form such a culturally relevant task group?

How will they make sure they have truly bonded with the people and culture?

Strategic planners see that they may need to arrange for a partnership with workers from another culture:

□ 7 **Task group leaders or mission agency leaders mobilize workers from emerging churches in the two-thirds world.**

In fields of a very different culture we partner with churches missionaries are culturally closer to the people we are focusing on and relate more readily to them. No amount of anthropological training to adapt to a new culture is as effective as being born in it or in a very similar one. The most effective evangelists for starting the kind of churches that multiply freely within a specific people group are those with similar background, politics, race, language, economic and social status, education, family size, rural or urban life-style and world view.

Ask: How are missionaries from churches with limited resources in the two-thirds' world mobilized?

Who develops the bridge between cultures?

How do we avoid forcing our culture and values on workers from another, or building dependency?

How can workers from other cultures get training for fields of restricted access?

Strategic planners see that workers first need training and deployment as bivocational "tentmakers":

□ 6 **Bivocational workers develop businesses or other means of support and residence in fields closed to traditional mission work.**

Only bivocational missionaries can reside in many—perhaps most--of the remaining neglected fields long enough to bring about church multiplication. Like Paul, they need cross-cultural church planting experience, task groups, formal commissioning and employment such as a small business that enables them to mix with the working class.

Ask: How are bivocational workers trained?

Who will develop bivocational work?

Strategic planners help sending churches to envision these shifts in mission approaches, to prepare and send the kind of workers who can reproduce churches in today's neglected fields.

Strategic Objectives for 'Sending Churches' and Agencies

□ *5* **Workers practice ministry skills and receive mentoring in sending churches, to prepare to reproduce churches in other areas.**

The skills needed may include those required for bivocational work, language learning where no formal training is available, incarnational evangelism, small group worship, organization of a congregation for organic body life, training leaders by mentoring behind the scenes and church reproduction.

Ask: Who models the needed ministry skills for workers who enter other cultures?

Where? How?

Strategic planners recognize the importance of these skills for the remaining neglected fields and make plans for the preparation of missionary trainers who are in touch with today's world.

□ *4* **Missionary trainers prepare to mentor workers in a way that will transfer to fields where institutional methods are impractical.**

Trainers keep in touch with field workers to know what for what skills new missionaries need. They also get practice with non-formal training methods by being mentored or cooperating with experienced mentors in the training of others. Western Seminary in Portland, Oregon offers such non-formal training. *(For information contact Dr. Galen Currah: Galen@Currah.com.)*

Ask: Who are the missionary trainers?

How are they prepared?

Strategic planners recognize that such specialized training is useless if a worker's mission agency fails to implement them. Therefor they also plan for a working relationship with agencies that can deploy workers with the right methods and the right coworkers in the right fields:

□ *3* **A cooperating mission agency deals realistically with today's world with its many neglected fields, including where bivocational workers must make disciple secretly.**

By the time a mission agency is in a position to orient a new worker, it is often too late. The worker has been exposed for years to methods and attitudes in the local church that hardly resemble those needed in the field.

Ask: How do sending churches cooperate with mission agencies to see that workers are deployed wisely?

Who will orient mission agency leaders who lack these strategic perspectives? How?

Strategic planners see that in order for an agency to develop an effective working relationship with sending churches, they need preparation and a challenge:

□2 Sending churches make their people aware of these guidelines and equip workers accordingly.

Churches help in the preparation of missionaries, since many of the skills they need cannot be acquired in institutional classrooms. They cooperate with training institutions and mission agencies to provide experience with needed skills for their workers.

Ask: How will leaders in sending churches communicate these guidelines?

Who will motivate and orient the leaders? How?

Strategic planners recognize that much advice for missionary training and field selection comes from organizations and individuals with a preconceived agenda. Therefore they discern between mere mission agency 'recruiters' and unbiased career counselors with no agenda for missionary candidates. Both are needed, but the unbiased mentoring should come first to avoid having workers trained in the wrong way, lined up with the wrong coworkers or sent to the wrong place.

□1 Unbiased mission career advisors and mentors coach churches and missionary candidates.

These counselors keep in mind all fourteen of these ministry areas, to enable potential workers to see where they fit in. But most counselors don't. Informal career counseling abounds, often by accident. For good counselors it won't be by accident; it will be planned and purposeful. They will help workers to keep their final objectives in mind as they assess their gifts, experience, resources, plans and working relationships, in order to plan future ministry.

Ask: Who will serve as mission career advisors?

Who will prepare them? How?

Strategic planners serve as, or train, unbiased mission career advisor to mentor church leaders and missionary candidates.

13-g Help Coworkers Evaluate Their Use of Ministry Time

Let us manage our limited time in a way that honors God. Reproductive evangelism and church multiplication take much time. To establish priorities daily to use our time wisely, we keep in mind Jesus' commands as the foundation for our God-given priorities (Ephesians 5.15-17).

Mark the clocks by guidelines below that you aim to deal with.

Delegate pastoral and evangelistic responsibilities to other leaders.

Let new workers do things. Once someone agrees to do something, avoid over-control of his or her work. Do not expect coworkers or your wife (or husband) merely to run errands for you.

Spend ample time with your family each day, and a whole day each week.

Take your Sabbaths. There was a time when you would have been stoned to death if you didn't. Do not let your family fear that they have to compete with your ministry for your time. If circumstances force you to miss your day with the family, make up for it without failure the next week.

Discuss your ministry regularly with your spouse and children so that they appreciate it and do not begrudge time you spend away.

Talk and pray with them about your plans (and theirs) before you travel and review with them what happened in both places when you return.

Avoid spending time arguing or discussing controversies.

New missionaries, seeking contacts, often cast their pearls before swine. We may enjoy an occasional friendly theological argument, but we must not get caught up in controversial issues. We discipline ourselves to avoid non-edifying details of theological discussions (remember Paul's warnings about foolish questions and genealogies; see 1 Timothy 1:4; Titus 3:9). Sometimes we cannot avoid a controversy. But we can avoid giving it too much time; keep doing the positive things you know God wants you to do. Don't feel you always have to prove yourself right. To always be right is dangerous.

Start immediately turning over long-range leadership responsibilities to local leaders.

Train adults who are potential leaders; give them more and more responsibilities as they prove capable of handling them. Let a new leader make mistakes. How he handles mistakes is crucial. If he learns from them, the mistakes become a blessing. If he tries to cover them up, look elsewhere for a leader.

Keep analyzing how you spent your time during the day or previous week.

Be ruthless in cutting from your work schedule (time spent in ministry) all activities--no matter how enjoyable--that do not move you toward your God-given goals. Avoid excessive television or other entertainment that fails to edify or unite your family.

Ask another person to monitor your progress.

No one effectively evaluates the use of his own time; we all need someone to hold us accountable to carry out our plans and God-given objectives.

If you are an excessively hard-working husband, ask your wife to schedule your appointments.

Does your wife feel insecure at times because of your time commitments? Does she (or the children) need to compete

146

with the Lord's work for your attention? if you are unsure, then they probably do--ask her about it! if the answer is yes, then authorize her to schedule your time, especially for activities that take you away from your home overnight or longer. If you often feel pressured, driven by guilt to have to fill every half hour of your time with work, you are taking on too many responsibilities; some of the things you are doing are obviously not God's will.

Give your wife authority to schedule regular sabbaths, the equivalent of one day a week spent with the family. Celebrate special events. Put off for a later week work that cannot be skipped.

Pray for daily self-discipline to follow God's priorities.

13-h Organize for Reproduction

With love born of the Holy Spirit, we organize the body of Christ to enable it to reproduce normally, doing the guidelines listed below. Mark any that need attention:

☐ **Build organization on relationships and worker's strengths.**

If a worker wins people to Christ, they will bond with him; arrange for him to lead and disciple them, or for them to join a small group in which he is active. If a worker disciples new believers well, let him be the one who shepherds or teaches them, or for them to join a small group in which he is active. If a worker trains newer workers well, let them continue in a group or projects which he leads or in which he takes an active part.

Let a worker earn 'promotion' by releasing his disciples and trainees for responsible ministries in a 2 Timothy 2:2 'mentor chain reaction.' A worker who disciples two others who disciple still others creates a chain in which he is respected as a discipler. If he has the gift of leadership, let him lead the new network; if not, let him work closely with a leader.

☐ **If you are a missionary from the outside, edify the growing body of Christ through your trainees.**

Do not do all the teaching, shepherding, and decision-making. Model it, then step back and let your 'Timothies' do the work in freedom as you coach them from behind the scenes. Enable others to begin discipling and shepherding in their homes. Provide Bible studies or reading schedules that are simple and easy to use in their homes or small groups.

Aim for mentoring chains (you train one and trains others). You might help your 'Timothy' set up a regular time of Bible study in his home and encourage him to help another newer believer do the same. These 'links' in a mentoring chain will keep multiplying if we pray and work hard to forge loving relationships at every link. New churches can wither on the vine when all the believers are linked directly to only one overworked church planter. They watch the church planter do all the work until he collapses exhausted.

☐ **Mentor able, mature men (*elder* types).**

Avoid training single, young men in pioneer fields as pastors. Train those who qualify as elders to shepherd. Paul lists the qualifications in Titus 1:5-9. In a pioneer field few men meet all the requirements, so we train the best ones that God gives us, using the scriptural guidelines as our criteria. They must be sober and able to teach. A new church in a field with no experienced pastoral leaders normally gets along better if led by several elders.

☐ **Organize in a detailed way *after*--never *before*--you know the specific things that the people need to do.**

Avoid rules and bylaws that do not come directly from Scripture unless you obviously need them at the time; discard them as soon as they are no longer necessary.

☐ **Keep evaluating your progress ruthlessly.**

We keep our eyes fixed on our goal, on the horizon. We also focus on the path as we go along, constantly evaluating our progress toward the goal. We pray and plan for breakthroughs when progress snags block progress. We explore new ways around the obstacles. As Scoggins discovered,

> **We found, in our experience with house churches, that such `horizon travel' leaves plenty of room for innovation, new initiatives, and a great deal of looking to the Lord!**

☐ **Deploy missionaries to use their *strengths,* not just to meet a *need* as other over-worked missionaries see it.**

Avoid placing new workers in an area simply because there is a 'need.' Where is there not a need? Let them minister where they can use their gifts and talents freely. Do not place them in a position simply to maintain the smooth operation of *programs.* Mission agency field supervisors sometimes fail to mobilize missionaries and national workers according to their gifts and experience. This error causes many to burn out.

☐ **Follow the biblical pattern of organization, arranging for loving cooperation among those with different gifts.**

The Western institutional pattern of specialization separates persons with different gifts or ministries. It forms independent and often competitive commissions, departments, or branches. Such organization can stifle church reproduction. We help people with very different gifts to find ways to cooperate that open new vistas for effective ministry.

☐ **Keep the vision alive and growing.**

The people in a task group or a church need a vision for what they believe God desires them to accomplish through their gifts. Once the vision is clear, we help each person to find his or her place in the ever-new 'horizon travel.' The vision needs fine-tuning as people come in with new spiritual gifts, to enable them to practice their gift-based ministries. The vision grows and shifts as we travel from one horizon to the next. God does not let us see the whole future but leads us from one horizon to another.

☐ **Enable volunteer workers to set their goals and performance standards.**

Encourage self-initiative, rather than pushing people by offering rewards for those who outdo others, threatening, using organizational clout or competition (rivalry is condemned in Scripture). Help workers to define their jobs and goals.

The underlying motive for true Christian service is love for Jesus who said, "If you love me, obey my commands" (John 14:15). When this discipling mentality of loving obedience is established in a church body, volunteer workers more easily visualize and achieve what God wants them to do.

☐ **Let mature shepherds with a servant's heart make crucial decisions for a church or group, rather than always taking a democratic vote or seeking a 'consensus.'**

1 Peter 5:1-5 and Hebrew 13:17 require obedience to our God-given shepherds. Therefore we do not rely on majority rule except for transactions requiring a congregational vote for legal reasons.

> **Scripture and history show that the 'majority' seldom votes for the cross-bearing, faith-stretching disciple's route. The 'majority' typically chooses a more secure, traditional, less demanding path—away from Scripture and Christ's guidelines.**

The Kingdom of God on earth (the church) is not a democracy. It is a monarchy. That's what the word 'kingdom' means! Jesus is our King.

Reproductive discipling requires loving authority, in which the strong leader is a humble servant (Matthew 20:25-28). Sometimes otherwise sound discipling programs crash because participants submit to majority rule within their church or denomination. Rule by the majority means that the sheep lead the shepherd. It is the abdication of godly, New Testament leadership. Let Jesus reign; human overseers are His 'under-shepherds.'

☐ **Develop church body life *between* new churches and groups.**

Church multiplication thrives on loving relationships between churches. Scripture reveals nothing of the independent spirit and 'autonomy' that some American missionaries impart to a new church. They may mean well, but come from a culture that idealizes individualism and personal rights above the welfare of the community.

Scoggins recalls:

> **We set up 'fellowships' consisting of several house churches. Each fellowship is a network of from two to six cooperating house churches. The leaders meet together regularly for fellowship, training and counsel. They discuss decisions that might affect the other house churches in the fellowship. The congregations all meet together, usually monthly. These working relationships between leaders serve to prevent a congregation from developing an ingrown or 'cultic' devotion to one strong leader. They also enable older elders to mentor younger ones. These congregational relationships reduce the number of failures of the house churches.**

Remember, your flock isn't the only one on this planet that God watches over!

The New Testament letters reveal cooperative, edifying body life *between* churches. Ephesians 4:11-16, for example, urges interaction not for one isolated congregation but for the cluster of closely-knit house churches that made up the 'church in Ephesus.' Christ's body is not a local congregation. The form of organization of the church in Jerusalem, like those in highly restricted fields today, resembled more an underground crime network than a modern, traditional church. Their leaders were considered as outlaws. In many of the remaining neglected fields we should not try to form large congregations, but an underground (in other words, criminal) network of unauthorized, tiny house churches. Criminals for Christ! Christian workers must be criminals according to the country's pagan laws, in order to obey God, as in Acts 4:19.

Healthy churches grow in *clusters* through multiplication, avoiding limitations imposed by physical facilities or legalistic control.

☐ **Trust the Holy Spirit to motivate new leaders.**

Do not fear that false doctrine will automatically creep into rapidly reproducing churches. History shows otherwise. Healthy, reproductive churches or cell groups are far more loyal to their mentors and obedient to Christ than their sterile, non-reproductive counterparts.

Missionaries who suspect false doctrine will creep in if they turn their backs overprotect the churches and provoke a rebellious spirit that opens the window for all kinds of rare birds to fly in and bring about the error they fear.

Every new church that is born has the same Holy Spirit, the same love for Christ, the same devotion to the Word of God as any other church. Why would God give it less of His Spirit? Just make sure you train the new pastors and elders in the Word of God. The only sense in which newer churches are necessarily weaker is immaturity; they are baby churches. Let them take their baby steps!

☐ **Do not overly fear a new leader's weaknesses (we all have them); rather, build on his *strengths*.**

Trusting the Holy Spirit, we build on what a potential leader can do; we release him to do it, instead of building rules around him to make him 'safe.' David was a great leader because God built on his strengths, not on his obvious weaknesses. We give responsibility to the men that God gives us. There is no perfect leader this side of heaven.

Scoggins emphasizes:

In our experience, strong men have strong weaknesses. If we develop good relationships between the leaders of a church, God uses other elders to offset those weaknesses. The strong leader does not become independent and proud; rather, he recognizes his need for his fellow elders and appreciates them.

Whether serving on a task group or in a church, the leaders need to set the pace in relying on others to help us in our weaknesses. As we become more aware of our own weaknesses, we become more willing to mobilize other leaders who also have glaring weaknesses. We find more and more that we need to rely on their strengths!

☐ **Delegate pastoral responsibilities.**

Let men with pastoral potential develop their gifts. Model pastoral skills for them. Give them the tools to study the Bible to teach its truths to others. Help them to make disciples at all levels, to multiply themselves and their church or group.

☐ **Help potential leaders to clarify personal objectives.**

Enable them to define their God-given goals for themselves and their people, and the little, intermediate steps to keep walking toward them.

☐ **Evaluate your progress by measuring results, not efforts.**

Define goals in terms of concrete results expected. Help the leaders of each task group, or church body to evaluate its progress in terms of *results*. Measuring *efforts* does not tell you if you are progressing toward your goals.

Efforts mean the things we do to win people for Christ and edify the church (meetings, classes, lessons, reading, ministries, etc.).

Results mean:
converts receive baptism,
  churches give birth to daughter churches or cells,
   workers start new ministries,
    families practice daily prayer,
     believers practice regular, sacrificial giving,
      new disciples take on ministry,
       new teachers and mentors apply the Bible.

Loving obedience leads to efforts made in the power of the Holy Spirit, which bring the results.

☐ **In pioneer fields use a simple worship form that new leaders with limited training can imitate at once and pass on to others whom they train.**

Use a culturally relevant worship style that new elders can lead with a minimum of supervision. If they are inexperienced, they should not do pulpit oratory. Do not even model it for them if possible or they will try it and it will make them proud. Let them celebrate the Lord's Supper weekly, read Scripture, exhort, and tell Bible stories or lead discussions about a Bible text that their mentors have helped them prepare.

☐ **Develop a midwife mentality for reproducing churches.**

If you work cross-culturally, help new churches to reproduce on their initiative, trusting in the power of the Holy Spirit. We do not cause the reproduction ourselves. The new congregation should take responsibility as soon as possible for giving birth to still other churches and for training their pastors.

Ironically, the stronger an expatriate church planting team is organizationally, the harder it is to keep its hands off the infant church and to let it take grow and initiative. Beware of unnecessary meddling!

☐ **Accept ongoing accountability only to those who encourage you in a ministry that uses your gifts and strengths, in fulfillment of what God is calling you to do.**

Prayerfully verify potential overseers' attitudes before committing your life's career to a particular project or organization.

☐ **Learn to disciple on all levels:**
    evangelize *seekers*,
        teach loving obedience to *new believers*,
            shepherd *growing Christians*,
                mentor *leaders*.

The world's remaining neglected fields need church planters and evangelists skilled in mentoring leaders. In Muslim and other fields where Christian gatherings are restricted--about one-third of the world's people--we work without classrooms or pulpits. A church that practices biblical discipling does not need a special program or department for evangelism. It is integrated into every aspect of the church's life, just as Paul includes it in the normal work of a pastor (2 Timothy 4:1-5).

13-i Note Plans to Organize for Reproduction

_____

_____

_____

_____

_____

_____

_____

_____

_____

_____

_____

14.
Church Reproduction
from the Viewpoint of a
Cell or House Church

Why crow about *house* churches ???
They're for the buzzards !   I want stained glass windows and my private perch !
Not some private nest !

Half of your wits remained up north when you migrated!

We say *'house churches'* even if a flock roosts in an office, warehouse or oak tree.

14-a   Keep Groups Small Enough for 'One Another' Body Life

This applies to separate house churches or cells tied to a larger body. We mention both home groups and house churches because, ideally, there should be little difference. We consider home groups or 'cells' to be a small church within a larger one. We do not consider them to be viable cell churches if the small groups are only 'Bible studies,' simply 'fellowship groups,' or merely 'ministry teams.' Both house churches and cells, by our definition, obey all the commands of Christ and do everything an obedient church would do.

Both house churches and home cell groups take advantage of the smallness of the group to practice New Testament 'one another' body life. Both aim at church (or cell) reproduction. Both normally train most of their leaders on the job.

The basic difference between house churches and home cell groups is how they identify with a larger body. House churches normally identify with a cluster of sister house churches, and have occasional united celebrations. Home groups or cells, as satellites of one larger body, identify mainly with it and also have united celebration with the other home cell groups, usually more frequently, often weekly, in the traditional Sunday Morning worship.

Christians in a conventional church enter into the dynamic church body life of a small group in two ways. One is by divorce. People tire of institutional, impersonal programs and find or form a house church, often taking with them much pain and a reactionary spirit. Another route avoids this painful division; a traditional church honestly faces its lack of relational, interactive church body life and forms vital groups small enough for it.

Both cell groups and house churches must partner closely with sister groups to meet New Testament requirements and stay healthy. Groups small enough for effective 'one-another' ministry within the group are *too small* to attain all of the vital spiritual gifts and gift-based ministries. Therefore they practice the one-another interaction *between* groups.

I don't trust home groups **!** Being small they'll attract hawks. And they'll invite *division* **!**

We fly into worse risk suppressing those whom God gives pastoral gifting.

Let them lead their small flocks within our larger one.

Your fear is simply lack of faith.

You should rather fear not doing what God's Word requires **!**

To fix Bible references about meeting in homes or houses in your mind, <u>underline</u> in these verses where they are mentioned:

Every day they continued to meet together in the temple courts. They broke bread in their homes and ate together with glad and sincere hearts. Acts 2:46

Day after day, in the temple courts and from house to house, they never stopped teaching and proclaiming the good news that Jesus is the Christ. Acts 5:42

From Miletus, Paul sent to Ephesus for the elders of the church. When they arrived, he said to them: "You know how I lived the whole time I was with you, from the first day I came into the province of Asia. I served the Lord with great humility and with tears, although I was severely tested by the plots of the Jews. You know that I have not hesitated to preach anything that would be helpful to you but have taught you publicly and from house to house." Acts 20:17-20

Greet Priscilla and Aquila, my fellow workers in Christ Jesus. They risked their lives for me. Not only I but all the churches of the Gentiles are grateful to them. Greet also the church that meets at their house. Greet my dear friend Epenetus, who was the first convert to Christ in the province of Asia. Romans 16:5

Paul, a prisoner of Christ Jesus, and Timothy our brother, to Philemon our dear friend and fellow worker, to Apphia our sister, to Archippus our fellow soldier and to the church that meets in your home: Grace to you and peace from God our Father and the Lord Jesus Christ. Philemon 1-3

Patterson found a culturally relevant to encouraged reluctant pastors to name home group leaders:

Forming small groups in Honduran churches at first went against their tradition, which favored the authority of one strong man. The patron or *jefe* was responsible to care for his people, like the rancher who provided the spiritual care of the village on his property and would build a small chapel. Our pastors instinctively feared that group leaders would usurp their authority.

As a result churches grew no larger than what one man could group around him. Churches led by one part-time lay pastor reached a plateau at around forty or fifty members. I gathered a group of pastors to discuss this. I lit a fire on the dirt floor of the chapel; the flames represented hell. I placed paper 'sheep' on several chairs a few feet apart and asked a pastor to guard them against 'wolves' that we named, who sought to steal the sheep from the chairs one at a time and throw them into the fire. The shepherd had to remain behind the chairs but could 'kill' a wolf simply by touching him. While the shepherd guarded one chair, a wolf would rob a sheep from another. Soon nearly all of the sheep were cast into hell. John Calvin would have winced at the theology, but it did make a point. I asked the pastors, who had the greater value, sheep or human souls?

We then asked the pastor to name an elder for each chair, to help him shepherd the sheep. When we turned the wolves loose again, they stole no sheep; instead, all the wolves met death. We read Jethro's advice to Moses in Exodus 18 to name group leaders, and prayed for God's leading. Soon small groups appeared in churches with renewed growth in numbers, service and spiritual virtues.

14-b Take Advantage of the Small Size of the Body to Do Reproductive Discipling

If you plan to form or lead a small group in which reproductive discipleship takes place, plan activities that enable it. Mark discipling activities that your house church or home cell group might practice, below.

ACTIVITIES FOR SMALL CHURCHES OR GROUPS

☐ **Evangelize in homes of friends and relatives.**

The best evangelist is the new believer. We mobilize newborn Christians to their unsaved friends and relatives what Christ has done for them. We keep the network of communication spreading. The most effective evangelists for children are fathers, mothers and siblings, in that order. We mobilize parents to disciple their children. We mobilize children to evangelize younger children.

It is easier to mobilize new believers to evangelize their friends through small, family-oriented groups.

☐ **Confirm each new believer's salvation without delay.**

Scoggins reports:

> **We teach new believers from Acts 2:37-41 three steps to confirm their salvation: repentance, baptism, and being added to the body of believers. We teach older believers their responsibility to shepherd new believers into the body. Since converts are being shepherded individually in love, we encourage them to do the same with those that come to faith through their witness. In some cases an older believer who leads another to faith through these early steps will baptize his 'disciple.' When a husband comes to faith some time before his wife, he may be encouraged to baptize her. When appropriate, we authorize fathers who lead their children to faith to baptize them.**

> **Disciples are taught by their mentors to become a part of the body. Since we emphasize the relational aspect of being part of the body of believers, we use a covenant to spell out the responsibility that believers have for one another as they become church members. When new believers understand that they are joining God's covenant people, their respective mentors recommend them**

for membership. The mentors affirm before the church the faith of the new believers and their readiness to contribute to the life of the body. Upon the recommendation of a mentor, a new believer affirms his or her desire to abide by the covenant, and the body affirms its desire to receive and nurture this new brother or sister. We pattern this covenant ceremony after the vows in a wedding and follow it with a feast to celebrate. *[The covenant is explained in more detail below.]*

When those who lead people to faith also disciple them into the body, discipleship 'chains' extend among new believers. Those who need help naturally go to their mentor. Likewise, mentors feel more responsible for new believers when 'their' believer gets into trouble.

Patterson observed how the Honduran churches effectively confirmed a new convert's salvation:

We discovered that new believers readily trusted that God had accepted them when God's people, the church, formally accepted them. They heeded His Word more eagerly after baptism. Normally the main pastor of the church or an authorized elder baptized them. This was followed by a joyful reception. We tried to give the same importance to baptism as the apostles did (Acts 2:37-42, *etc.*).

☐ **Mobilize fathers to shepherd their families.**

Fathers should pray with their wives and children, read the Word together, and tell their children Bible stories. Scoggins's churches offer daily family reading schedules with questions about what they have read. Practical questions show how the Word of God applies to individual, family, and group needs.

☐ **Help fathers of families and mentors to apply the Word of God continually to their loved ones.**

We give them the tools to discover the meaning of a Bible passage instead of simply telling them what it says. They study it and explain at the next discipling session what they found. For example, we don't simply assign Exodus 18 to our group leaders, but ask them to examine it to find out why group leaders were necessary for Moses, and why our church needs them today. (Note that all the Bible studies recommended in this book ask you to look for something.)

Appendix F provides a list of readings for you, your family or small group, from the whole Bible. It links texts to the practical application, suggests things to find in each passage and indicates stories to tell children.

☐ **Help members of the group to obey all the commands of Jesus, including celebrating the Lord's Supper regularly.**

We can serve Communion in small groups or together with the entire church. Small groups are stronger if they celebrate Communion as a group. Group leaders see that all their members take part in the Lord's Supper regularly. We celebrate it with the solemnity it deserves, following a time of self-examination and confession of sins. We ask the Holy Spirit to use it, to speak to us and strengthen us through its God-ordained drama and mystery.

☐ **Leaders of the group train apprentices as assistant leaders.**

The assistants help lead the groups and start new groups. The church grows by addition and multiplication. Growth by addition adds converts to the existing body; growth by multiplication creates nuclei around which new members are easily added. A new daughter church or a newly formed home group attracts seekers more readily than a large group of mature Christians. The easiest way for a new group leader to get started is to serve as an apprentice to a more experienced leader.

☐ **Arrange for new leaders to gain experience by leading group discussions.**

Inexperienced leaders can start teaching in an effective way simply by asking relevant questions about a Bible passage after their group reads it.

Some questions to apply a Bible passage to our lives:

- What does God want us to do?
- What promises does it have?
- How can it help us to be more like Jesus?
- How will we put it into action? With whom? When?

☐ **Form a new group each time an old one grows large.**

A group is too big when it can no longer give attention to each member's needs and ministry. Experience shows that a group becomes too big somewhere between seven to fourteen adults, depending on the number of leaders and how the people relate to each other.

☐ **Group leaders meet regularly (preferably weekly) with whoever is training and overseeing them.**

This trainer helps the leaders plan their next meetings. He does not force all groups to follow the same path or teach the same material. This hinders the leaders' ability to meet needs and ministry opportunities as they arise. He holds them accountable to carry out evangelism and edifying group activities, and to see that all their people receive discipling from someone.

☐ **Cultivate loving fellowship within the group.**

Give personal, loving attention to seekers and new Christians. Deal with them as a family when possible.

☐ **Deal with common personal needs and apply the Word of God to specific individual or family problems.**

Arrange for counseling within the groups for personal or family problems, such as grief after a death, drug or alcohol addiction, broken family relationships, divorce, or injured emotions.

☐ **Help members to discover and practice their different spiritual gifts (evangelism, prophecy, mercy, giving, faith, healing, etc.).**

Scoggins relates:

> **We emphasize to small house churches that all the spiritual gifts needed for effective nurture of the body are not available in a single church. As a result our house churches network together so that gifts can flow between the churches. This is especially important in the ministry of counseling, or what we call 'soul healing.' We find it true in other areas as well.**

☐ **Pray for one another.**

We pray especially for the lost, the sick and those oppressed by demons. We give personal attention to, and pray for, any person present who might feel left out. This may require forming still smaller prayer groups during part of the meeting time.

☐ **Give offerings for special projects.**

In a small group that is not a house church, the church of which it is a satellite normally does the accounting of these funds.

14-c Be Spiritual Midwives; Assist with the Birth of Churches or Cells

Give lots of loving help to very young groups or churches. Like any newborn infant, they need much tender care.

Neglect of items below commonly aborts groups and churches before their can achieve normal birth. Mark any that you plan to give attention:

☐ **Visualize a clear model for the kind of church body you want and what God wants it to do.**

Ask God to help you visualize by faith the new body doing these activities. Otherwise, you cannot *lead* the people because you do not know where God wants them to go.

To start a healthy church or cell, begin at once to act like a church--obey all of Jesus' commands. Do not simply have a Bible study. You will deal with the Word, but the group exists to do the other ministries also that the Word requires. Plan for a definite, formal beginning and end to each worship time. Celebrate the Lord's Supper regularly with solemnity. Give offerings.

Scoggins found how to share and confirm a church's vision:

> Each of our house churches develops a vision statement that attempts to see about six months into the future. They write it with specific goals for reproduction (starting new evangelistic gathering groups and reproducing disciples, leaders, and new congregations) as well as activities that enable the church to progress toward these goals. Several times in the course of the six-month period the group will have a 'health check' to evaluate its progress and vision and to bring new members up to date with the vision.
>
> In Rhode Island we found that men tend to warm up to a vision. There seems to be a pioneer spirit in men that needs to be stretched. from the outset of evangelism, we try to explain the vision God has for His Kingdom, its expansion, and their place in it. Men tend to be strongly drawn to such 'Kingdom' evangelism. Perhaps this is the response Jesus points to in Matthew 11:12: "From the days of John the

163

> Baptist until now, the kingdom of heaven suffers violence, and violent men take it by force."
>
> An example from physics helped me explain this. Moving objects generate friction, which slows down the object. A similar form of friction develops in human institutions. Churches tend toward maintenance activities as opposed to growth activities that bring constant change.
>
> But Christ has given the church marching orders: Advance! the Kingdom of heaven is at hand! from evangelism onward, we must present this God-centered call to those who would be His people if a vital reproducing Christianity is to be sustained.

☐ **Keep evangelizing after the birth takes place.**

Don't stop harvesting when you begin public worship services! Do not count on your newly begun worship services to bring in outsiders. Aim to gather people from the same culture and social level.

☐ **Share pastoral responsibilities and hold volunteer workers accountable to do their jobs.**

Keep training new leaders on the job as assistants. Follow the guidelines in Titus 1:5-9 for selecting elders, to recognize assistants who are ready to lead their own groups.

New believers can also lead new 'gathering' groups made up of their friends and relatives, provided that a more experienced believer coaches them behind the scenes.

If you detect competition between the elders, workers or trainees, stomp on it firmly at once before it creeps any farther. Help them to apply the teaching of Philippians 2:1-18 on humility and respect for others.

Help each leader and his wife to agree on *her role* in the ministry.

☐ **Avoid discouraging new workers with too many chores.**

In small groups, limit refreshments to something simple; do not make it hard to host the meetings. Avoid serving meals, except for special occasions. Take turns caring for the children if they distract.

Hold small group meetings in the house of someone besides the main leader so that no one thinks that the host owns the group.

Scoggins cautions against meeting too often:

> **By keeping meetings to a minimum, we avoid overstaying our welcome in a particular home. We try to have only one community meeting weekly in a central home. We hold other meetings for gathering (evangelism) and ministry in other homes as the Lord directs.**

☐ **Be creative in how you apply the Word to the needs and level of spiritual maturity of the members of small groups.**

Be sensitive to the fears and doubts of new members. Bring assurance of God's grace and forgiveness.

Do not simply study the Bible. Apply it also. Let God's Word guide us as we deal with specific current needs and ministry opportunities.

Avoid long sermons. Encourage group participation in the studies. Include children and young people.

Use other ways of teaching God's Word besides lecture. Encourage spontaneous discussion, telling stories, simple drama, composing poems or songs about the topic and words of exhortation.

Try interpretive reading; assign the conversation corresponding to different people in passages with dialogue to as many readers.

Scoggins found how to teach in small groups:

> **We found that lectures are counterproductive to learning. Our people learn far more by interacting with the Word in a discussion. This works especially well when they have had a reading schedule to follow in their homes during the week. Sometimes a lecture is called for, however, for larger meetings to instruct more mature believers in matters of general concern.**

☐ **If you are meeting in homes, avoid meeting too often or too long in one home.**

Let's not wear out our welcome. Also, avoid moving so frequently from one house to another that people lose track of where to meet.

☐ **Avoid too many outside speakers**

Regardless of how 'good' they may be, outsiders who come with objectives foreign to your group can erode the will of your people to persevere in their God-given tasks.

☐ **Prohibit *business* dealings (selling insurance, etc.) and *political* discussions during meetings.**

☐ **Impart a vision for reproducing home groups, especially to new believers.**

☐ **Imitate the example of the apostolic church in its use of homes.**

Ministry in homes, including the celebration of the Lord's Supper, appears in Acts 2:46; 5:42; 20:20; Romans 16:5; Philemon 2.

14-d Offer *'Gathering Meetings'* for Seekers

A 'gathering group' normally has one or two families or a few singles. It is for seekers. It is not for worship or in-depth Bible studies. Older Christians who know their Bible well and have already overcome the problems common to new Christians can leave the seekers feeling ill at ease. They should not come to a gathering meeting unless they are helping in some definite way or bringing unsaved friends.

New leaders, even new converts, who are discipled behind the scenes by a more experienced believer, sometimes lead these temporary groups for seekers. We simply mobilize converts to witness for Jesus to family and friends, and to follow them up in small 'gathering groups.' We keep holding these informal gatherings until the 'vein of gold' runs out. That is, when a convert's entire network of friends and relatives has heard the Good News and either responds or rejects it.

Sometimes a gathering group is born when an unconverted seeker who is the head of a household begins reading Bible stories to his family or in some other way teaches the Word or prays with them. Usually this occurs under the guidance of a discipler.

Those who receive Christ in a gathering group may form a regular home group or new church, or join an existing home group, as circumstances allow. They may merge with other gathering groups to form a home group or new church.

An 'outside' church planter may lead gathering meetings at first. But he turns leadership over to a new local leader as soon as

166

possible. It normally works better if the new leader is head of a household and receives coaching from behind the scenes.

We do not extract converts from their social circle by turning them over to a congregation that fails to relate well to their community. We keep discipling them in gathering groups until they are grounded and can form a group identified with the local neighborhood or social network. This new group might be part of a larger church or become a separate house church, as conditions warrant.

When heads of households come to Christ, we help them start new gathering meetings for their family unsaved friends. Do everything in a way a newer leader can imitate at once, to keep it flowing. We do not stop holding evangelistic gathering meetings to ground or consolidate new believers. They have the best contacts for new gathering groups.

If you lead a gathering group, *model servant leadership* in a way that new leaders can imitate. Before a convert's social network becomes 'mined out' start another gathering group with those converts who have connections in an entirely new 'vein of gold.'

14-e Verify Circumstances that Indicate if House Churches or Cells Are Needed

When would one start a house church with the intention that it remain indefinitely as a house church and not seek a building?

When do we purposefully aim to multiply small churches? A common Western assumption is that the lack of a lot of people in one building means failure. This is not from Scripture. The early church in Jerusalem, like that of Ephesus and other cities, was a cluster of tiny house churches. So where do the assumptions come from, that we must have a building, a large crowd in one place, that we must pay at least one professional pastor full time or that he must be trained in an institution outside the church? The are culturally based traditions. The assumption that the Spirit of God needs these things is contrary to faith; it often damages the Church and frequently stifles growth and reproduction in Christ's body.

Our decision to form, remain as, or discontinue a house church should not come from feelings *pro* or *con* about buildings. No inherent virtue or evil attaches either to church buildings or to house churches. Scripture mentions that the early Christians met both in the Jewish temple (in the outer courtyard) and in houses. God gives us liberty to do both. Our motive should rather be to obey Jesus and allow God to keep the work growing and reproducing, without restricting it in any way.

Under some circumstances house churches offer more freedom to mobilize new leaders and put into practice spiritual gifts. In other circumstances church buildings offer opportunity. In some societies churches reproduce more rapidly when they have buildings. In some third world countries believers build humble chapels at very little cost out of materials available locally, involving no limitations or delay. In some fields when a church outgrows a small chapel, they build another nearby, often with a style that is more acceptable to the culture than the structures put up at first by foreign missionaries. They normally multiply this way more easily where churches have a *plurality of elders* and sister churches remain in close contact with each other in order to maintain relationships between brothers in Christ when a new church forms.

Scoggins learned from experience the value of having shepherding elders:

The plurality of elders enables older leaders constantly to train younger ones. When new churches begin, these older elders, perhaps in a different church, still serve as a discipler for the younger men. This networking of leadership between churches serves to give stability to the leadership and the congregations in which they serve. It will also counter the independent spirit that often fosters competition between churches. Where the leadership is networking closely together in a cooperative spirit, there is less sheep stealing. People rather move from one church to another with much encouragement and blessing as we see God's hand employing the resources of one church to edify another.

Our goal is to remove all barriers to what the Holy Spirit might desire to do. If He desires to bring explosive growth and reproduction, we want to use ministry methods that are flexible enough to grow with Him and not restrict His blessing. Such methods need plans for multiplication and not simply addition. We want to give liberty for the Spirit of God to mobilize workers to evangelize and edify, without restrictions imposed by buildings or the lack of them. In some cases, a rapidly growing house church may see a building as a detriment to growth; later they might decide that a building would be helpful. Unfortunately, many Western churches seldom consider the alternative to building; their cultural inertia moves them toward centralizing rather than decentralizing.

How do we discern the circumstances that favor house churches over erecting, expanding or renting a building? People often overlook objective criteria when they decide to build or to meet indefinitely in homes. The indications of the need for house churches vary from culture to culture. We list common guidelines below to recognize when to opt for house church multiplication. Mark items that apply to your church:

☐ **You lack funds for a building.**

As obvious as this is, the house church option is often overlooked, when money is lacking to rent or build. The financial burden very often causes new churches to fail, especially in urban areas, where a house church cluster could have cheerfully and easily solved the problem. Scoggins recalls:

> **A driving force in our decision to start house churches was our limited resources for renting or building in an urban area. Most people living in urban areas have limited resources, and land values are high. As a result we settled on a house church strategy to keep financial pressure from dictating the policy of the church. Too often money becomes the deciding factor in what does or does not get done. In our house churches the financial question became irrelevant.**

☐ **Hostile authorities persecute churches.**

Where churches must gather underground house churches often thrive. In Muslim fields, China and southern Asia millions of believers meet in tiny house churches. The most widespread people movement of all history, in China, takes house churches for granted.

☐ **You lack funds for *full-time* pastoral leaders.**

Western Christians often associate salaried, professional ministry with church buildings and the larger congregations that attend them. They also associate costly centralized organization with a building. Decentralized organization with strong inter-church organization often yields a vital network of house churches. When money is lacking for paid staff, let us prayerfully consider the house church option. Scoggins recalls:

> **None of the elders in our house churches are supported. All are bivocational and supply the needs of their families through normal jobs (from doctors to truck drivers). Since each elder oversees**

only three or four families, this is not an excessive burden.

☐ **You lack the 'critical mass' needed to launch a growing church in a building.**

Churches that opt for centralized organization, paid leadership from the start and a building need around fifty committed adult believers to begin public worship. A smaller number gets them off on the wrong foot; they lack the personnel to maintain the image and programs needed to attract more people to that kind of church. House churches, in contrast, can start with any number of believers. In Scoggins's experience, a house church often starts with two or three families.

☐ **You have the *vision* to form a *cluster* of house churches.**

An isolated house church seldom survives long, as Scoggins observed:

> **Independent house churches are fraught with dangers. They easily develop cultic tendencies that go unchecked, since there is no accountability beyond themselves. They usually fail to reproduce and become ingrown. They also often become self-centered and elitist; God's Spirit is no longer able to use them. They collapse, leaving in their wake a string of broken, embittered believers. For these reasons, we focus on starting networks of cooperating house churches rather than isolated house churches. Interaction between house churches brings stability and perspective. In times of blessing, we can share resources with others that are struggling. In times of trial, others are there to help us.**

> **The capacity to multiply depends on the leaders' ability to train new elders as co-pastors to keep up with the growth and multiplication. A church planting task group lacking this ability cannot provide leadership for an ongoing movement of church multiplication. An effective task group thinks in terms of reproducing house churches. Just one house church is like one baseball player facing the other task group's nine alone. A house church needs the warmth and identity of a cluster of sister house churches in close fellowship with it. They meet together for a united celebration (perhaps once a month), and their leaders meet even more frequently to coordinate the work.**

☐ **You have the ability and desire to form an inter-church network between churches, keeping relationships intact as churches multiply.**

Women generally feel more threatened when continued growth by multiplication forces them to break existing relationships. They can maintain these relationships, however, through inter-church organization. People must be available in a mother church who are experienced or can be trained to disciple newer Christians and leaders in the daughter churches, including women and teenagers.

☐ **You have the ability to keep children actively participating in worship or to take care of them some way.**

Sometimes several house churches or home groups will cooperate to provide childcare.

☐ **You can arrange for teenagers from several churches to gather.**

This may require inter-church cooperation.

☐ **Your leader can resist opposition to a house church.**

Where traditions are very strong in favor of buildings, people sometimes stubbornly assume that a building is necessary, regardless of obvious, compelling reasons to the contrary. Leaders must not allow the two philosophies to clash. If they open the door even a crack to consider a larger building, such people will insist on it without thinking it through.

Deeply embedded traditions sometimes keep people from feeling that they have worshiped seriously unless they have done so in a church building. In spite of conscientious biblical instruction on the true meaning of worship, they simply cannot adapt to a house church. A church planter must be sensitive to this mentality; if his flock will not follow him into a house church, he must chose between keeping his flock or his ideal. He may have to allow for a building, even though circumstances indicate that it could hinder the work later on. It's still better than losing his church at in its infancy. In more traditional societies, a cluster of house churches needs at least one strong, popular leader who successfully stems this tide.

☐ **You recognize *danger signals* that warn when keeping people as *one* church centered in a building is stifling freedom in the Spirit.**

 Circle bombs below that may be warning that your people should not be confined to one facility.

 (Danger Signal) **'Maintenance' replaces outreach.**

We smell danger when we give more thought and energy to keeping existing programs running smoothly than to reaching out to the neglected community. Programs exist without 'sunset clauses' (about when to terminate them) or any commitment to evaluate their continued effectiveness. A church's activities simply take on a life of their own, whether or not they accomplish the purposes for which they were initiated. When someone suggests scrapping a program, more noise is made about who might be offended and whom we might lose than how we can better win the lost!

 People complain about investing tithes and offerings in material buildings.

Sometimes, even though funds for buildings are available, a congregation places higher priority on giving to ministries or workers. Their conviction is often due to a healthy reaction against excessive institutionalization. House churches allow them to achieve large church growth and maintain non-institutional priorities at the same time.

Scoggins speaks from experience:

> **Generally in a house church, offering money is allocated to *people*. Most of our house churches use only about 20 percent of the giving for administrative purposes. The rest goes to benevolent needs and missions.**

New workers 'walk on eggs' to avoid offending others in order to develop or expand a ministry.

An organization is too big or too centralized when newer members--or older members desiring to do something new--have to play church politics to avoid hurting feelings, breaking rules, or offending persons in power. This condition is also common in house churches whose leaders are legalistic or power hungry. Sadly, there may even be a lack of interest and fervor in following up newcomers.

Often, in large churches with attendance of a thousand or more, the amount of evangelism done outside the church in the community drops practically to zero. This also happens in some older, ingrown house churches.

People express frustration because their ministries are being restricted or they are not allowed to do what God has gifted them to do.

Such complaints from otherwise non-critical persons may indicate that a building (or the centralized organization associated with it) is restricting freedom in the Spirit to serve and exercise spiritual gifts. These complaints may be God's voice for us, urging us to consider starting more daughter churches or cells in houses.

Leaders complain of exhaustion. Ministry is a chore rather than a joy.

Planning sessions revolve more around keeping the organization running smoothly than around spiritual and pastoral concerns.

Leaders spend more time discussing how they can improve or protect the image of the church, save or raise funds, maintain programs or avoid problems, than making plans of a pastoral nature for edifying specific people and dealing with new opportunities.

Rules proliferate.

Staff spends too much time revising constitutions, bylaws, or other policies in order to maintain control, safeguard from possible dangers, and avoid problems. Leaders rush to surround innovators with rules to protect the smooth-running machinery of existing programs. Non-leaders complain (to each other) that the church is run by human policies instead of being led by the Holy Spirit; they fear to suggest changes lest they be considered divisive.

Innovations take longer.

It takes longer to open doors for new ministries; channels for decision become bureaucratic, and leaders are more concerned with how things operate than for whom or why. Decisions made from the top down discourage individual initiative. Often leaders make great decisions that never get implemented because of apathy on the part of the congregation. The alarmed cry resounds, "We don't want to make a mistake!" as if no decision or delayed decisions are not mistakes.

Another cry is "We don't want to move too fast"--as if it is never wrong to move too slowly. The book of Acts shows that the Spirit of God often moves rapidly. What would be your church's response if 3,000 were added in one day? Might some older members groan and complain until many left through the back door, then sigh with relief as things get back to 'normal' with nothing new happening?

Potential leaders are *competing*.

New workers must 'fight to the top' for a position in which their spiritual gifts can be used freely--a complaint also heard in house churches if leaders over-control.

The percentage of members in places of leadership declines.

A chronic shortage of leaders in touch with the local community stifles outreach.

A church fails to train and reproduce enough of its own really effective leaders for essential ministries, especially ministries that mobilize new believers for evangelism of their friends and relatives.

The church must rely more and more on *paid* staff.

Paid workers complain that volunteer workers or leaders can no longer be counted on for key positions.

 Programs receive more attention than people do.

 Funds for buildings and paid staff are become a major concern and topic of discussion by leaders.

People feel bullied into giving more and more. Other areas of pastoral concern get less attention in business or board meetings.

 Unsaved visitors seldom return.

Non-Christians and visitors seeking a new church sometimes fail to find friends who readily receive them into the group, or they feel that their spiritual gifts are not wanted--also a problem in house churches if they become ingrown.

 Sterility replaces reproduction.

New small groups and daughter churches are a thing of the past.

 Even heroic attempts to form effective home groups are futile.

A large and growing church needs more and more small groups that give real pastoral care on a personal and family level. These small groups draw in new converts and mobilize new leaders for growing needs. When a church fails to mobilize small groups in spite of heroic efforts by its leaders, it has probably long since passed the time when they should have begun multiplying house churches or cells.

If many of the above danger signals apply to your church, prayerfully consider and plan for cells for those who want them. Don't *push* those who cling to the status quo. Let them lie beside still waters. Work with the other sheep that follow.

Hey, some of these dangerous menaces swoop down on home groups and house churches, too //

Of course.
But we unruffle feathers easier in small flocks.
And when a rooster falls off his high perch he won't drag as many other birds down with him.

14-f Be Content with Being a House Church if that Is how God Leads

Be happy with the goal of multiplying a cluster of small churches, and do not to try to act like a large church, or plan secretly to become one large church. A cluster of house churches can rent a building if God so leads and meet as often as they like in united celebration. They might pay a pastor to help coordinate the entire network of churches and help train leaders. In the meantime, be content to be a good house church. Act like a small congregation and enjoy the close fellowship of a little community.

House churches are devastated when a leader uses them as a stepping stone to a larger church. He might secretly aspire to pastor a large church that pays a good salary. He inevitably leads a house church into an impasse: they cannot grow large enough in a house to afford a building, but they become too large for the house. This becomes impossibly painful if the leader discourages starting new house churches, fearing that members will leave his congregation to join a new church and leave him even farther away from his goal of a traditional church.

Such a leader pushes a house church into a building before it can afford it and also fails to use a style of teaching, worship, or organization that fits small churches. He also uses a style of leadership that is not appropriate for small churches and that other potential leaders cannot imitate, making it difficult to multiply more churches.

14-g To Multiply, Prepare New Leaders on the Job as Apprentices

We prepare new leaders more easily if we enable all heads of families to pastor their spouses and children. This family approach produces new leaders who are overlooked in traditional churches. Many new shepherds emerge, making it possible to multiply churches.

14-h If you Meet as a House Church, Be Positive Toward Other Churches

Some house churches hurt themselves by developing an independent spirit. They assume that *not having a building* makes them more spiritual. This attitude commits the very same error for which they criticize others. It assumes that a building makes a significant difference one way or another in our relationship with God. It doesn't. Our *attitude* toward other Christians, however, makes a crucial difference.

If we rely on having a building or *not having one* instead of on the Holy Spirit for our power in ministry, we fall into the same error. Spirituality comes from God alone. He can walk through church walls or break them down as He pleases.

14-i Make Use of Small Groups to Help Entire Families to Participate

Here are some ways in which families can worship together in a small group:

❖ Prepare **younger children** before worship time to sing, recite poems or Psalms, read or recite verses or act out Bible stories.

❖ Prepare **older children** to take part in Bible study discussions. Have them find things ahead of time in the passage to be used.

❖ Help **adults** also to act out Bible stories; this has a great impact. They can also give testimonies, pray for one another, share experiences, ask and answer questions, exhort and admonish.

CAUTION

Don't force shy newcomers to participate. Some won't return. Overly eager leaders make them use their wings before they're ready. Spontaneous participation is *learned*.

❖ Arrange **chairs** in a circle or horseshoe. This helps people to sing and discuss the Word of God more freely.

❖ In **new churches** or **cells**, study and practice the biblical 'one another' relationships between members and leaders.

The carnal attitudes, ambitions, power struggles, selfishness and indifference in larger churches also arise in small churches. In fact, they arise *more readily*. The intimate family atmosphere makes it harder to hide them! The greater opportunities to lead and serve also bring them out quickly. Welcome this. The intimacy and flexibility of the small congregation facilitate correction as problems arise.

Much of the Bible teaching during a church's first year and certainly as long as new leaders are developing should deal frankly with these carnal attitudes in a family atmosphere of loving acceptance. Scoggins' new groups spend weeks applying the New Testament 'one another' verses to their group life, especially to relationships between members in preparation for *covenanting* together as a house church.

14-j Affirm Loving, Family-Like Church Body Life with a Covenant

A covenant affirms briefly what the group is and does. Small churches should covenant together to love, forgive, nurture and minister to one another as a family. Scoggins uses a covenant to confirm a new church's birth:

When a new group prepares and signs this covenant, we consider the church to be born. The covenant--call it what you may--is not a traditional constitution with legal overtones. It defines how members live and serve the Lord as a caring body. The emerging group deals with every detail of it. They analyze each point slowly in Scripture and discussing it openly and prayerfully, before asking every member of the group to agree upon it. Make sure a new church in embryo understands God's covenants in the Old and New Testaments, so they can covenant together to define the kind of church they will form, and how they will behave toward each other as members.

This covenant is not to define doctrine nor prohibit sins. It is positive, emphasizing their love, forgiveness and ministry for each other. As mentioned above, the churches should study and discuss the 'one another' passages in the New Testament for several weeks while they are learning to work together and recognizing their new leaders. During this time, as they make decisions and explore their gift-based ministries, the carnality of the members and the weaknesses of the leaders always become apparent. This helps them to discuss and write their covenant in a context of reality, struggle and progress, which makes it practical for future guidance. The house church, thus born through a process of joyful and tearful struggle, continues as a *closely-knit family type community.*

Group member might enjoy writing the group's covenant. If not, provide a model covenant that they only need to study and affirm. Some groups write this agreement as poetry; others have set it to music. Some people consider it legalistic to have to sign pledges; in this case avoid the signing. Simply ask them to join in the discussion to affirm their agreement any way that they want.

Here is an example of a model covenant. The numbers refer to ways, explained below, that the group can study, discuss and put into practice its guidelines:

Our Group Covenant

We join our hearts to pledge in love[1]

That we'll obey our Lord above[2]

Who heals, forgives, unites, uplifts[3]

And helps each one to use his gifts;[4]

To serve each other and be served;[5]

And pass the joyful news we've heard

To those outside this family

So they'll find love eternally.[6]

1 *(1st line of the covenant, above)* The *first line* emphasizes that the group covenants with God *together*. We need each other to do His will; we do not approach Him as private individuals. We are a spiritual family, walking with God in joyful harmony. Explain what a Covenant is. You or one of the older children might tell the story of David and Jonathan from 1 Samuel 18, who formed a covenant of lasting friendship. Also, you or another adult might relate how Israel entered into a covenant with God when they agreed to obey the Ten Commandments that He gave through Moses, (Exodus 20).The group will study and agree as a body on each numbered phrase in the Covenant.

2 *(2nd line)* Discuss *obeying* Jesus. Go over His basic commands.

You might ask someone to read Acts 2:37-47, then ask the group to name things that the 3,000 new Christians of the first New Testament church did in obedience to Jesus.

They should find that the new believers repented, were baptized, received the apostle's teaching and shared it with others to win them to Christ, broke bread, had loving fellowship, gave generously and prayed.

Then, agree as a group to obey and help each other to obey Jesus' commands.

3 Discuss the things that Jesus has done for us and praise Him for it.

4 Discuss the different spiritual gifts and help each member to make plans to discover and use his to minister to others.

You might study Romans 12:4-10, 1 Corinthians 12:4-11 or Ephesians 4:11-16. Section 6-h lists different God-given gifts mentioned in the New Testament and the ministries that they enable us do.

5 Discuss our interaction as a body as we serve one another in love.

Section **6-f** lists the different "one another" verses of the New Testament.

6 Discuss the last three lines of the covenant, which deal with our joyful duty of sharing our faith with others.

Relate the accounts of His sacrificial death and life-giving resurrection.

Pray for people who need Christ.

If you write your covenant, let it contain a pledge to obey Jesus' commands, and to serve one another with our different God-given gifts. Keep it brief. Go over each part of it as you form the group; when new people join, let someone review it with them. It might be the basis of Bible studies for the first few weeks.

14-k   Leaders from each Church Meet Often to Coordinate Area Activities

Arrange for leaders of the churches in your area to form an 'overseer board' (call it what you want) to meet often, for cooperation between the churches. In some cases a network includes both house churches and conventional churches in a friendly, mutually helpful alliance. Their elders arrange for the churches in their network to meet together regularly at convenient intervals for united worship and celebration, community projects and to serve one another as needs and opportunities arise.

14-l   Multiply Wisely

Discuss this reproduction from the beginning of a new church's life, especially with new leaders.

When a house church grows too large for good interaction (normally around three or four families or 14 adults) let anyone who wants to go with a new group do so. Don't force them. The new group covenants together to confirm the new house church or cell. Call it *multiplication,* not *division.*

Don't simply divide the original group down the middle. Usually only a small part of the original group goes with a new one. Perhaps only one couple serves as the nucleus of the new group. Others might help them do evangelism but remain with the original group. Let everyone pray for it. Seek agreement, including wives of the main leaders.

Sometimes a gifted church planter who is not of the original group comes for a short time to furnish initial leadership.

During the birth stage and often for more than a year, the new group receives intensive, loving nurture from the parent church, which gives this care as long as they need it. The more experienced members of the mother church keep mentoring the leaders and workers of the daughter church. Women in the mother church keep discipling women in the daughter church.

For rapid house church reproduction, aim for more than one leader (elder or co-pastor) in a church. Normally a more experienced man will have helpers who are his apprentices. If an experienced church planter leads the group at first he turns over leadership to new, local leaders as soon as possible. The longer he waits, the harder it is. He and every elder he trains should always be training 'Timothies' as apprentices. Each trainee should also begin soon to train his own Timothies in the same church or daughter churches.

Often two or more church planters work together to start a new church. After the initial gathering or evangelism stage sometimes all but one of them move on to work in another area. The one who stays trains the first new leaders, then he also moves on. When leaving a church in the hands of new leaders, a church planter should make a clean break from any public leadership so that the new leaders feel free to take full responsibility. He continues, however, to mentor them *behind the scenes* as long as the need it.

14-m Note Guidelines and Plans for Home Groups or House Churches

Note plans to form and develop home groups or house churches. Do this with your coworkers if possible:

_____

_____

_____

_____

_____

_____

_____

_____

_____

_____

_____

15.
Church Reproduction from the Viewpoint of a
Mother Church
(Sending Body)

Start daughter churches ???

First, let's help our own flock grow bigger and bigger. That's something to crow about--big success !

Don't even *think* of starting new flocks like the Antioch pigeons did, until we've built a strong home nest here !

But we've been building our nest for years !
You'll never think it's large enough !
We'd never do what Jesus says in Acts 1:8 !

Find in Acts 13:1-3 how God moved a 'mother' church to send a church-based missionary task group:

In the church at Antioch there were prophets and teachers: Barnabas, Simeon called Niger, Lucius of Cyrene, Manaen (who had been brought up with Herod the tetrarch) and Saul. While they were worshiping the Lord and fasting, the Holy Spirit said, "Set apart for me Barnabas and Saul for the work to which I have called them." So after they had fasted and prayed, they placed their hands on them and sent them off.

15-a   Form Task Groups with Those who Have God's Apostolic Gifting

God promises a church people gifted as *apostles*--the missionary gift (Ephesians 4:11-12). We mobilize these people to use their gift to reproduce churches by putting them to work using their gift. We release them to disciple the neglected nations (people groups). We help them training new workers by first working with neglected ethnic groups nearby.

How does a 'sending church' prepare and send a task group that reproduces the church in a neglected area? Let us clear away some smog first by stating what a church does *not* need in order to multiply *if we follow New Testament guidelines.*

A reproducing church does ***not*** need:

- **large membership** (small churches partner with sister churches).
- **a paid 'missions pastor'** (he could help, of course),
- **an experienced 'missions committee'** (again, it would help),
- **much money** (it helps in budget-oriented societies),
- **a high-powered executive** to recruit and push folks to work,

Churches in virtually every major culture group often multiply without any of these things.

A reproducing church ***does*** need:

- **A firm vision** that it belongs to the living, reproducing body of Christ and therefore receives from God all that it needs to reproduce (He gives all living things the power to reproduce),
- **Determination to discover members with the needed spiritual gifts**, especially the apostolic gift, to lead a church planting task group. If we nurture these gifts within the body, the Spirit of God lets us know when to separate a task group, as He did for the Antioch church in Acts 13. Any obedient, healthy church body reproduces *normally* when it uses of the spiritual gifts God has given to it.

184

Patterson found how to convince the Honduran churches to reproduce:

> **At first our Honduran pastors insisted it was the missionary's job to start new churches. But at the rate we were going that would have taken two or three thousand years to plant churches in all the villages in our area. So we had another meeting.**
>
> **I explained that a mission agency was not what God intends to reproduce churches. Churches reproduce churches. I was not going to plant any more churches, but I would help them do it.**
>
> **They drew on a large piece of cardboard a rustic map of the villages and pueblos in the area. Each worker signed his name by those for which his church would be responsible. Each worker prayerfully committed himself to mobilizing a church planting task group from his church. This was a turning point in our work; God used it to give the vision for multiplication. The national workers held the reins; I was their servant.**

How can you help your home church to develop a task group with this mentality for church reproduction? Church-based task groups sent by a loving, caring church (or by several churches working together) usually have a higher view of a church's ability to reproduce. They see it as normal. If they work together before going overseas, harmonizing their gifts and building relationships, they will have a great advantage. Workers sent out by their church usually maintain stronger accountability to it. God is reawakening this vision of church reproduction in Western churches that take Acts 13:1-3 seriously. Mission agencies can more easily mobilize workers for church reproduction if they are sent as task groups by a church or several churches in partnership.

15-b   Deploy Bivocational Workers

If your church cannot support members who are gifted as apostles, this does not mean that it has to stop sending them. Neither does it mean that you must seek financial aid from other churches. Bivocational (self-supporting) work is an option for those who are gifted as apostles. It is the best way to work among most of the remaining neglected peoples. Consider asking businessmen in your church and others with cross-cultural experience to develop plans for your 'tentmakers' to support themselves fully or in part. Be creative!

A word of caution about combining business with church planting. As a general rule, pastors and missionaries make lousy businessmen. Likewise, businessmen often make lousy pastors and church planters. The solution is to work as partners in the spirit of 1 Corinthians 12, not alone. Each does what God has gifted him to do. They may both work in the church as well as the business but the main overseer of each is the one with the corresponding ability.

15-c   Provide Unbiased Mission Career Counseling

Help your home church to arrange career counseling by a mentor that is unbiased (that is, who has no motive to recruit for his favorite agency, training approach, method or field. Otherwise missionaries candidates, advised only by recruiters and promoters of mission agencies and training institutions, will continue to be channeled by default into existing programs and keep clustering in fields already reached.

Let us not perpetuate the present imbalance: nearly all new missionaries go to fields that already have national, indigenous churches that are fully capable (often far more capable) of reaching the rest of their people. Few missionaries enter those areas where authorities are hostile, even though that is where the need, and often the response, is greater, and where most of the remaining, totally neglected populations live. Let us inform potential missionaries honestly of all options.

15-d   Help Workers to Love and Appreciate God's Church

Church planters must love the church and its ministries in order to plant healthy daughter churches. Some have had a negative experience in a stagnant church, or have never attended a warm, active church. They lack a clear concept of what they are planting. Some workers on church planting task groups come from *parachurch* organizations that are not churches. These need serious training for church planting, with a good church model. They cannot gain all the necessary church planting skills in a classroom.

For people who lack solid experience in a loving church with normal church body life, we recommend a *temporary training church*. Let them practice small group worship including the Lord's Supper, family oriented evangelism and apprenticing leaders on the job.

Some schools provide lectures on different aspects of church planting. If students lack experience in a reproductive church, lectures alone will not prepare them. The teaching may be excellent but the *model* is also essential for churches to reproduce. Practicing one's spiritual gift (in this case the gift of teaching by a lecturer) without harmonizing it with the use of other gifts given to the church body is a bad model that can hinder church reproduction. Speakers who present evangelism, development, or other ministries without integrating it in the church body as 1 Corinthians 12 requires, can make it harder for students to plant churches, even though their teaching *content* is accurate.

186

15-e Pray for God's Help to Grow by Multiplication as Well as by Addition

Most church planters find it helpful to map their vision. Please get a large piece of paper and do it now. It may look like the diagram below.

Add the names of the churches, even through they do not exist yet.

Also add also the names of workers that you hope will cooperate, under each church:

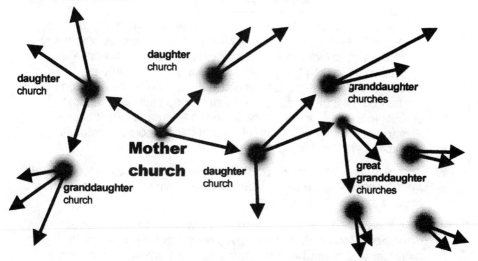

Find in Acts chapters 13-14 how a mother church (Antioch) commissioned its apostles and how they remained accountable to it:

While they were worshiping the Lord and fasting, the Holy Spirit said, "Set apart for me Barnabas and Saul for the work to which I have called them." So after they had fasted and prayed, they placed their hands on them and sent them off. Acts 13:2-3

From Attalia they sailed back to Antioch, where they had been committed to the grace of God for the work they had now completed. On arriving there, they gathered the church together and reported all that God had done through them and how he had opened the door of faith to the Gentiles. And they stayed there a long time with the disciples. Acts 14:26-28

Church planting is essential for widespread evangelism for several reasons:

1. **Most populations are best evangelized by planting many small churches.**

2. **People in small, new churches do more personal evangelism.**

After a congregation reaches a comfortable number for its ministry, further growth in numbers causes a *decrease* in evangelism in proportion to the amount of members.

Now Hear This !

Do not be tempted by the false 'success syndrome' that shouts 'bigger is better.' The hard fact is that the percentage of ministry time given to evangelism and other shepherding ministries in proportion to the membership *decreases drastically* as churches grow larger and become well funded. The average member of a *megachurch* does almost no evangelism. Most people who join a very large church are already Christians, attracted from smaller churches that cannot compete with its expensive, more attractive programs.

3. **When a new church is planted near another church, generally *both* churches gain more new people** provided they respect biblical ethics and do not 'steal sheep.'

4. **God blesses churches that make a sacrifice to reproduce.**
   Churches often weaken themselves temporarily to give birth to daughter and granddaughter churches. Others resist reproducing because they think it is too difficult. Once they make the sacrifice, however, they usually find it easy and joyful!

   Missionaries with ample training and resources sometimes hesitate to start a new church because they feel the need for more money, education, or official backing. They are suspicious when they see uneducated converts start churches without these advantages. New believers who simply trust the Holy Spirit to convert their friends in another neighborhood or town often give birth to new churches quite apart from any missionary's efforts.

A church that gives a good part of its time, ministry, prayer and funds to multiplying daughter churches will, in a generation, easily win ten times as many people to Christ than if it concentrates all its energies inward. The multiplication is exponential, a chain reaction. It creates a movement of people for Christ such as has been witnessed where pastors let it happen with a sacrificial spirit, begging their strongest tithers and worship leaders to leave and help start a daughter church nearby.

15-f Give Missionary Trainees Practice in Effective Witnessing

A sending church prepares its missionaries to witness for Jesus with the power of the Holy Spirit. It perseveres in intercession for the unsaved, trusting God's power to transform those who receive His forgiveness (Romans 1:14-17). It communicates the essential gospel. This is *the Good News*—the historical facts of Jesus' miraculous life, sacrificial death and life-giving resurrection that the Holy Spirit uses to bring people to faith and repentance in all cultures (Luke 24:44-48; 1 Corinthians 15:1-8).

A sending church can train its foreign missionary task groups by planting churches among nearby ethnic groups, fulfilling the Great Commission in its own 'Samaria' (Acts 1:8).

A sending church looks for those with the itchy feet, cross-cultural apostles gifted to go and multiply churches. They may be businessmen, engineers or teachers. A congregation should imitate the Antioch church. It recognized and sent out the first long-range apostolic task group (Paul, Barnabas, and John Mark) with prayer, fasting, and laying on of hands (Acts 13:1-3, 5).

A good sending church will seek a healthy balance between sending career workers and short term ones. A short term is good for testing spiritual gifts, enrichment and surveying a field. Short-term workers also help with temporary projects that do not require much cultural sensitivity. But career workers are needed for a movement of church reproduction, workers with the commitment to go and do what Jesus says, no matter how long it takes.

15-g Plan Activities to Help a Church Reproduce

It helps to develop a checklist of key activities for a sending church as a *Progress Chart* or checklist. Do it together with your coworkers. The list below is just an example; we hope your chart will have more items to fit the particular circumstances of your church and some neglected people group. Mark items that you aim to give more attention to.

☐ **Inform the church body of its God-given task.**
Instruct the entire congregation to obey Jesus' Great Commission, to disciple all nations, by cooperating in some way. Ask all teachers and small group leaders to help communicate this duty.

☐ **Mobilize the church to reach Jesus' four areas of focus.**
Arrange for people in all ministries, classes, departments or groups to pray, give and share information for their missionary outreach. Help them to identify the areas where Jesus says to be witnesses (Acts 1:8), *Jerusalem*, *Judea*, *Samaria*, and the *ends of the earth*.

Jerusalem = our own local race and culture.

Judea = people of our culture in nearby communities.

Samaria = peoples of other cultures nearby.

Ends of the earth = distant, neglected people groups.

☐ **Adopt a neglected people group.**
Study neglected fields to adopt, pray for, and start churches.

☐ **Recruit workers for home and overseas ministry.**
Encourage businessmen, for example, to start, advise or serve businesses that provide entrance and residence in otherwise inaccessible fields.

☐ **Train workers.**
Mobilize missionary candidates in local cross-cultural church planting and New Testament mentoring. Help all ages to participate in some kind of mission service. Children can learn about, pray for and prepare for future mission service of some kind. Let them participate frequently in mission related projects.

☐ **Send missionary task groups.**
Task group members remain accountable to their church to reproduce churches in the chosen field and to serve in a ministry that maximizes their spiritual gifts and natural strengths. A church-based task group might include members from like-minded sister churches.

☐ **Commission missionaries for apostolic ministry.**
After prayer--and fasting if you like--lay hands on those that the Holy Spirit separates for foreign outreach, as the Antioch church did in Acts 13:1-3.

☐ **Pray.**
Continually pray for the task group and the people it trains.

☐ **Support the mission work.**
Keep giving sacrificially to support missionaries and meet needs as they arise.

☐ **Mobilize bivocational workers.**
Fields of restricted access need career 'tentmaker' church planters who are experienced in cross-cultural church planting, including businessmen. Small businesses especially can enable church planters to be in touch with the common people, who are generally the most responsive. Self-employment makes the missionaries believable with the local people. If they see you hanging around without earning your living they assume you are a CIA agent, paid proselyter, racketeer or simply lazy.

Appendix D shows a more complete Example of a Progress Chart for a Mission Action Group in a Sending Church

15-h   Note Plans to Mobilize a Sending Church

Write plans for your sending church, with its leaders.

_____

_____

_____

_____

_____

_____

_____

_____

_____

_____

_____

_____

_____

_____

_____

_____

16.
Church Reproduction from the Viewpoint of
Trainers of Pastors or Church Planters

Don't train so many leaders for our flock *!*

They'll challenge our pecking order.

We'll lose out to those with bigger beaks *!*

Mentor new leaders lovingly as Jesus did and they'll be loyal to you.

But distrust them as you say and they'll be suspicious and disloyal.

Find in Titus 1:5 principles for mobilizing a church planter:

To Titus, my true son in our common faith: Grace and peace from God the Father and Christ Jesus our Savior. The reason I left you in Crete was that you might straighten out what was left unfinished and appoint elders in every town, as I directed you.

Find in Acts 18:24-28 an example of mentoring *behind the scenes* and the results:

Meanwhile a Jew named Apollos, a native of Alexandria, came to Ephesus. He was a learned man, with a thorough knowledge of the Scriptures. He had been instructed in the way of the Lord, and he spoke with great fervor and taught about Jesus accurately, though he knew only the baptism of John. He began to speak boldly in the synagogue. When Priscilla and Aquila heard him, they invited him to their home and explained to him the way of God more adequately. When Apollos wanted to go to Achaia, the brothers encouraged him and wrote to the disciples there to welcome him. On arriving, he was a great help to those who by grace had believed. For he vigorously refuted the Jews in public debate, proving from the Scriptures that Jesus was the Christ.

16-a Train Church Planters and Pastors on the Job, as well as formally

Two *Efforts* Needed to Train Leaders as Churches Mature

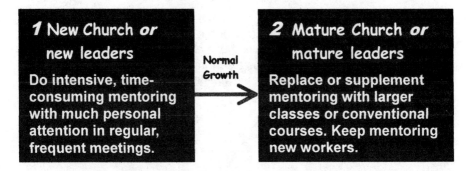

To multiply churches in pioneer fields we train pastoral leaders within the movement itself in the churches. New churches and workers require much personal mentoring. As churches mature they need less attention. A Jesus left the twelve on earth to serve without His spiritual presence, as Paul left Timothy in Ephesus and Titus in Crete, likewise mentors taper off the intensive, time-consuming, personal work with a worker as he matures. More mature workers for well established churches should benefit from more formal, classroom training.

We require new pastoral students to serve in a serious shepherding ministry during their training. They lead and disciple others, to edify their small groups or congregations as Ephesians 4:11-16 requires. One might start with his family. Then, as they mature, we also train them in a more formal way. This requires two training efforts, one for new trainees, and another for mature ones.

Patterson observed problems in training programs that rely exclusively on formal institutional teaching for a pioneer field:

> **While coaching church planting task groups in third world pioneer fields, when they send potential pastors away for training, few return. The few who did made these errors:**
>
> ❖ **Most of them failed to relate to their people because of a condescending attitude.**
>
> ❖ **Most insisted on the same unrealistic training for other pastors.**
>
> ❖ **Most failed to build the *Paul-Timothy* relationships with others that they taught, repeating their 'classroom only' experience.**
>
> ❖ **Most failed to help others use their gifts. Their churches neglected mercy ministries, church planting and discipling.**

Most brought back a domineering leadership style acquired in the classroom--teachers often rule with total control.

If you work in a pioneer field, someone on your church planting task group needs the skill to train pastors for the kind of churches that multiply. A church planting task group should have at least one worker with the gift of teaching by mentoring, who was also trained on the job. He should plan to stay as long as it takes to equip national pastors to train the newer pastors.

Training on the wing is OK for lay leaders.

But to keep students' undivided attention and train *real* pastors, we need an ivy-covered campus separated from the evil world and the flocks that would distract them.

You want us to take trainees *outside* of the Body of Christ and the community where real life goes on, to *shelter* them ?

Patterson saw the need for pastors in a pioneer field to mentor newer pastors on the job:

> Our new Honduran churches urgently needed pastors. For a missionary to train all the pastors on the job was too slow. We arranged for more experienced pastors or elders from a nearby church to train others. When we yielded to tradition and imported pastors from the outside, they slowed things down. They had excellent Bible schooling but lacked a concept of training pastors on the job for church multiplication. They resisted starting daughter churches with such arguments as:
>
> "Converts from other villages can come to my church!" (Even if they had to walk ten miles).
>
> "The funds available will be spread too thin if we start more churches!"
>
> "We'll lose control if these new pastors work beyond where we can give them supervision! They will teach false doctrine!"

Our only serious doctrinal problems occurred in churches led by these formally trained pastors. Not satisfied with our local, non-formal training resources, they sometimes read the wrong books.

More significantly, they hindered their churches from reproducing. Whenever a new man came from the outside we had to fight the old battle all over again! We learned the hard way--to multiply churches, train leaders *within* the movement; do not import them!

Scoggins also discovered the value of training leaders on the job:

One of the first responsibilities of our church planters is to seek out those men who are leaders, then mentor them in the skills of leadership. Usually the church planter teaches the basics of the Christian walk to potential leaders, then helps them pass it on to other newer believers. The church planter immediately sets up such discipleship chains from the moment there is more than one male believer. The same is done with women; older women teach the younger. Leaders are trained to shepherd by doing it, as opposed to studying it only in books.

If we are starting a cluster of house churches in a new area and there is already another house church nearby, we often ask the leaders of the existing house church to train the emerging leaders in the new house churches. This way the churches develop strong relationships and much greater stability over the long term. In this way we also develop leaders on the job; more experienced leaders mentor newer ones, who begin at once mentoring even newer believers (the difference in spiritual age may be more one of character than actual duration of their faith).

Churches in pioneer fields grow and reproduce more rapidly by training leaders on the job. Bible Institutes and seminaries have their place but not in most pioneer fields. For formal training in the churches should be well established so that students know what they're training for. Also the economy should be affluent enough to allow mature 'elder' types to leave their jobs to go study (otherwise they send their teenage sons). Also, the level of education should be high enough for the intensive training.

New churches often grow out of small evangelistic groups or home Bible studies with an evangelistic thrust, provided their leaders receive pastoral training in the process. If a church trains leaders for these evangelistic studies and for shepherding those who come to Christ through them, it is far easier to grow and reproduce churches or cells.

To reach a large population an inner city church often needs to reproduce many small groups or cells (tiny churches within the larger one) rather than separate house churches. It is easier to multiply groups within their ethnic group, economic level, and subculture. In a multi-ethnic area, we are to witness for Jesus also in our 'Samaria' (nearby, different ethnic group).

To work with another ethnic group, it normally works better to plant a separate church or cell with its own elders. If you share the same building with another ethnic group, have a clear agreement for its use, and be sure to discuss arrangements with people who enjoy working cross-culturally. Otherwise the potential for misunderstanding is great; cultural bullying results. You may not hear offended people complain; they simply stop coming, or bringing their friends.

If we bring people from a different culture into our congregation, conflict often arises from the differences. Inevitably, the more dominant culture cancels out the other. This is why the apostle Paul complained so vigorously in his letter to the Galatians. To ask converts to assimilate into a different culture cancels any hope of a strong movement for Christ in their original culture because the evangelism itself fights against their culture and creates a wall--a self-defeating policy. We must not extract people from their culture but help them set up a sister congregation that can reproduce within their culture.

The need to train many as apprentices of more experienced leader becomes obvious when you seriously try to reproduce. As you organize to train leaders, aim for the church to grow not only by addition (bringing converts into an existing body) but also by multiplication. Let each trainee form a small nuclei or core group to which converts are easily added. Converts are far more likely to follow through if assimilated at once into a new group or church with other new Christians with whom they readily identify.

As you train leaders, help them to work closely with others whose spiritual gifts are helpful for enabling churches to multiply, such as:

Faith--for the vision,

Evangelist--for personal evangelism, like Philip the evangelist who presented Christ to people on a personal level,

Apostle--for cross-cultural church planting, like Barnabas the 'sent one' who equipped leaders in other cultures (Acts 14:3, 13-14),

Pastor--for elders to shepherd the flock,

Teacher--for true disciplers who equip the saints for the ministry.

16-b   If Experienced Workers Are Lacking, Name 'Provisional Elders'

Find how soon Paul established leaders in new churches in pioneer fields, in Acts 14:21-23:

> They preached the good news in that city [Derbe] and won a large number of disciples. Then they returned to Lystra, Iconium and Antioch, strengthening the disciples and encouraging them to remain true to the faith. "We must go through many hardships to enter the kingdom of God," they said. Paul and Barnabas appointed elders for them in each church and, with prayer and fasting, committed them to the Lord, in whom they had put their trust.

Find how Paul delegated the job of naming and establishing elders, and what kind of man an elder was to be, in Titus 1:5-9:

> The reason I left you in Crete was that you might straighten out what was left unfinished and appoint elders in every town, as I directed you. An elder must be blameless, the husband of but one wife, a man whose children believe and are not open to the charge of being wild and disobedient. Since an overseer is entrusted with God's work, he must be blameless--not overbearing, not quick tempered, not given to drunkenness, not violent, not pursuing dishonest gain. Rather he must be hospitable, one who loves what is good, who is self-controlled, upright, holy and disciplined. He must hold firmly to the trustworthy message as it has been taught, so that he can encourage others by sound doctrine and refute those who oppose it.

In pioneer fields missionaries frequently serve churches that need to be led and protected from wolves but lack experienced elders. Paul the apostle had the same need. He had to name and quickly train relatively new believers as elders in the new Galatian churches (Acts 14:23). Some call these new leaders 'provisional' elders, meaning they are temporary and because they have not yet been *proven* as Scripture requires.

Scripture warns not to lay hands suddenly on new leaders, that is, not to name someone to a position of pastoral leadership while he is still weak in his Christian life (1 Timothy 5:22). To define the word 'suddenly' let us recall the practice of Paul whom God inspired to write it. He commissioned elders in Galatia where there were none yet, far sooner than would have been prudent in his mature home church in Antioch; it had an ample number of experienced leaders (Acts 13:1).

Naming *provisional* elders is appropriate for churches or fields with no experienced leaders available. We take into account that spiritual responsiveness seen in persons whom the Holy Spirit has prepared even before they know Christ, such as God recognized in Cornelius in Acts 10:1-5.

16-c Chart Progress in Developing Ministries that the New Testament Requires for a Church

To train pastors to be *shepherds*, it helps to use a *Progress Chart* as a checklist to record vital church activities that their people are practicing. The elders of a new church in a pioneer field are normally mentored behind the scenes by members of the church planting task group, a pastor or elder from a mother church. Their *Progress Chart* for a new church might include the following activities:

☐ Witness for Christ and call the people to repentance and faith,

☐ Baptize and receive converts in a loving way into the body,

☐ Celebrate the Lord's Supper and worship as a body,

☐ Pray and develop personal and family devotions, intercession for the lost, the sick and the needy, and spiritual warfare,

☐ Give and develop joyful stewardship of all God has given us-- time, talent and treasure.

☐ Teach the Word of God, as well as church history and doctrinal studies that help interpret and apply the Word,

☐ Cultivate loving relationships among members of the body, and with other churches or cells,

☐ Love needy neighbors in a practical way,

☐ Organize for members to serve with gift-based ministries,

☐ Form special ministry groups as needed and as ministry opportunities arise,

☐ Watch over the flock to drive off wolves, correct the unruly and detect straying lambs,

☐ Administrate with order (for example, authorize a treasurer to pay monthly expenses with a church budget),

☐ Reproduce daughter churches,

☐ Counsel those with personal or family problems; bring reconciliation, healing and forgiveness to limping lambs,

☐ Strengthen marriages and family life,

☐ Send missionaries to neglected fields.

See Appendix B, *Example of a Progress Chart for a New Church* for a more detailed list and explanations of the activities.

16-d Relate what you Teach to the Life of Students' Churches or Ministry

Scripture requires that we *apply* the Word to the work. We both *hear* and *do* it (Matthew 7:24-27; James 1:22-25). Teachers can apply the Word at once if they:

❖ **Listen** first to those they teach, for the needs and ministry opportunities of their churches. If a teacher does not have time for this, he can name helpers as temporary mentors.

❖ **Select teaching content** that supports current needs and opportunities, which you heard about when you *listened*. As Jesus said, we are to bring forth from our treasure of knowledge things old or new (Matthew 13:52). We don't use the same standard lesson plan for every student.

❖ **Assign reading** or other studies that support the activity that the student's congregation or small group is developing.

❖ **Provide Bible reading schedules** for families to follow in the home, with practical discussion questions.

For ***Bible Readings*** that cover the whole Bible in a menu form that intersperses the Old and New Testaments, and relates the reading to today's life and to church activities is provided in **Appendix F.**

These readings link Old Testament passages that appear to have little bearing on today's world to New Testament passages that reveal the bridge between then and now.

They also indicate Bible stories for children. You can select passages that keep their attention during family reading.

❖ Teach with the specific purpose of *equipping the saints for the work of the ministry* (Eph. 4:11-12). This requires focusing on the members of the church body, their God-given gifts, duties, needs and opportunities. This fails if *all* leadership training takes place in an institution apart from the student's church.

We supplement church-based pastoral training with formal theological education where conditions warrant it.

Conditions favorable to institutional theological education:

● **There is a high enough level of education**. Uneducated students cannot assimilate the intensive study.

● **There is a high enough level of affluence**. In poor societies the 'elder' types whom we should train as pastors cannot leave their jobs, families or fields, so they send their sons and daughters who are too immature to serve as pastors.

- **There are enough well established churches**. Unless students have a model of a well organized church in mind they cannot associate the classroom theory with church life and pastoral work.

- **Experienced pastors or shepherding elders model servant leadership**. Pastoral trainees also serve as models for the flock, for a godly life. The congregation is to imitate them. A classroom professor alone is an inadequate model.

Scoggins discovered the need to model the pastor's heart and work:

Pastors prepared in formal, resident seminaries often provide an effective model, but sometimes they do not (especially if that is the only way they have been trained). Our experience with formally educated pastors shows that they still need to learn careful, personal shepherding in order for their pastoral skills to embody more than theory.

We have also found that a low ratio of sheep to shepherds helps to maintain spiritual vitality. Jesus worked with a 12:1 ratio; our experience confirms this to be a practical proportion.

Section **16-v** below has a comprehensive list of helps to relate what you teach to the life of your students' churches.

For tools for Christian mentoring that applies to Word of God to our lives, see ***www.MentorAndMultiply.com***, prepared by author George Patterson.

16-e Build Up the Church of the Pastoral Student, Not Just the Student

Trainers teach to *edify the body*, to *convert, equip and lead*, not just to communicate the Word because we love to teach (Matthew 7.24-27; Ephesians 4:11-16; 2 Timothy 3:16-17). This requires that we use the teaching gift in harmony with the other gifts given to the body by the Holy Spirit (1 Corinthians 12:31-13:2).

Scoggins' churches help their people to use their gifts:

We have found that our teaching must equip the saints to do the work of the ministry (Ephesians 4:11-12). We begin preparing our leaders with our vision statement for growth and reproduction. From there they figure out what equipping will be necessary to carry out the task. Reading schedules and teaching plans grow out of this evaluation. We emphasize that

God's purpose is to extend His Kingdom; thus our teaching must be not only theoretical but also practical, applied to the building of the Kingdom.

1 Corinthians 12, Romans 12 and Ephesians 4:11-16 all reveal that *no spiritual gift justifies its independent use as an end in itself.*

Teaching is a much-abused gift, often used independently from other gift-based ministries of the church body in violation of God's instructions for using gifts.

Teachers in the 20th century were probably more careless than other than other types of ministers, in neglecting to harmonize their work with the other gift-based ministries. They used the Bible primarily as the content for their teaching and preaching, rather than as the norm for how they taught or preached. Most of them ignored the Bible's teaching on the need to minister in an interactive, highly relational and experiential way in the church body (Romans 12:5; 1 Corinthians 12:1-12, 18; Ephesians 4:1-13). Patterson found that simply to teach the Word without relating his work to the other ministries of the body was not productive:

> **Twice since leaving Honduras events have convinced me that we must teach in a relational, experiential way, applying God's Word to the immediate needs of the people. In Uhrsleben of eastern Germany, shortly after the fall of communism there, I asked residents one Sunday afternoon why they didn't attend their town's church. A friendly man invited me into his house, pleased that I cared about his spiritual life. I remarked, "I visited your church and saw very few people apart from the pastor's family. Is it because during the communist regime they destroyed your faith?"**

> **"Ach, nein! We Germans are too stubborn to let them destroy our faith! They only proved that their atheistic beliefs debase and destroy healthy society. The problem is that the church people do not minister in a relevant way to today's Germany. They still live in the days of Luther."**

> **"So what should they do? I'm teaching pastors here this week and I want to be on target."**

"Tell them to do what you're doing now. Listen to us. Talk to us. Love us. Not just sit in that chapel and prepare doctrinal homilies."

I recalled that the chapel was over 800 years old. We discussed the needs of the village and I commended him, "You seem to be genuinely concerned for his town."

"I'd better be," he revealed. "I'm the mayor."

The other case was similar. A church planter explained why he was starting churches in northeast Portland where many churches already served the population.

"I evangelize postmoderns," he explained. "They come to Christ and I take them to the church down the street. But they don't continue. Unless they have a church background they don't connect. The preacher preaches down at them from a huge pulpit in a non-relational way that is alien to them. They love Christ but fail to find the friendship they seek."

He added more examples of converts who could not bear more than one or two visits to a church that offered little care, social interaction or personal discipling.

Post-modern culture entered Western Europe a generation before it came to America. Many churches, concerned with teaching liberal theology, failed to reach out. The new generation wanted a more relational and experiential church life—precisely what God demands in the New Testament but they did not find it. Thousands of churches became nearly empty. Where half of the people attended church after World War II, a generation later less than five percent did. Now post-modernism is hitting American churches like a tidal wave. It is emptying many of them and will continue until they provide a more relational experience. With God's help many churches are making a healthy shift toward small groups for greater interaction and a more loving, family atmosphere. Perhaps more than anyone else, we who train church leaders must model the humility and love needed to harmonize different gift based ministries in a relational body.

16-f To Train Pastors in a Particular Field, Get the Skills you Will Need for It

Learn to mentor leaders by *being* mentored. If you do not have this experience and need it, arrange to meet regularly with a mentor with experience in the type of ministry that you pursue. Do not try to learn reproductive mentoring only from books or lectures. While being trained this way as a leader, you should also mentor *other* potential leaders. Do as Paul told Timothy in 2 Timothy 2:2: "That which you have heard of me among many witnesses, commit to reliable men who are able to teach others also."

The 2 Timothy 2:2 Mentoring 'Chain Reaction'

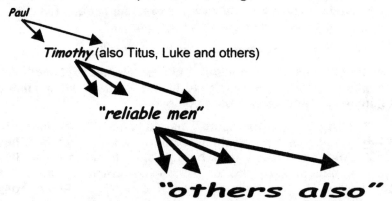

Paul

Timothy (also Titus, Luke and others)

"reliable men"

"others also"

Many Western pastors and missionaries lack the skill of mentoring new leaders as Christ and His apostles did. You may need to look around for a person who can mentor you. You may want more than one, for different ministry areas. You might arrange this with a pastor or worker who will:
model skills for you,
 meet regularly with you,
  pray with you,
   listen to your reports,
    help you plan what your people will do immediately,
     help you strategize for long-range objectives,
      recommend studies that support your plans,
       help you network with other leaders.

> *Above all...* Avoid mentors who try to fit you into their program or agenda !

A mentor need not be very experienced in your field but must agree with your objectives and help you:
 use your spiritual gifts,
  discern new or better ministry opportunities,
   build on your experience and strengths,
    think through your plans,
     monitor your progress objectively.
You may need two mentors, for different needs.

To train pastors in a field that outlaws missionary work you need to mentor them behind the scenes, in private or very small groups. To go the field without acquiring this skill first is as about as wise as trying to fly a jet fighter without any training.

In our zeal to help our trainees gain skills we must not neglect the need to build Christian character in practical ways. Scoggins reminds us:

Wise church planters know that God's call is to be faithful-- not always productive. Faithfully walking toward the goal is as important as achieving it, for it is the process that shapes and molds us. Someone has said, "God is more interested in the work He is doing in us than the work He is doing through us." Good works as seen by God proceed from a transformed heart and life. Thus family activities, which appear to have no direct relationship to your official church ministry, may indeed be far more important than this ministry, especially when a lonely wife or child asks you to do something with them.

16-g Use Progress Charts as you train leaders.

A *Progress Chart* lists the competencies, aims and activity plans of the your student. It helps you and the leader you train to evaluates progress and see at a glance what is still lacking. For examples of a progress chart for individual workers, a new church, a field task group and a mission action group in a sending church, see *Appendices A, B. C and D*.

Meet regularly and help your trainees develop and work through their *Progress Chart*s. You share the responsibility for their effective ministry. They, in turn, may help you in your ministry. You might ask your trainee to give spiritual care to some people in your church or group.

A *Progress Chart* should include not only what your trainees will do but also what those whom they shepherd or train will do. They use the chart to guide them toward their God-given goals, short-range plans and long-range objectives.

Why should a leader list what his people will do? He cannot be a leader unless he leads. He cannot lead unless he takes people from one place to another. That may be to start a new ministry or improve an old one. Moses received a list of activities that God wanted His people to do. He used it not only to lead the people to the Promised Land but also to equip elders and help the people obey God's laws.

Some teachers think they are leading when they *teach*. But if we only pass on information, we do not lead. Some think they lead because they enforce rules. That is not leading in God's kingdom according to Christ (Matthew 20:25-28). The only way to lead His people is to know first where He wants them to go, then help them get there. It helps to list in a

Progress Chart what God wants one's flock to do. Joshua was a great leader because he knew exactly what God wanted His people to do and led them in it.

To help your trainees plan activities for their people, be ruthless in eliminating vague, spiritual-sounding activities that do not move people toward their God-given goals. It is weak, for example, to list as an objective "Build spiritual character." We all want to build character, of course, but the wording is too general. *How* do we build character? We flesh it out. For example, we might include in our activity list to work on each aspect of the Fruit of the Spirit listed in Galatians 5:22-23. We might ask in a mentoring session,

"How will you build patience? Who do you need to have more patience with? Who can help you?"

Your trainee replies, "I'll practice on my teenage son by not getting angry the next time he forgets to turn the lights off when he leaves a room. My wife will be glad to pray with me about it and help me."

In less literate societies a *Progress Chart* might not be a written checklist but something that serves the same purpose. Patterson helped the nationals make plans without the paperwork:

Honduran leaders, especially uneducated village elders, hated paperwork. They didn't care to check off ministry activities on a written list. So I helped them learn about key Bible persons and the activities that are associated with them. They focused on what the model person did. Examples:

Abraham	**faithful prayer warrior,**
Peter	**evangelist,**
David	**poet and singer who people to higher dedication,**
Priscilla	**house church hostess, servant and discipler,**
Lydia	**businesswoman and hospitable hostess,**
Barnabas	**care giver,**
Dorcas	**compassionate helper of the poor,**
Timothy	**shepherd and trainer of other shepherds,**
Titus	**trainer of new elders for new churches,**
Philemon	**reconciler who hosted a church in his home and welcomed back as a free brother his runaway slave,**
Abigail	**giver, who contributed material goods to meet an emergency,**

206

| Jesus | healer, who prayed for the sick, |
| Paul | discipler, who corrected erring Corinthians without condemning them. |

Some found it easier to imitate the activities and virtues of the biblical models.

16-h   Help your Pastoral Trainees Train Newer Pastors

Find in 2 Timothy 2:1-4 principles and examples of reproductive mentoring:

You then, my son, be strong in the grace that is in Christ Jesus. And the things you have heard me say in the presence of many witnesses entrust to reliable men who will also be qualified to teach others. Endure hardship with us like a good soldier of Christ Jesus. No one serving as a soldier gets involved in civilian affairs-he wants to please his commanding officer.

If you train pastors, seek mature men--elders as the biblical describes them. Look for mature, serious heads of families who will begin at once to shepherd their people. Elders are to be able to teach (1 Timothy 3:2). This includes training other pastors, who train still others (2 Timothy 2.2; 3:14-17). Scoggins, like Patterson, diagramed the 2 Timothy 2:2 chain for his leaders:

We use a diagram based on 2 Timothy 2:2 to keep track of our mentoring chains. ("And the things that you have heard me say in the presence of many witnesses entrust to reliable men who will also be qualified to teach others.")

Link 1: Missionary *Paul* teaches:
Link 2: Timothy, his trainee, who teaches:
Link 3: '*Reliable men*,' who teach:
Link 4: '*Others*.'

We use these guidelines to organize mentoring chains; we keep track of the relationships within the body and see how far the training is extending down the chain. For multiplication-type growth, the chain must extend at least to a third link.

16-i Help Participants to Make Commitments Needed to Multiply Churches

Churches multiply when the persons who participate in pastoral training make their corresponding *commitments*:

Participants	Commitments
Churches	Reproduce daughter churches
Pastors	Train their 'Timothies' (new pastors, leaders)
Pastoral students	Shepherd others while they study, applying at once what they learn. Train their own pastoral 'Timothies' to extend the training chain reaction.
Pastoral trainers	Require students to be active in pastoral work while they study (start a church or home group or help to pastor a church), applying what they learn at once. Listen first as students report their people's progress or problems, to relate the Word and other teaching to their work and their flocks.

16-j Follow Biblical Guidelines to Mentor Leaders-in-Training

To imitate Jesus and His apostles in the way we train leaders, we will:

1. Require obedience above all else to Jesus' basic commands and the other requirements of the New Testament,
2. Train on the job while starting or developing churches, relating the theory and practice,
3. Harmonize gift-based ministries, including that of training pastors, by cooperating closely with those who use other spiritual gifts,
4. Foster loving relationships between teacher and trainees.

The truly biblical pastoral trainer, like our Lord and His apostles, shares responsibility for the effective ministry of his student and gives personal attention to the details of his ministry. The student should give something in return. The teacher is to be open to receive as well as to give (Galatians 6:6). The Western concept that maturity means attaining financial independence is foreign to Scripture.

16-k   In Training Sessions, Respond to Each Student's Needs

The acronym 'LEAP' recalls the essentials for a training session.

*L*isten and plan

*E*valuate

*A*ssign

*P*ray

Listen And Plan

Listen to each trainee's reports of both progress and problems and help him plan fieldwork to be done before the next session. Keep a copy of his plans, to evaluate at the next session.

Role playing to prepare for new situations can help; students talk through what they will do for confrontation, discipline, shepherding or counseling, before they have to do it. They discover and deal with their weaknesses before they help others.

Evaluate

Check on work and reading done (look over answers written in workbooks or ask questions). Trainees may give a short talk on something they have studied, or a summary of what they plan to teach their group.

Assign

Assign reading in Scripture or other books that corresponds to the trainees' immediate plans for their church, group, or persons they are discipling.

Pray

Each participant prays and is prayed for. Pray for God's guidance; ask also for help to carry out plans made.

16-l   Assign Reading that Supports a Student's Pastoral Work

Assign reading for Bible knowledge, doctrine and church history, etc., that corresponds to any activity that a trainee develops with his people. Record this reading in his *Progress Chart* under the corresponding activity. Examples:

❖ When the student helps his people to obey the commands of Christ, assign reading about our Lord's *deity*. Jesus requires our obedience to His commands precisely because He is *all-powerful* in heaven and on earth (Matthew 28:18-20).

❖ When assuring believers of God's grace, assign reading dealing with justification, the promise of eternal life and Christ's intercession.

❖ When naming deacons to care for the needy, assign reading about the social duties of the church.

If topics in a theological textbook do not include how to relate them to people's lives or to pastoral ministry, they probably are not worth assigning, no matter how interesting.

Verbal reports on reading are usually better than written. Trainees relate how the material applies to their spiritual life, family, church, and ministry. Oral reports develop verbal skills; trainers can respond at once to things that need correction or comment. Good mentors ask questions that enable trainees to grow in their ability to think and respond quickly, as well as to reflect on the principles behind their plans. (Examples: Why do you want your people to do that? What biblical principle does it follow?)

16-m Use Materials on the Trainee's Level, that Deal with His People's Needs

Often theological training programs started by Western missionaries, including Theological Education by Extension, begin on an educational level way too high. For materials that combine pastoral training with church planting and all other New Testament ministries, especially for fields where institutional training is impractical, we recommend *Train & Multiply* ™, Project World Reach, pwr@telus.com. For details see Appendix E *Materials for Training Leaders in a Movement of Church or Cell Multiplication*, second item.

For a tool to train missionaries that deals with the circumstances of today's neglected fields, we recommend **Disciple the Nations**, an interactive e-textbook on CD ROM by George Patterson and colleagues experienced in church multiplication in diverse fields. For information see Appendix E *Materials for Training Leaders in a Movement of Church or Cell Multiplication*, first item.

16-n Evaluate Training Terms of Students' Effective Current Ministry

We rate our teaching and preaching by the *results*, not by our *efforts* or the *efforts* of our students. We help our students to measure their progress not only in growing knowledge but also in converts baptized, changed lives, new churches and ministries. If they are not getting the results you believe God wants for them, you may need to change your method of teaching or the items on the *Progress Char.* It should deal realistically with the activities that really matter for the student and the people he serves. It should record progress in their pastoral work and studies that they complete.

Scoggins discovered the value of good evaluation of teaching:

> **Good teachers are brutal in their self-evaluation and also listen well to the input of others. Once an elder in one of our churches was complaining about his congregation. "I just preached one of the best messages of my life," he moaned, "but the people slept through it!" He failed to make a brutal self-evaluation from the congregation's perspective.**

16-o Be Creative in Communicating God's Word

Jesus and the Old Testament prophets used creative ways to communicate God's message including symbols, vivid illustrations, poetry, drama, questions, narrative, parables, irony, pithy proverbs and riddles. Try different methods of teaching. Do not overlook story telling, drama, dance, music, poetry, ritual, and symbolism.

If working cross-culturally, avoid importing evangelism and teaching methods from other cultures or educational levels. Use methods that converts or workers can immediately imitate to pass on the teaching to others.

A form of story-telling that is easy for most literate people is dramatic Bible reading. For Bible stories with dialogue, ask persons to stand and read the conversation of one of the people in the story. A narrator reads the portions that are not spoken as dialogue, skipping phrases such as "and he said."

Six readers, for example, can voice the conversations in John 9, of the following persons in the story:

1) the **disciple** who asks Jesus why the man was born blind,

2) the **Lord Jesus**,

3) the **blind man**,

4) the **Jews**,

5) the **parents**.

6) a **narrator** (reads text that is not dialogue).

16-p   Model Skills for Students

Jesus commanded His disciples to do only what they had seen Him do first, in a way they could imitate. To train pastors we imitate Jesus if we want them to reproduce. No one individual can model all the skills that students need; we seek other mentors to model skills we lack. We arrange internships or whatever will enable students to serve as apprentices or 'Timothies' to observe good models. For churches or cell groups to reproduce spontaneously, we do everything in a way that students can imitate at once. Paul told the Corinthians to imitate him as he imitated Christ (1 Cor. 11:1).

Some churches train bivocational church planters by starting daughter churches in a different, nearby culture. With this cross-cultural experience their workers are more apt to multiply churches when they go abroad. Sometimes businesspersons take on apprentices or in some other way help prepare bivocational workers for a field that needs 'tentmakers.'

We model vital ministries in a way that new shepherds can imitate us. Jesus, Paul and his coworker Barnabas all modeled these skills for their students who included Luke, Mark, Titus, Timothy, Aquila and Priscilla, Philemon and many more. Plan and arrange for new leaders to observe you or another worker doing these common pastoral tasks.

Check ministries for which you or another trainer aim to **model skills**:

To extend Christ's Kingdom on earth:
- ☐ **Evangelize**, reach converts' family and friends
- ☐ **Help the needy**, with material needs (integrate with discipling)
- ☐ **Reproduce** cells or daughter churches
- ☐ **Penetrate neglected fields** and people group

To enrich our prayer life and deepen our personal relationship with God:
- ☐ **Intercede**, pray for healing, and wage spiritual warfare
- ☐ **Watch** over and develop member's spiritual life and character

To help lame or straying lambs:
- ☐ **Counsel** and encourage any with personal or family problems
- ☐ **Strengthen marriage and family life**
- ☐ **Correct** without condemning, watch for straying lambs and wolves
- ☐ **Deal with demonic oppression** and influences

For edification of the church body and training:
- ☐ **Teach** in a way that equips *doers*
- ☐ **Disciple** on all levels
- ☐ **Practice stewardship** for wise use of *time*, *talents* and *treasure*
- ☐ **Train** leaders and helping them to train others,
- ☐ **Lead** worship
- ☐ **Cultivating fellowship** within the church body.
- ☐ **Worship** in a way that engages all in active participation,

including for small group and the Eucharist.

After modeling these skills and activities, let your trainee do it with freedom. Trust the Holy Spirit. Let them make mistakes. Let new leaders take their baby steps. Get out of their way! It's their inner motivation that counts, not perfection in their efforts.

A reproductive model often requires materials that students can study and use with their students, who pass them on to still others in a 2 Timothy 2:2 chain reaction. Many Western missionaries use materials that do not lend themselves to such reproduction, written on too high an academic level, too expensive, too abstract, too Western or contain an unbalanced emphasis on knowledge that hinders relating content to other gift-based ministries.

Scoggins' churches use materials in a way that facilitates a reproductive chain reaction:

We found that small, portable paper booklets of from four to six separate studies that fit neatly inside a Bible are practical. When we do a study with one person, we can give the booklet to that person and ask him or her to do the same study with another person. We needed to develop methods of discipleship that were easily transferable and did not require a seasoned professional teacher or pastor. Discipleship is an art, and we improve our ability with practice. It's easy to become the 'expert' that no one else can approach and everyone admires, but the result is that one person does all the discipling; there is no reproduction.

> ## *Importantísimo !*
>
> If your main spiritual gift is teaching, you must work closely with others who can make the chain reaction occur.
>
> Simply teaching in the traditional way will never, by itself, do it! Blend your gift with other birds whose gifts include leading, helps, discernment, compassion and evangelism.

16-q In Pioneer Fields Use Equipment that Is Available to Those for whom you Model Pastoral Skills and Methods

Except for special, occasional events, avoid high-tech, expensive projectors, computers, or any other equipment your people lack it. Such reliance on technology destroys your model, robs national workers of initiative and kills spontaneous reproduction. In most pioneer fields Western missionaries must discipline themselves to avoid 'Broadway' attitudes toward expensive, entertaining musical instruments for worship and dependency on budgets and technology. Some short term Westerners tote along such a quantity of amps and silicon that they give the impression that the power of the Holy Spirit extends only to the end of their electrical cord!

16-r   Avoid Modeling Values Rooted in the Paganism of your Own Culture

Westerners must avoid exporting to churches of other lands all their cultural values. Many things are held in high esteem in the West that weaken God's work in other fields. Western values that can be dangerous when exported include the following.

Western Value	Result in Non-Western Society
Entertainment	Entertaining worship, including music that is considered frivolous by mature people
Tolerance of bad influences	Obscenity, violence, fornication, homosexuality and nudity in the media, tolerance in the church
Size	Superficial evangelism methods, excessive fear of offending in teaching
Instant gratification of desires (availability of commodities, consumer-oriented marketing)	Immediate acquisition of the latest *things* and fads offered in the Evangelical market

Financial success	Commercialization of church programs, evangelism and healing campaigns, sacred concerts, seminars, etc.
"Official" credentials, often described in terms of "excellence," or "highest standards."	Gifted pastors who cannot get the formal training cannot celebrate Communion, and less gifted men with man's credentials chase the latest educational fads.
Compartmentalized organization	Excessively program-oriented church organization fails to harmonize gift-based ministries
High technology	Contented enslavement to electronic equipment and communication
Hedonism—'what feels good *is* good'	Easy toleration of sexual liaisons that destroy families, drug abuse
Equality of the sexes	Disparagement of the biblical male role in marriage
Democratization (all govern)	Lack of oversight by a group of godly, mature elders as taught by the New Testament
Individualism	Keeping one's relationship with God excessively private, failing to deal with converts' relatives and friends
Independence	Evangelism by extracting individuals socially from among relatives and friends whom God wants them to love and reach, in violation of the Acts 16:31 principle
Unity based on conformity	A Babel-like passion for unifying cultures, at the expense of destroying the weaker ones
Rationalism—'belief = *understanding*'	A rationalistic approach to sacraments and the Word

These and many more Western values restrain and sometimes paralyze church reproduction when exported by insensitive missionaries. This is the modern version of the Galatian error of forcing elements of one culture on Christians of another. Such legalism hinders the free flow of God's grace. Converts must experience *two* conversions, one to Christ, another to some aspects of a foreign culture and its values.

And meanwhile the old dragon laughs !

16-s Develop a Caring, Long-lasting Relationship with Pastoral Students

Coaching people in Christian love for serious ministry motivates and mobilizes them more powerfully than using organizational pressure. It also provides a channel between a mother and daughter church through which love and power flows to help new churches to grow and develop.

Such mentoring is not always 'one on one;' Jesus personally discipled twelve. It is personal in the sense that we share personal responsibility for our student's effective ministry. Scoggins cautions:

Developing a discipling relationship with new leaders is like building a bridge. You want to build it strong, because someday it may have to bear the weight of a freight train driving across it!

I once did a study on Jesus' interaction with His disciples. He spent three years working with them. But He saved much of His reproof and correction of them until the last week of His life. He built a very strong bridge because he knew that it would eventually have to bear an extremely crushing weight (compare Matthew 16:21-23).

16-t Augment Mentoring with Teaching in Larger Groups

To personally mentor leaders requires a group small enough to give careful attention to each one. Such discipling takes too much time to continue it indefinitely with each trainee. So we also meet in larger groups for common issues, encouragement and ongoing training for mature leaders. We keep balance in our training by providing both types of meetings. You can combine both by meeting all together, then separating for smaller group mentoring sessions, if you prepare the mentors.

16-u   To Plan Ministry Details, Keep Students of the Same Level together

In small mentoring groups we do not mix students of different social, economic, or educational levels unless they are already mixing easily. In less educated societies such mixing can seriously stifle the initiative of less educated or poorer workers.

16-v   Review Helps to Combine Doctrine and Duty

Jesus and His apostles applied at once what they taught to the life of their disciples, the community and the church. Wise teachers relate biblical and other teaching at once to its corresponding practical duty.

The following list is a review for some of the guidelines. They are important enough to warrant the recap. Mark items that you aim to give more attention, to apply your teaching to your students' ministry. Skip the rest:

☐ **Help new leaders of a church or group to envision what God wants their people to do. Plan these activities, then add the supporting theoretical studies.**

> People of faith look ahead, focusing on where God is leading them and planning accordingly. Set realistic goals and plan the little, easy-to-take steps to reach them. Stagnant churches live in the past; future plans are vague.

> Scoggins' churches learn to think ahead:

> > **We encourage every church to have a written vision statement that has a specific reproductive goal with corresponding activities for evangelism and edification that will enable the group to achieve it.**

> When you meet with students pray, listen to their ministry reports, help them plan ministry for the next week or two and assign studies that support their plans.

☐ **Give priority to Jesus' foundational commands and provide biblical studies to help your people obey them.**

☐ **When you help plan activities for a church, provide studies that support them.**

> Add to activity plans the biblical studies, doctrines, history and any other study material that support it.

> For curriculum that thoroughly weds evangelism, church multiplication and pastoral training, examine *Train & Multiply*™. Prepared originally by George Patterson and improved by the editing

218

of SEAN, Int'l with help from other experienced cross-cultural church planters, Train & Multiply ™ has proven to be effective in a variety of cultures. See Appendix E *Materials for Training Leaders in a Movement of Church or Cell Multiplication*, second item, for further information.

☐ **Keep revising the *Progress Chart* or checklist of activities that you use to monitor a student's flock's progress toward their objectives.**

We frequently revise a *Progress Chart* to deal with new needs and objectives. This makes it easier to select studies that support them.

We emphasize this New Testament guideline again:

> *Teach or assign reading in response to the immediate needs and ministry opportunities of your student's flock.*

In effective training sessions communication flows two ways. Students report what their people are doing; the trainer responds with biblical counsel that applies immediately to the needs and opportunities facing the students' church or group. Scoggins found it helpful to encourage students develop their own plans:

> **As students progress in their understanding of ministry and church or cell reproduction, they eagerly develop their plans for training others. Normally this occurs when they begin reproducing themselves in their Timothies. As they develop another leader, they add another link to the discipling chain, promoting themselves in a way by becoming a mentor and developing still more leaders.**

☐ **Deal frankly with a student's shortcomings or poor attitudes.**

Mistakes due to inexperience are a normal part of learning and are often better overlooked. But mistakes due to bad attitude or pride are another matter completely. Scoggins deals with such attitudes at a deeper level:

> **Problems often appear at the behavioral level when a new leader begins practicing a new ministry. Errant behavior is often only symptomatic of deeper problems at the motivational or affection level of one's personality. We**

also teach pastors to be sensitive to motives rather than merely to behavior.

Charles Spurgeon said that a preacher must change the affections of his congregation, not just their behavior. A good parent is not satisfied with a child whose behavior merely conforms to the code but desires one whose character (affections and motives) embraces the code. Jesus pointed out the source of sinful behavior--the heart. It is our heart that needs regeneration and then must go through the normal cycles of repentance and renewal.

☐ **Help new leaders to define their vision and plan ahead.**

We help students define their long-range goals and list the steps that lead to their fulfillment. Do this as you would place stepping stones across a shallow stream, close enough so that one does not have to leap too far and fall.

Help students to trust the Holy Spirit as they plan to deal with obstacles, and not to come to you for help every time. Do not fear that you will lose control. You are more apt to lose control of those you keep on too short a leash.

To help new leaders envision reproduction, Jesus' parables illustrate how churches grow and multiply similarly to grain. In just a few years of reproduction, one rice grain planted in good soil will multiply enough to feed the entire human race. Every time we look at grass, trees or flowers, or eat a meal, we are enjoying the fruit of God's miraculous reproductive power. All creation reminds us daily of how our Father makes every living thing reproduce! Like grain, the church has its own God-given power to grow and multiply.

We humans cannot *make* a church grow; we only sow, water, and cultivate it in faith; God gives the growth (1 Corinthians 3:6). But when it comes to reproducing His living Body on earth, Christ limits His infinite power to our weak faith! So we ask him steadily to give the increase, to bring people into His kingdom and grant us the Holy Spirit's power to do our part.

☐ **Train new pastors to solve problems by dealing with root causes rather than symptoms and discern the difference.**

Patterson observed how detecting underlying causes rather than external symptoms helped to cure damaging behavior:

A devout Honduran pastor was disturbed because the señoritas in his church kept running off to live in 'common law marriage' (without the blessing of church or state). He failed to discern the real cause, which was poverty and

220

despair. In his area the girls of marriageable age were often underfed, unwanted and miserable in the little village huts they shared with oversized families. They saw no hope for a better future. But the pastor, looking only at the external symptoms of the problem, assumed erroneously that the girls were motivated by sex. He preached incessantly against the sin of fornication.

The pastor's scolding only dealt with symptoms and did not deal in love with the underlying and painful cause. It had the opposite effect from what the pastor wanted. He unwarily kept the idea of a possible way of escape from their plight before the girls' troubled minds. It became evident that his church was having more cases of fornication than other churches in the same depressed area, whose pastors did not make it a major point in their preaching.

The other pastors noticed the root cause of the problem and took a more positive approach. They helped the youth visualize a better future, work together to create, train for, or find better employment. They helped them ponder how to achieve wholesome marriages, with far fewer cases of promiscuity.

☐ **Do not so fear false doctrine or bad practice creeping in that you chain leaders to needless rules and policies.**

Rules growing out of fear stifle spontaneous growth and development. They also provoke a subtly rebellious spirit in our trainees and coworkers that eventually opens the door to the errors one fears. When we establish a permanent rule for a church with no explicit basis in Scripture, we will probably find later that it limits the free working of the Holy Spirit.

Scoggins' people learned to avoid dogmatic rules that would have hindered the flow of God's grace:

We have found that a group of leaders meeting together will often see more clearly the issues involved than an outsider can. Church planters, unless they live permanently in the community and plan to stay in the church, are considered as outsiders.

A woman who was already a believer wanted to join one of our churches. She had come to Christ years ago while reading the Bible with her teenage girlfriend. After reading that they should be baptized, they went down to a nearby quarry and baptized each other!

Was the baptism valid? The group debated for hours.

Was baptism done only by the church, or are private baptisms valid in unusual circumstances? Can women baptize? Can non-ordained people baptize? They discussed the mode of baptism (sprinkling versus immersion) as well as the number of immersions (one of the brothers had come from a church that immerses three times forward) and infant baptism.

It was fascinating to watch these men, who were untrained by human institutions, deal with the issue by turning to the Scriptures. They finally agreed that if it was done from a heart pure with the desire to be obedient, then it was probably acceptable to God and would be acceptable by their fellowship of churches. They thought it through with no input from outside church planters or traditionally trained pastors.

I was impressed with how fully they explored the issue and with the effect on the congregation. I have been to many ordination counsels and can't remember such a thorough illumination of this issue in its practical import.

Patterson recalls a similar case of avoiding fear-based policies:

A devout Roman Catholic girl and her boyfriend were attacked by a shark while swimming off the coast near where we lived. She dragged him ashore and saw that he had only moments to live; he was losing blood rapidly from large gashes. She asked him if he wanted to affirm his faith in Christ, then took seawater and baptized him in the name of the Father, Son, and Holy Spirit. She feared that her church might disapprove, but faith overrode her fear.

Some questioned the validity of the baptism, both Protestants and Roman Catholics. The bishop, however, declared the baptism valid even though not done by an ordained priest. The girl believed that the Holy Spirit led her and felt the freedom to do it, uninhibited by tradition, as many would have been, including some Evangelicals.

☐ **Write or get textbooks geared to the local needs and educational level of your people.**

Textbooks by less educated writers can be very effective when prepared for a specific people's needs and on their level of reading comprehension. Such books can help more than books that erudite scholars have written for another time or culture. Scoggins affirms the importance of relevant reading:

We found it very helpful to put together little pastoral-

222

level study booklets that deal with Scripture passages on a particular, currently needed topic. These booklets are set up as daily reading schedules; each week focuses on a specific sub-theme of the topic. It starts with a question, with seven days of reading, each day focusing on a passage or two.

For instance, we have a booklet on *spiritual warfare.* Each of five weeks' lessons focuses on an aspect of it:
- The Reality of the War,
- The Focus of the War (the Church),
- The Enemy,
- The Schemes of the Devil; and
- The Agents of the Evil One.

We have developed many such booklets as the needs arose to deal with different aspects of the victorious life and development of the churches.

☐ **Mobilize for ministry the members of a church or small group.**

Normally it is easier to mobilize people for ministry if the group they serve with is small. It is easier yet if it is also new. Scoggins found ways to mobilize people for ministry:

One of the study booklets we have created is called *Finding your Place in the Body.* Once a person has been shepherded into the body and understands that we 'have been saved to serve' (Galatians 5:13), we use this booklet with them to study spiritual gifts and their application in the body. We use this study in conjunction with the vision statement to help new believers to pray and seek how God has equipped them to help the body attain its vision. This reinforces the ongoing teaching that the church is a community of people who have been given something by God to be passed on to someone else.

When a church reaches an unwieldy size (i.e., too large to effectively mobilize most of its members), we reorganize. The congregation should either separate members to start a daughter church nearby or form small ministry groups or sub-congregations where members can be mobilized to help give pastoral care to each other on a personal and family level. We found that for best shepherding, group size is ideal at from eight to twelve adults. Some groups may exist more for outreach and others for edification.

☐ **Base training at all levels on loving obedience to Jesus Christ.**

To lead people into loving obedience we establish it from the beginning as the foundation for all discipleship and ministry. Obedience comes before discernment (John 7:17). If we teach heavy Bible doctrine before one has learned simple, loving, childlike obedience we jeopardize his commitment to Christ.

Scoggins saw the beauty of obedience in action:

We have observed that maturity comes from practiced obedience (Hebrews 5:12-14). We try to avoid the paralysis that arises from teaching heavy Bible doctrine to potential leaders before they can apply it and learn to live in simple, loving, childlike obedience. Our Western tradition for developing leaders is to prepare a theological student for every contingency. In the process, he sometimes gets the idea that professional proficiency comes from ever-higher learning rather than from going to the Master.

This contrasts with the on-the-job training Jesus gave His disciples. He sent His apprentices out where they often failed and evaluated their learning of both doctrine and pastoral skills as they worked. In Jesus' model, leaders learn by *doing* and *studying* (always related) rather than by theoretical instruction in the doctrines of the faith in a classroom only. Paul's attitude toward his own teaching echoes this approach; he acknowledged that it was to be evaluated only by the lives and work of those he trained (1 Corinthians 3:1-9; 2 Corinthians 3:1-6).

Leaders often seek more training because of a feeling of inadequacy. Before doing detailed doctrinal training (as important as that is), we train them first to depend upon the Lord. I have noticed that some seminary-trained leaders rely upon their books and theologians, rather than upon *the* book and its Author.

In rapid reproduction of churches, traditional seminaries cannot keep pace with the need for leaders, especially for lay elders. Also, seminary-trained leaders seldom have the flexibility to disciple leaders on the job, keeping up with the moving of the Spirit, because they prefer to train others the same way they were trained. I was trained within a church in a personal discipleship relationship and therefore rely upon this method. Some seminarians have insisted that my training was inadequate. They encourage men in their churches who are called to the ministry to go away to seminary, thus failing to train the large numbers of elders at the time they are needed to shepherd truly reproducing churches.

224

❑ **Keep gearing the training--week by week and month by month-- to current needs and opportunities.**

Patterson saw missionaries over-educate new pastors in some ways and neglect current needs in other ways:

A Honduran pastor working with another denomination had been extensively educated in Guatemala. He heard about the little comic books that we developed to teach serious theology on a pastoral level for less-educated people. He called on the phone to ask me to mail him some of these training booklets.

He explained, "In seminary I learned wonderful things from the Word of God. The only problem is, having returned to my church of semi-literate peasants, I find I can no longer communicate to them."

He read a few of our booklets and later wrote, "This is what I want. Send me the rest." Later he thanked us for helping him get back on the same cultural wavelength as his own people.

Churches often follow the only training model they know--the traditional classroom. They aim to learn more and more doctrine, but without practicing the ministries that correspond. We avoid creating the long-eared 'hearers only' that James 1:22 warns about by being and training *doers* of the Word.

Teaching theory only, without enabling students to apply it immediately, numbs discipling and stifles mobilization of church members in ministry. The fact that many do it does not justify its perpetuation. It sidetracks sincere workers who fear they cannot obey until they learn all the theory. We are always learning more, and will do so for all eternity!

Our trainees should learn and serve at the same time, as the disciples of Jesus and Paul did. Such training brings reinforces true humility because trainees rely not on previous learning but the Spirit of God at work in the body of Christ.

❑ **Mobilize non-academic pastors or shepherding elders for uneducated societies.**

The working classes of the world need thousands of non-academic lay pastors who are trained on the job. Churches among the poor and uneducated thrive and reproduce with non-academic pastors and elders, trained by godly pastor-mentors. Such movements often stagnate or decline when they start to depend on outside institutions to train all their pastors. A similar problem would develop if all the soldiers in a campaign were prepared by West Point to be generals but no riflemen. We need both, but in a sane proportion. Among the apostles the ratio was one out of twelve; only Paul had formal academic training, with Gamaliel. In most pioneer fields we can meet this need by training new pastors by extension education that follows biblical discipling principles.

 Let us clarify this point.

> **The authors approve formal academic training.** George Patterson teaches at Western Seminary. But we lament the damaging assumption that all pastors need it. Both history and contemporary observation show that formal training can provide only a small fraction of the shepherds needed. They also show that if institutional training is the *only* preparation one has, his pastoral work will be deficient. This deficiency is even more noticeable in pioneer fields.

Scoggins found the value of non-formal training for pastors:

> **In Rhode Island our house churches have relied on shepherding elders trained in our churches by experienced pastors. We have men who have been ordained who have never attended college and some who didn't even finish high school. We even have two who never entered high school. But they are good shepherds, seasoned by experience in the world, who love the Lord and His people.**

16-w Note Plans to Train Pastors or Missionaries

Please note plans for training leaders, following New Testament principles. Do it together with your coworkers if possible:

_____

_____

_____

_____

_____

_____

_____

_____

_____

17.
Church Reproduction
from the Viewpoint of a
Church Leader

A leader with the largest flock in town will hardly enjoy dividing it to form another !

That depends on his motives.

If he only wants to rule the roost over more subjects he's not a true leader in the Kingdom of God, according to King Jesus.

And don't say *'divide.'* It's so negative !

Say 'multiply.' Let a few with eager wings carry the mother flock's vision, faith and life to form a tiny nucleus for a new flock.

If you have never read carefully 1 and 2 Timothy and want to understand church multiplication from the viewpoint of a church leader, please do so now. Look for what shepherds are to do with their people.

To embrace church multiplication for the first time, your people and their leaders need preparation. This preparation is not only intellectual but includes attitudes toward leadership. Scoggins dealt with attitudes of many new leaders when churches started multiplying:

We found that at the early stage of planning for multiplication, a pastor or church planter must deal with his 'flesh.' Western culture worships success and efficiency. We fear failure and try to avoid it at all costs. As a result, new leaders tend to over-control, inhibiting the spontaneous leading of the Spirit through the flock.

God, in His wisdom, allowed me to be trained as a research scientist. A researcher accepts that for every successful experiment there are many failures. Each failure is crucial because, when analyzed, it moves us further toward the successful one. When success occurs, it is almost anticlimactic, since the failures have been pointing to it, defining it, like a loop being drawn tighter and tighter around what we are seeking to grasp. In other words, we learn more from our failures than our successes. This is true both for us and for our disciples. We need to give them plenty of room in which to fail and show them how to evaluate their failures in light of God's sovereignty, helping them to see that every failure opens an opportunity for growth.

Another thing I learned from research is that, although a scientist starts with a hypothetical solution to a problem and progresses toward it, the real strides forward in research occur when forward progress is blocked and we try completely new ideas. This is frustrating since it is unexpected and may take weeks, months, or years to discern the new direction to go.

How many churches simply keep walking a treadmill to nowhere because they fear to try new directions? Instead of making radical changes, they somehow justify making the vital, reproducing Christian life into a routine of maintaining programs. Often even pastors back this mundane routine, praising the rut the church is running in. They fear to give the congregation the flexibility to try new things by faith, including risking failure, in order to restore the walk of faith. Where leaders desire to control the direction of the church, one can often predict where the church will be years from now simply by looking at where it is not going now. How sad that some churches allow the Holy Spirit, the supreme agent of

change on the earth today, less flexibility than a scientist is allowed in a laboratory!

17-a   Help your People Do Gift-Based Ministries

How do we measure the health of a church? Ephesians 4:15-16 reveals it as the "proper working of each individual part." Leaders sometimes assume that they cannot mobilize more than a minority of their people for service. But balanced, obedience-oriented discipling, especially in small groups or house churches, often leads to a high percentage of members in active service. At first many people come to church only to get their needs met. But we help them graduate from this infant stage in their spiritual life. Jesus and His apostles called their trainees to a life of unselfish, sacrificial service. This service comes from our love for God and others (Galatians 5:13). As love grows, so does our service. Effective service also grows by having the assurance of a clear conscience through Christ's sacrifice (Hebrews 9:14).

Scoggins learned from personal experiences to encourage people to serve:

> **Discipleship, or following Christ as we serve in His Kingdom in such a way that we become like Him, is progressive. Some respond immediately and make rapid progress, entering quickly into service. We have seen progress so rapid that a man has gone from being saved to being a strong leader in less than a year. Obviously, God has been preparing such persons for service in His Kingdom even before they were saved. Praise God for such Kingdom people!**

> **But others bring with them many scars from this world, which are healed through illumination by the Holy Spirit, repentance, and renewing of the mind. These stumble forward with fits and stops and require much healing before they can contribute significantly to the Kingdom. But even during this crippled stage they can be serving in some way; their contribution should be recognized and appreciated. They can pray for the leaders and the needs of the body and often will have words of encouragement for the downhearted. Some of their healing will come as they contribute their part in the kingdom.**

> **I have a retarded brother who, despite his mental handicaps, has been quite a challenge to me. One day he asked me who would preach the gospel to people like him? His concern challenged me. Children who know Christ also need to see themselves as contributors to the Kingdom. A Jewish boy in Jesus' times was considered a man at age twelve and was expected to carry out his religious duties in**

the synagogue. We often have no place for children to serve until after they graduate from college! Maybe that's why we lose so many. They do not see service in God's Kingdom as a part of their life. Instead church is a place where they are entertained and served. When the world offers better entertainment and more attractive opportunities to do things, they are seduced.

In our house churches we sometimes have 'affirmation meetings,' where members of the congregation mention how they have seen others minister in the body. This encouragement helps spur others to greater ministry. Little teaching is done at such meetings, but the ministry of helps, encouragement, reproof, and compassion are made more visible; otherwise they often go unnoticed.

All of us ought to be progressing measurably in our walk with the Lord. Those who are not need to recognize that something is wrong. If our children stop growing, we take them to see a doctor; likewise those who have experienced new life in Christ ought to keep growing. We cannot accept 'nominal' growth as normal in a reproducing church.

We need to detect and oppose the 'convenience volunteer' when we mobilize our people for ministry ("I will do ministry when it is convenient--when it is not, I have my own things to worry about"). In God's army there are no such convenience volunteers, only conscripts. Unlike the volunteer militia in the beginning of the American Revolutionary War who went home when the going got tough, we are 'regulars' who have been drafted for the duration of the war. For us there is no turning back! Those who will not move forward need our help in order to remove Satan's barriers.

Scoggins corrects these who continue to resist sacrificial service:

We help them to see that the church is like a big boat pulling away from the dock. You either move on, or you will be left behind by your own choice. Some churches hesitate at the dock while timid members make countless excuses for not getting on. Eventually even the most committed grow weary waiting for their brothers to make up their minds, and join the uncommitted standing on the dock watching the boats go by.

Disciples who show progress need to be encouraged to go forward and given more responsible ministry, on the principle that "he who is faithful in little will also be faithful with much" (Luke 19:17). We include them in our meetings when we initiate ministry, plan, and set objectives so that they feel that they are 'in' and not simply subordinate to the elders and paid

staff.

The primary goal of leadership is to equip believers and coordinate efforts of the members of the body for its edification and reproduction. Leaders who simply enforce rules rather than help others to minister hinder normal reproduction.

Some churches find it hard to turn over key positions to volunteer workers. Staff complains, "You can't count on them." Yet other large churches enjoy an abundance of reliable volunteer workers. Why the difference? The leaders of churches with many volunteer workers do not hesitate to challenge members to loving obedience to Christ. They praise their efforts and are patient with new workers. They do not polarized the congregation into an elite paid staff versus those who attend church to get their needs met and give offerings to pay the staff to do the work.

17-b Let Organization Grow out of Relationships and Intentions to Serve, Not the Other Way Around

Determine first what God wants your people to do, then organize for it. Don't reverse this order or impersonal structures will dictate how you do ministry. Good church organization is flexible; like a living body it continually adapts. It conforms to our understanding of what God wants our people to do. In a healthy church this understanding grows and changes as we grow in understanding of God's Word and observe changes in our community. We invite failure when we pour new plans into the old wine skins of an organization originally set up for different times and people. A shepherd who does not know the activities that God wants His people to do in the future cannot lead them toward their fulfillment; he can only teach and enforce rules.

Common enemies of reproductive organization:

❖ Methods and organizational structures set up to do things other than what needs to be done now.

❖ Over-control (workers do not feel freedom),

❖ Delegating with too many safeguards, rules and policies,

❖ Building the work around the organization rather than building the organization around the people and their gift-based activities,

❖ Placing leaders of highly reproductive house churches under the supervision of a traditional regional church board (instead of overseers that understand church reproduction and desire to continue it),

❖ Failure to maintain relationships with those who start another church or small group. Wives and teenagers are often more motivated by relationships than a vision for reproducing groups.

To allay fears of breaking relationships, maintain them with occasional united celebrations and fellowship activities for members of all churches or groups. Also, arrange personal discipling for both members and leaders of the new groups by the leaders of the parent group. Mobilize older women to disciple younger, and others including young people to disciple those in the new groups who are newer in the faith (Titus 2:3-4).

Scoggins found how to keep organization fluid:

We have found that house churches can reproduce rapidly, thus requiring regular changes in organization and relationship building. Monthly meetings that include members of the entire network of churches help to keep up old relationships. In addition to monthly meeting of all the churches, we also have weekly men's prayer meetings, women's meetings, and youth meetings. Discipleship chains often extend from one church to another, especially when a new house church begins.

Organizing for normal, spontaneous reproduction requires flexible, open-ended organization (in which churches or groups are free and encouraged to reproduce themselves, without being tied to rules imposed by a controlling board or grandmother church). Each church is a 'whole new ball game,' entitled to make its own rules for its own ministry--and to make its own mistakes. The best organizational structures for the multiplication and continued fellowship of churches and groups grow normally out of the loving relationships already developing in the process of training assistant pastors in the churches or groups.

We should verify at least quarterly which ministries need attention. Wise leaders keep an eye all vital ministries. Appendix B is an *Example of a Progress Chart for a New Church* with key ministries, for regular evaluation.

17-c Note Plans to Periodically Evaluate Ministries

_____

_____

_____

_____

_____

_____

18.
Church Reproduction
from the Viewpoint of a
Mission Career Advisor

Find in the book of Jonah both good and bad attitudes for a cross-cultural missionary, which wise mission career advisors can help us avoid.

18-a   Provide Unbiased Mission Career Coaching

Churches, schools and mission agencies should provide unbiased counsel so workers can follow the Holy Spirit's leading with freedom. Otherwise, missionaries and agencies get an unbalanced focus. They neglect fruitful ministries and fields by channeling workers into familiar programs and clustering them in fields with excessive concentrations of workers.

An unbiased career advisor bears in mind the entire scope of mission work from sending churches to very neglected fields. Patterson observed cases of grief caused by poor career counseling:

> **The need for unbiased, comprehensive mentoring for new missionaries became evident after I listened to complaints from several persons who received counseling from recruiters for mission agencies or training institutions. These counselors meant well but their advice was biased. They recruited for their organization, field, or ministry, sometimes without knowing well the person's calling and gifts. The family disasters and career failures that resulted from such counseling were heartbreaking. We need the recruiters, but not until potential career missionaries have accurately assessed their gifts and the options offered by a global view of the entire spectrum of mission work.**

The different categories of people that need to be mobilized and their tasks appear in Section **13-f**.

18-b   Keep Reviewing your Church or Organization's Mission Outreach to Arrange Orientation and Training for Current Needs, Resources and Opportunities

Advisors in a local church should review their church's missionary outreach at least annually, to review progress and make suggestions.

If you mobilize persons or groups in a sending church, consider these activities and mark those you plan to deal with:

☐   **Train potential missionaries.** Missionaries, including short-term workers, bivocational workers and partners from two-thirds world churches, need special training. For many pioneer fields someone on the task group needs the skills for:

  ❖   **Business or other vocational skills** (apprenticeships may work)

  ❖   **Training pastors** on the job rather than in an institution.

234

- ❖ **Low profile, incarnational evangelism.**
- ❖ **Discipling new Christians** for obedience.
- ❖ **Leading worship for small groups** (in pioneer fields most churches start as small home groups).
- ❖ **Training new missionaries from two-thirds world churches** on the job.

  Normally missionaries should receive training in their own country or in the new field. Serious problems often result when training in the West moves missionaries from poorer economies into a higher income bracket from what their churches can pay, or from that of their compatriot coworkers. It also often weakens the advantage they otherwise have of being culturally closer to the people than Western missionaries. We make an exception for experienced, mature leaders who are authorized by their church or denomination to receive higher education in the West for specialized work.

- ☐ **Mobilize missionary trainers.** Many trainers need more experience with mentoring skills required in today's neglected fields. These skills include reproducing small churches cross-culturally and training leaders by discipling them on the job. They may need to learn how to deal with two-thirds world workers and cross-cultural entrepreneurs.

- ☐ **Explain to your church how to prepare and send church planting task groups.** Leaders of a sending church should plan or the church body to adopt and disciple a neglected people group.

- ☐ **Help mission agencies to send task groups that are equipped with the needed pastoral and vocational skills.** For many of the remaining neglected fields, mission agency administrators must bring together small business managers, entrepreneurs, mentors of pastors and workers from the two-thirds world in the same task group. They should do this in cooperation with sending churches.

18-c Let People Serve out of Love for Jesus

Make sure a career worker serves out of a desire to obey Christ--not because an organization demands it. If they aim to serve overseas, verify their commitment. Is it to go and simply do what Jesus says? Or is it to spend a measured amount of time overseas to simply satisfy their conscience, people of influence in their lives or a desire for adventure?

For more detailed activities for a sending church see Appendix D, *Example of a Progress Chart for a Mission Action Group in a Sending Church.*

18-d Note Plans for Mission Career Guidance

Arrange for an unbiased mission career advisor—one that is not trying to recruit for any program or organization--to help new workers think through their plans. Do this planning with coworkers if possible:

_____

_____

_____

_____

_____

_____

_____

_____

_____

_____

_____

_____

_____

_____

_____

_____

APPENDICES

APPENDIX A.

Example of a *Personal Progress Chart* for a Married Worker Preparing to Serve in Vietnam

(Activity Checklist)

Confirm our commitment (my wife and I) with prayer, and in consultation with experienced mentors.

Date begun _____ Commitment confirmed_____

Explore opportunities to discover and practice our ministry skills, in order to focus on the type of ministry that God has for us. Help start a new church within another culture nearby to get experience in different ministries and cross-cultural work, and a better understanding of our abilities and limitations.

Date begun _____ Ministry skill confirmed_____

Discuss, and agree upon, my wife's role in the ministry.

Date begun _____ My wife's role at this stage in life verified_____

Define relevant criteria and decide if we should form and lead a church based task group from our own church and sister churches, or join one already formed.

Date begun _____ Task group involvement confirmed_____

Define relevant criteria and decide if we should work with a missionary organization with experience in Church Multiplication in Vietnam or develop a private business as base of operations.

Date begun _____Organizational involvement confirmed_____

Define relevant criteria to investigate people groups in northwestern Vietnam in order to select one that is both neglected and responsive

Date begun _____ Responsive people group identified_____

Define relevant criteria to decide if we should work with an export business or some other bivocational approach.

Date begun _____ Bivocational work confirmed_____

Practice training small group leaders by apprenticing Fred and Sam in my small group and, if the Lord wills, help them form new groups.

Date begun _____ Practice confirmed_____

Practice 'incarnational evangelism' with heads of families.

Date begun _____ Practice confirmed_____

Date arranged _____ Internship completed satisfactorily_____

Pay off my college loan.

Date completed_____

Start learning the language; find a helper who speaks it.

Date begun _____ Practice verified_____

Get Nancy's teeth straightened.

Date begun _____

Get on a family health plan.

Date done _____

Help Mom and Dad accept emotionally, my call to go overseas.

Date begun _____ Done_____

APPENDIX B.

Example of a *Progress Chart* for a *New Church*

The chart lists ministries that the New Testament requires for a church. Each ministry is dealt with on three levels: *beginning*, *growth* (i.e., ongoing ministry), and *reproduction* (advanced).

Do not go through these ministry levels one after another in order. Use the chart as a 'menu' by selecting items that fit current needs and opportunities. Don't simply work through it. Initiate or improve any of the ministries as the opportunity comes. Although the 'Reproduction' level is listed third, God may bring fruition about any time through a ministry. We must be ready to move with Him.

Make Disciples

Beginning level. Learn and observe all of Jesus' basic commands (review the Gospels)

Growth level. Leaders mentor newer leaders, including those for daughter churches and new home groups.

Reproduction level. Pastoral trainees (elders) take on more and more pastoral responsibility in new churches or groups and train newer leaders. (Study Titus)

Pray

All levels. Pray and praise God daily, privately and as a family. Practice regular congregational prayer. (Study those Psalms that are prayers)

Evangelize

Beginning level. Members witness to friends and relatives; converts are baptized (study Acts chapters 1-2; Acts 8).

Growth level. The church sends out task groups to evangelize.

Reproduction level. Leaders help daughter churches mobilize members to witness for Christ (study Acts 2:36-47; Acts 10 and Acts 13-14).

Worship

Beginning level. All churches celebrate the Lord's Supper.

Growth and reproduction levels. Congregations practice all essentials of corporate worship (praise, confession and assurance of forgiveness, application of the Word, Eucharist, prayer, giving, and fellowship). They also celebrate sacred seasons of the church year.

Fellowship

Beginning and growth levels. All members cultivate loving fellowship, forgiving and asking forgiveness for all offenses, building all organization on loving relationships (do a topical study on passages dealing with love, unity and fellowship).

Reproduction level. Each church or group as a body maintains loving, cooperative inter-church (inter-group) relationships, including regular united celebrations with sister churches or groups.

Shepherd

Beginning and growth levels. Watch over the spiritual life of the flock. Help parents and new teachers relate Bible stories dealing with vital doctrines, family and church needs. Give member care; correct personal or family problems patiently and humbly without condemning.

Reproduction level. Small group leaders train assistant group leaders who form new groups (study 1 and 2 Timothy).

Reproduce Daughter Churches or Cells

Beginning level. Pastors mentor newer pastors for new churches

Growth and reproduction levels. Mother churches (groups) mobilize daughter churches and new groups to multiply. Help daughter churches to start granddaughter churches. (Study Acts chapters 13-14.)

Teach to Edify

Beginning level. Teachers and pastors teach in a way that their disciples can imitate their teaching style and teach others.

Growth level. Believers do inductive Bible studies to interpret correctly and apply God's Word to their lives and ministries.

Reproduction level. Teachers prepare assistants on the job as new Bible teachers for new small groups and daughter churches. Pastors train newer pastors (you might want to use *Train & Multiply™*; in this case see Appendix E *Materials for Training Leaders in a Movement of Church or Cell Multiplication*, second item).

Grow in Christ, Develop Christian Character

Beginning level. Members cultivate the hope that purifies, for new life in Christ.

Growth and reproduction levels. Leaders seek daily guidance by the Holy Spirit. Family heads shepherd their families for growth in Christ.

Practice Christian Stewardship

Beginning level. All members give in faith, trusting in our Father's heavenly reward.

Growth level. Elders discern worthy projects and workers to support, channel giving through the church, develop a budget and teach giving.

Reproduction level. Members give sacrificially to reproduce other churches at home and abroad.

Organize

Beginning level. Elders integrate different ministries in one loving body, and practice the New Testament 'one anothers' within *and between* groups and churches.

Growth level. Group leaders and new elders provide *total* pastoral care.

Reproduction level. Small groups multiply themselves and their ministries in mother and daughter churches.

Mobilize for Global Outreach

Beginning level. Leaders teach to discern and pray for neglected fields.

Growth level. Churches recruit and prepare missionary task groups.

Reproduction level. Churches send task groups to start churches in ripe, neglected fields.

Strengthen Families

Beginning level. Families develop loving communication between spouses and children.

Growth and reproduction levels. Parents practice loving Christian discipline in the home. Elders and older Christian women counsel spouses, couples, or children with problems and help fathers to shepherd their families.

Serve the needy

Beginning level. Believers and the church as a body obey Jesus' Great Commandment to love our neighbor in a practical way.

Growth level. Deacons or deaconesses develop ministries that mobilize many to help the sick and needy.

Reproduction level. Churches or groups alleviate injustice and poverty in other communities and fields, including through daughter churches there.

Appendix C

Example of a *Progress Chart* for *Field Workers*

If you lead workers to plant new churches, you should find it easier if you prepare a *Progress Chart* with activities and guidelines. Mark items that you plan to give special attention.

Activities for Starting a New Church

☐ **Prayerfully select and focus on the neglected people that you plan to disciple.** Study a people group to determine its most responsive segment. Normally this is a segment of the working class.

☐ **Focus on people who are culturally similar to you and your task group members--*Or* add to your task group workers from other fields that are culturally closer to the people.** This is especially important at the start when outsiders must do the evangelism.

Introducing a church style that is too Western can delay church multiplication for many years. If possible find helpers from other, closer cultures who do not have to make as large a cultural leap.

If your church 'adopts' a neglected people and prays for it, God will give members the apostolic gift to send to disciple them.

☐ **Recruit task group members committed to complete the job.** Workers must commit to do simply as Jesus says, to disciple a people group, no matter how long it takes or what sacrifice is needed. If your church is small, work with other churches to form a task group.

Short-term service is helpful for temporary specialized service, enrichment and to discern one's gifts and calling, but not for permanent church multiplication.

☐ **Bond with the people and their culture.** Workers should live with the people they are discipling and identify socially with them--not with other missionaries or foreigners. The missionary's deepest social needs, apart from his own family, should be met by the people.

☐ **Bind Satan.** Pray in Jesus' all-powerful name to bind Satan and his demons in your area. Our Lord defeated them utterly by in His death on the cross and in His resurrection.

☐ **Filter out nonessentials.** Avoid non-transferable methods, attitudes, and equipment--including ways to teach, witness and worship.

☐ **Bring God's hope to those who suffer from brutal class discrimination.** The oppressed in most fields are the most responsive, but avoid messy politics. For the initial penetration of areas with hostile authorities, seek to live among people who want change and do not cling to the *status quo*. Also, seek to reside where authorities do not watch closely.

☐ **Maintain fervent prayer for the unsaved and for converts.**

☐ **Seek the 'man of peace' that Jesus mentioned.** Look for responsive heads of families and friends or relatives of believers, who can introduce you to the community and provide contacts.

☐ **Witness for Jesus.** Begin, if possible, with heads of families. Help seekers to repeat to their families Bible stories that show Jesus' death and resurrection, through which we gain forgiveness and eternal life.

☐ **Baptize.** Baptize entire families without unnecessary delay,.

☐ **Break bread.** Celebrate the Lord's Supper with the new believers in regular worship. Do not require them to go to a distant church for it.

☐ **Teach new believers to obey the commands of Jesus** and apply the Word of God to their lives.

☐ **Organize.** Name elders, train and mobilize them to shepherd their people (Acts 14:23). They are to help their people use their God-given gifts in the different ministries that the New Testament requires.

☐ **Agree on each worker's spouse's ministry.** Couples talk it over now and again when a change in status follows birth or children or when they develop into a less dependent stage of maturity.

☐ **Keep doing evangelism in the homes**, especially after starting public worship services.

☐ **Make worship an edifying, meaningful celebration.** Prepare well, planning well ahead of time, even for a tiny group.

☐ **Give responsibility to the local leaders.** Avoid over-control or ongoing control from the *outside*.

☐ **Teach Christian stewardship from the start.** Avoid permanent subsidies from the outside for pastors. Let the people support their leaders. Let leaders serve voluntarily as Paul did (2 Thess. 3:6-12).

☐ **Arrange for each new worker to report regularly to a capable mentor(s) who sincerely cares for the worker and his ministry.**

☐ **Mentor new leaders as Jesus and His Apostles did.** Imitate their model. In a pioneer field, do not send inexperienced leaders out of their community to receive pastoral training. Disciple them on the job. Let more experienced pastors train newer ones. Use materials geared for this (Appendix E *Materials for Training Leaders in a Movement of Church or Cell Multiplication*).

APPENDIX D

Example of a *Progress Chart* for a *Mission Action Group* in a Sending Church

We recommend that a sending church form small groups to train missionaries in skills needed for today's world. These skills include small group worship, family-oriented evangelism, mentoring new leaders and church organization that allows all members to serve one another with their different gifts.

The activities in this chart are for a mission action group that mobilizes a church body for global outreach. Mark those that apply to your work:

Prepare for a *Mission Action Group*
(or whatever you prefer to call it)

☐ **Prayerfully seek the support of the elders or leaders of the church, especially of the senior pastor if there is one, for a Mission Action Group. Arrange accountability to them.**

☐ **Recruit committed volunteers for the Mission Action Group.**
Aim for representatives from each department, class, ministry, or small group in the church. They take back to these people information, prayer requests and reports of needs, to keep the entire church body aware. Do not allow the church to polarize around two parties: those who promote foreign missions and the indifferent.

Launch the Mission Action Group

☐ **Orient volunteers to their individual tasks.** Help workers to define their job descriptions and arrange accountability.

☐ **Arrange for the group to meet regularly to function as a small church within the larger one.** They worship, celebrate the Lord's Supper, and do everything else that Jesus and the apostles ask churches to do. They especially help missionary candidates to practice skills for ministries they will need to do in future fields.

☐ **Plan activities** to regularly inform the entire church body. Keep the church praying for workers and their preparation, and for missionaries on the field and the neglected people they work with.

☐ **Help mission action group workers to communicate in a way that relates to the age, spiritual maturity, and nature of any people that they teach.** A worker with children would tell stories. One with teenagers might plan mission-related projects or field trips.

☐

Provide Tools, Contacts and Guidelines for Workers

☐ **Catalog available resources for mission awareness and mobilization.** Provide tools for increasing mission awareness and mobilizing volunteer workers.

☐ **Network with other churches.** Share with these churches ideas and resources; encourage and pray for each other.

☐ **Cooperate with supportive organizations.** Work with mission agencies, missionary training schools and denominational leaders that support your church's activities.

☐ **Use training materials that are geared to church multiplication for missionaries and new leaders on the field**, including where conditions do not favor institutional education. For recommendations see **Appendix E** *Materials for Training Leaders in a Movement of Church or Cell Multiplication*.

Suggested Activities for a Twelve Month Cycle

This is an example only; you should prepare your own agenda to fit your circumstances. We do not mean to limit the activities for any month to those mentioned below. We suggest that you give the activity special emphasis during the month and keep practicing the others also.

☐ **Month 1. Arrange for informed prayer by each class or small group in the church**. You might use *Global Prayer Digest*.

☐ **Month 2. Teach a comprehensive biblical perspective.** Use Old and New Testament passages on God's plan for the nations (use related sections in *Perspectives on the World Christian Movement*).

☐ **Month 3. Teach giving for world outreach and arrange for it. Encourage 'faith promise' to allow individuals and families to give as God leads them to specific missionaries.**

☐ **Month 4. Present a comprehensive historical survey.** Investigate what God has done throughout the history to extend His kingdom on earth (You might use Tucker's from *Jerusalem to Irian Jaya*).

☐ **Month 5. Arrange for local mission work.** Evangelize and start churches among an ethnic group nearby.

☐ **Month 6. Heighten awareness of worldwide mission work.** You might use *Target Earth* or Patrick Johnstone's *Operation World*, William Carey Library, Pasadena.

☐ **Month 7. Arrange for ministry career guidance by unbiased advisors** who help workers to explore the entire range of options open to today's apostles for starting churches in neglected fields.

☐ **Month 8. Review and evaluate the past and current mission outreach of your own church.**

☐ **Month 9. Develop more effective training for mission work.** Determine what further training career and volunteer mission workers need. Provide training in small groups that use models that are transferable to the fields where workers plan to serve.

☐ **Month 10. Impart a cultural orientation for global outreach.** Help others in the church to appreciate other cultures and God's love for the nations with their distinctive characteristics. You might use related sections in *Perspectives on the World Christian Movement*, William Carey Library, Pasadena.

☐ **Month 11. Plan and pray for the church to reproduce daughter and granddaughter churches at home and abroad.** You can easily use this book as a manual for training potential task group members.

☐ **Month 12. Mobilize, commission, send and uphold workers.**

APPENDIX E

Materials for Training Leaders in a Movement of Church or Cell Multiplication

For a list of materials, mentors, tools and downloads see **MentorAndMultiply.com** by author George Patterson.

1. For Missionaries

Disciple the Nations. For training materials for **missionaries** based on biblical guidelines that foster church multiplication in pioneer fields, as well as cell multiplication in established churches, we recommend this **CD-ROM.**

Disciple the Nations is an interactive e-textbook written as a fast-paced novel based on actual field events. They are woven together in narrative form for enjoyable reading and enhanced learning--the next best thing to being on the field. You select options voiced by characters in the story, to compete with an adversary. If he outscores you in any of 24 episodes he appears on the screen to laugh at you. You do that phase over. The program tracks progress in over 100 areas of pastoral work, biblical guidelines and cross-cultural communication. The reading is equivalent to a book of 300 to 400 pages, depending on how much you explore supplementary information.

Disciple the Nations helps you to work through increasingly difficult skill levels to make disciples under widely diverse field conditions. It also helps you to combine church planting and evangelism with pastoral education by mentoring, for new workers in fields where institutional training is impractical.

Development of this tool took 12 years of gleaning information from dozens of fields and Christian workers.

To view full information:
http://www.westernseminary.edu/mrg/disciple/

For a live human contact DiscipleNations@Servants-Inc.org.

2. For Training Pastors and Other Leaders

For training materials for *pastors, small group leaders and church planters* that are based on biblical guidelines that foster church multiplication in pioneer fields, as well as cell multiplication in established churches, we recommend *Train & Multiply*™.

Train & Multiply ™ *(T&M™)* is a basic pastoral training curriculum comprising 65 small textbooks with ample illustrations. But it goes far beyond these written materials; it is a New Testament discipline based on Christ's and the apostles' leadership training models. It has proven to be effective for multiplying churches in many fields and is available in several languages. It uses the 'menu' approach to teaching, and is especially helpful for new pastors and leaders of all educational levels.

George Patterson is the original author of Train & Multiply™.

For information on this education tool, which combines church planting and evangelism with pastoral training by mentoring, visit www.TrainAndMultiply.com.

For information about translation or licensing for reproduction rights, contact Project WorldReach, pwr@telus.net or LloydNiles@TrainAndMultiply.com

Project WorldReach
474-800-15355-24th Ave
Surrey BC
Canada
V4A 6R4

For help on troubleshooting in the field contact author George Patterson, Gpatters@WesternSeminary.edu. or GeorgePatterson@TrainAndMultiply.com

APPENDIX F

BIBLE READINGS

For Family Devotions and Small Group Discussion

We arranged readings under activities that Scripture asks us to do, to help you apply it to the lives of your family or small group.

Readings, covering the entire Bible, are listed on three levels starting with simpler texts.

Before reading or telling a Bible story, tell hearers what to look for. Suggestions for what to find follow the word "FIND" for the Bible passages. For example:

> FIND:
> *In 2 Chronicles 1:6-12 what a leader of God's people should ask in prayer.

Before reading 2 Chronicles 1:16-12, you would ask participants (or do it yourself if you are alone) to listen or look for "what a leader of God's people should ask in prayer."

After reading, ask questions to help group discussion:
What important truths did you find? What do they teach us about God?
What was hard to understand?
What does God want us to do about what we just read?
What is your plan?

Prepare! Group participation is stronger if you study a passage at home, then lead or participate in the discussion of it, when you meet as a small group or family.

Stories for the whole family. Asterisks (*) indicate *stories* for children as well as adults. They sometimes indicate portions of a story that might be too long to read to children in its entreaty. The list repeats some Bible stories, including those that appear in two or more Gospels. We learn by repetition; for children it is essential.

Aim for spiritual growth. The readings cover the entire Bible. They appear under activities on three levels, so that you can repeat an activity on a more advanced level, rather than studying it only once.

Use the list below as a menu. Select readings according to the needs or interests of your small group, family or personal walk with Christ.

BIBLE READINGS -- LEVEL 1

Seek God's will and plan accordingly. (LEVEL 1)
FIND:
*In 2 Chronicles 1:6-12, what a leader of God's people should ask in prayer.
*In Matthew 26:36-46, how we submit in prayer, to the will of God.

Triumph through Prayer (LEVEL 1)
FIND:
*In Genesis 18:16-33, how Abraham triumphed in prayer.
*In Luke 18:1-8, how the widow triumphed with her pleas.

Tell Others About Jesus (LEVEL 1)

FIND:

In Genesis chapters 1-3, how Adam caused all mankind to fall.

    *In chapter 3, how the devil tempted Adam and Eve.

*In Genesis 4, what was sacrificed for a man's sin, why Cain was mad.

*In Matthew 4:1-11, the difference between Adam and Jesus, in their response to temptation.

*In Mark 14:1-9, how we should feel about Jesus when we think of how and why He died.

*In Mark 14:10-31, what Jesus said and did when He showed us how to celebrate Communion.

*In Mark 14:26-31 with 66-72 (after Jesus' arrest), how Peter broke his promise to God.

*In Mark 14:32-42, Jesus' supreme act of obedience to His Father

*In Mark 14:43-52, how they arrested and tried Jesus, why they sentenced Him to die

*In Mark 15:1-20, what they did to Jesus before they killed Him

*In Mark 15:21-41, things that happened when Jesus died

Be Baptized and Added to Jesus' Church (LEVEL 1)

FIND:

In Genesis chapters 5-9,

    a) why the Most Holy God gets angry with people,

    b) what He did in Noah's time.

       *In 6:9-14; 7:1-24; 8:15-22, find how God saved some people, who, why and what else was in the boat

In Exodus chapters 14-15, how the Israelites escaped from slavery.

    *In chapter 14, what God did to save His people from Pharaoh, the angry king.

In Acts 16:19-40, several things that happened that started the new church in Philippi.

    *In verses 19-34, who received baptism, when, and why.

In Rom. 5:12 through 6:14, how baptism in Jesus leaves us changed.

Pray for the Sick and Demon Oppressed (LEVEL 1)

FIND:

In 2 Kings 4, several unusual things that happened.

    *In verses 17-37, how Elijah dealt with the dead child.

*In Acts 16:16-18, What Paul did to cast out the demon.

In Ephesians 6:10-20, the purposes of the different pieces of the armor of God.

Make it Easy to Tell Others About Jesus (LEVEL 1)

FIND:

*In Joshua 1:1-11, how we should think, to conquer for Jesus.

In Genesis 10.1 through 12.3 (compare with Galatians 3:8-9 & 13-14), how nations began and how they will be blessed.

    *In Genesis 11:1-9 and 12:1-3,

        a)   how God separated the people of different nations,

        b)   through whom He would bless all nations.

In Luke 10:1-24, what Jesus orders us to do as we announce His kingdom.

In Luke chapters 23-24, the basic story of the good news of the gospel.

    *In 23:1-25, why the king and governor let the religious leaders turn Jesus over to be killed.

    *In 23:26-43, what Jesus said when He was hanging from the cross.

    *In 23:44-56, what the Roman Captain thought about Jesus, where Jesus was buried.

    *In 24:1-12, how they first knew that Jesus had risen from the dead.

    *In 24:13-35, how two disciples recognized the risen Christ.

*In 24:36-44, how the risen Lord proved to His disciples that He was not a ghost.

*In 24:45-53, what we should explain to others about Jesus, and where He is now.

*_In_ Matthew 13:24-43 and Rev. 20:11-15, what will happen to people who reject God.

Learn to Live the Christian Life Victoriously, by Faith (LEVEL 1)

FIND:

In Genesis chapters 12-19, important things that Abraham did.

*In 12:1-3 & 7-9, God's promise to Abraham.

*In 12:10-20, Abraham's foolish lie.

*In 13:1-18, how Abraham avoided a quarrel with his nephew.

*In 14:1-24, how Abraham freed his nephew.

*In 15:1-21, what Abraham did, that God considered him to be just, what God promised.

*In 18:1-15, why Sarah laughed and what the angel said about it.

*In 18:16-33, how Abraham saved his nephew again.

*In 19:1-29, what happened to some very bad people.

*In Matthew 28:16-20, what a new disciple of Jesus is to do.

In 1 Tim. 3:16-17, the purpose of all Bible teaching (see v. 17).

*In Mark (the entire book), major events in the life of Jesus (jot them down). _(Nearly every chapter has stories that are excellent for children.)_

Love God and Our Neighbor in a Practical Way   (LEVEL 1)

FIND:

*In 1 Samuel 24, how David showed his love for his enemy.

*In Luke 10:25-37, how we show true Christian love for our neighbor.

Read and Apply the Bible to Our Lives (LEVEL 1)

FIND:

In Nehemiah 8 (*verses 1-6), what was done so that the people applied the Bible to their lives.

*In Matthew 7:24-26, what happens if we learn the Bible without practicing it.

*In Matthew 15:1-20, how we corrupt ourselves, if we use the Bible incorrectly.

In 1 Peter 1:22 through 2:3, what the Word of God does for us.

In Rev. 22:18-19, a warning against changing Word of God.

Get along with Our Brothers in Christ and Worship Together (LEVEL 1)

FIND:

In Genesis chapters 20-36, good attitudes toward God, for worship.

*In 21:22-34, what Abraham and Abimelech did, to live together in peace.

*In 22:1-18, how God tested Abraham's faith.

*In 24:1-67, how God provided a wife for Isaac.

*In 25:27-34, how Jacob tricked Esau into giving him his rights as first-born (for a special inheritance).

*In 27:1-40, how Jacob tricked his dying father into giving him his brother's blessing.

*In 32:22-32, how Jacob and his descendants received the name _"Israel."_

*In 33:1-20, what Jacob did so that his brother Esau would forgive him.

In Exodus chapters 16-17 (compare John 6), with what attitude we are to receive what God provides.

*In Exodus 16:1-35, how God provided food for His people in the desert.

*In Exodus 17:1-7, how God provided water for His people in the desert.

*In Exodus 17:8-16, what happened when Moses' arms fell, what they did about it.

*In John 6:1-15, how Jesus provided food for the people in the desert.

*In John 6:22-69, the food and drink that lets us live forever

In Exodus chapters 25-27 and 33:7-10, the form of the old sanctuary, priests' duties.

*In Acts 2:36-47, what they did in the worship services of the first church.

In 1 Cor. 11 and Hebrews 10:25, guidelines for attending and celebrating worship.

Celebrate Family Devotions (LEVEL 1)

FIND:

*In Joshua 24:15 and Job 1:5, what Joshua and Job did with their children.

*In Luke 18:15-17 and Ephesians 6:4, what we should do with the children.

In John (the entire book), stories of Jesus, to tell to our families. *Nearly every chapter has stories that are excellent for children.*

Organize the Church (LEVEL 1)

FIND:

*In Exodus 18:13-27, how they shared the pastoral work.

In Nehemiah chapters 3-4, how they divided the work among many.

In 1 Corinthians chapters 12-13, how the work of the Body of Christ is coordinated.

*In Acts chapters 1-12, examples of how God disciplined and governed His new church *(Nearly every chapter has stories that are excellent for children).*

Develop Loving Fellowship in the Family of God (LEVEL 1)

FIND:

*In Genesis 37-50 (select key portions) Joseph's love for his family (relate his adventures).

*In Matthew 26:17-30, what Jesus orders us to do in worship.

In John 13:34-35, Eph. 4:31-32, 1 John chapters 1-5, guidelines for fellowship.

In Ephesians (select key portions from the entire book), guidelines to cultivate love for God and others.

Visit and Encourage our Brothers in Christ (LEVEL 1)

FIND:

*In Genesis 18:1-15, what the visiting angel promised Abraham and Sarah.

*In Acts 9:36-43 (compare James 1:27), why Peter visited Dorcas.

Develop Generous Stewardship (LEVEL 1)

FIND:

*In Genesis 14:17-24 (compare Malachi 3:10), what Abraham gave to the priest Melchizedek.

In Exodus chapters 35-36, why Moses prohibited that they give more offerings.

*In Luke 21:1-4, how God calculates the amount that we give to Him.

*In Acts 8:4-25 (compare 2 Cor. 9:6-8), the correct attitude for giving.

Prepare to Serve Christ (LEVEL 1)

FIND:

In Exodus chapters 1-10 (compare 2 Tim. 2:2), how God prepared, called and used Moses.

    *In Exodus 1:1-22, why Pharaoh wanted to kill the children.

    *In Exodus 2:1-10, how the baby Moses was saved from Pharaoh.

    *In Exodus 2:11-25, why the man Moses ran away from Egypt and how he found friends.

    *In Exodus 3:1 through 4:17, how God called Moses and what He sent Him to do.

    *In Exodus 5:1 through 6:1, how Pharaoh hardened his heart against God.

*In Exodus chapters 6-11, how the different plagues effected Pharaoh and the people. *All these chapters have stories for the children; be sure to emphasize the last plague, the death of the firstborn, in chapter 11.*

In 1 Timothy, find basic guidelines for shepherding others.

Mobilize New Pastoral Trainers (LEVEL 1)

FIND:

In EXODUS chapters 12-20 (compare Titus 1:5), how Moses mobilized others to lead.

*In 12:1-36, how the death angel death knew when to pass over a house

*In 12:37-51, what the original Passover feast celebrated,

*In 13:17 through 14:31, how God rescued His people from the Egyptian army

*In 18:13-27, what Jethro told Moses to do, to shepherd all the people

*In 19:1-25, how God prepared the new elders and His people, to receive His law.

*In 20:1-21, the main commands of God for His people of the *Old Testament*

In 1 and 2 Timothy, how Paul prepared Timothy to lead (principles of leadership).

Train Those Who Have the Apostolic (Missionary) Gift (LEVEL 1)

FIND:

*In Genesis 12:1-3 (compare Matthew 28:18-20), the promise to bless all nations.

In Acts 10, guidelines for missionary work.

BIBLE READINGS Level 2

Develop Prayer in the Church (LEVEL 2)

FIND:

In Daniel, examples of the faith of Daniel and his companions.

*In 1:1-21, how Daniel and his companions stayed in good health

*In 2:1-49, what the king's dream meant, what happened when Daniel explained it

*In 3:1-30, what God did for the three boys who prayed to the one true God

*In 6:1-28 (compare 1 Thessalonians 5:17), how Daniel showed faith and courage.

In Daniel 9 (compare Ephesians 1:15-23), what the leader asks for his people.

In John 17, what Jesus asked for Himself and for us.

In 1 John 1:8-10 through 2:2, guidelines for the confession of sins.

Take the Good News to New Places and People (LEVEL 2)

FIND:

*In Joshua 10, the example of obedience when Joshua conquered the idolaters.

In Isaiah 52:13 through 53:12, old prophesies of the redemptive work of Jesus.

*In Matthew 13 examples from God's natural creation of how churches grow and multiply.

*In John 4, the vision Jesus wants us to have, for harvesting peoples in other places.

*In Acts 8:26-40, an example of how to use the Bible to witness for Jesus.

*In Acts chapters 13-14, guidelines for a missionary team sent by a church (Both chapters have stories that are good for children).

*In Luke (select key portions from the entire book), the most important events in the life of Jesus (jot them down). *(Nearly every chapter has stories good for children.)*

Strengthen the Church and Plant New Churches (LEVEL 2)

FIND:

*In Joshua 1, how Joshua was commissioned to be the commander, and how he prepared the troops.

In Matthew chapters 26-28 (compare Galatians 1:6-12), all that Jesus did, to save us from our sins and establish His church.

    *In 26:1-13, what a woman did to prepare Jesus for His death and burial
    *In 26:14-29, how Holy Communion was established
    *In 26:36-46, what Jesus did not want to do
    *In 26:14-16 & 47-56, why they found it easy to arrest Jesus and what He did
    *In 26:57-68, what happened at Jesus' trial, and why the High Priest got angry
    *In 26:30-35 & 69-75 and 27:1-2, what Peter did, that he regretted later
    *In 27:3-10, what happened to Judas
    *In 27:11-31, what Pilate did to defend Jesus, and the result
    *In 27:32-44, what Jesus' enemies said to mock Him as he hung nailed to the cross
    *In 27:45-61, things that happened when Jesus died
    *In 27:62 through 28:10, what the greatest miracle of all time was
    *In 28:16-20, what Jesus commands His church to do

*In Acts 2, what the Holy Spirit enabled them to do to form the church.

Make Disciples (LEVEL 2)

FIND:

In Exodus chapters 21-40, rules for the discipling of the ancient nation of Israel.
    *In 31:18 through 32:35, why God wanted to destroy the people and what Moses did to change God's mind

*In Mark 3:13-19, reasons why Jesus named the twelve Apostles.

*In Matthew, guidelines from Jesus' example, for making disciples. *(Nearly every chapter has stories that are good for children.)*

Apply Basic Doctrines to our Lives (LEVEL 2)

FIND:

In Genesis chapters 37-45, in what ways were the lives of Joseph and Jesus similar?
    (Joseph was a "type" of Jesus; his life contained many parallels with that of Jesus.)
    *In 37:1-36, why Joseph's brothers envied him and what they did to him
    *In 39:1-23, why Joseph was put in prison
    *In 41:1-55, how Joseph came to be governor
    *In chapters 42-45 (select portions of a length that children will pay attention to),
        a) what Joseph did to save his brothers,
        b) things he did (or that happened to him) that also happened to Jesus.

*In Exodus 20, the basis of the old covenant, which the people could not keep.

In Romans, steps in the Christian life toward maturity.

In Colossians, guidelines for a life of truth and holiness.

In 1 Thessalonians, examples of counsel to encourage our brothers in Christ.

Face False Teaching or Wrong Church Practices (LEVEL 2)

FIND:

In Exodus chapters 32-34 (review--compare 1 John 4:1-3), why God wanted to destroy His people, what Moses did for them.

In Jeremiah (the entire book), how God uses leaders to deal with error (list several things).

In Obadiah (the entire book), how God punished rebellious people in the Old Testament.

*In Acts 5:1-11, how God punished liars in the New Testament.

In 2 Thessalonians, the main error that Paul corrected.

In 1 Peter 1:1-12, how to think about problems and persecution

In 1 Peter 1:13-25, results of following God's Word

In 1 Peter chapters 2-5, several guidelines for victorious living and leading others

In 2 Peter, 2 and 3 John and Judas (the entire books), guidelines for avoiding error.

Face Opposition and Persecution (LEVEL 2)

FIND:

In 1 Samuel chapters 17-22, several ways in which David dealt with unjust opposition.
   *In 1 Samuel 16:1-13, how God chose David as a leader of His people.

In Joshua, examples of how Joshua faced the enemies of God.
   *In 1:1-18, how God prepared Joshua to lead His people.
   *In 2:1-24, what Rahab did to help God's people, and what they promised her.
   *In 3:1-4:9, the order in which they crossed the river, to conquer the promised land.
   *In 6:1-27, their tactics for attacking Jericho.
   *In 7:1-26, the cause of their defeat at Ai, and what they had to do to correct it.
   *In 8:1-29, what happened the second time they attacked Ai.

In Lamentations (select key portions from the entire book), how Jeremiah lamented the fall
   of Jerusalem.
*In Mark 14:53-65, what Jesus did when they persecuted Him, and why they sentenced
Him to death.
 Matthew 5:11-12; 10:17-20, what to do when we are persecuted.
*In Acts 7:1 through 8:1, why they killed Stephen, how they did it, and who stood there
approving of it.
*In Acts 9:1-35,
   a)   what God stopped Saul from doing.
   b)   what Ananias did.
   c)   what Saul did as soon as He could see.

Mobilize the Congregation for Discipling and Serving (LEVEL 2)

FIND:

In Deuteronomy, reasons to know and obey the Word of God.
   *In 1:19-46, why God punished His people making them wander 40 years in the
      desert.
*In Deuteronomy 6:4-9, what the Israelites were to teach their children, and how often.
In Acts 2:46-47, where they taught the Word, and with what results.

Gather for Public Worship *and* Special Celebrations (LEVEL 2)

FIND:

*In Exodus chapters 12-13, how they celebrated the Passover the first time.
In Leviticus chapters 1-22, the form of the worship service of the Old Testament.
   *In 10:1-20 with 16:1-7 & 15-19,
      a)   why Aaron's sons had to die,
      b)   rules made afterwards, for entering the most Holy Place.

In Numbers chapters 5-10, different rules for leading Old Testament worship.

In Numbers 6:22-27, a blessing for ministers to give God's people

In 2 Chronicles chapters 5-6, things that happened in a special worship service.
   *In 5:2-14, how they worshipped God, and how He responded
*In Matthew 17:1-13, how God glorified Jesus before His disciples.
*In Mark 14:1-31, the importance of the Last Supper.

Appreciate God's Presence with Us (LEVEL 2)

FIND:

In Matthew chapters 1-2, major events before and after Jesus' birth
   *In 1:18-25, what the angel told Joseph to do.
   *In 2:1-23, what the wise men gave Jesus, why Joseph took him and Mary to Egypt.
Luke chapters 1-2, events related to Jesus' birth that Matthew did not mention.
   *In 1:26-38, what the angel told Mary, and what she answered.

*In 2:1-20, what the angels told the shepherds and what they did.

*In 2:21-35, what Simeon said about the baby Jesus and about what would happen to His mother Mary.

*In 2:39-52, what happened when they visited Jerusalem.

*In 2 Kings 4:8-37, blessings for both Elisha and the Shunamite, due to his visit.

In Matthew 10:5-15, guidelines for visiting and evangelizing.

*In 2 Kings 4:8-37, blessings for both Elisha and the Shunamite, due to his visit.

In Matthew 10:5-15, guidelines for visiting and evangelizing.

*In 2 Kings 4:8-37, blessings for both Elisha and the Shunamite, due to his visit.

In Matthew 10:5-15, guidelines for visiting and evangelizing.

In Matthew chapters 21-28, the main things that happened during Holy Week (the week before Jesus died)--(list them).

* In Matthew 21:1-11, what happened when Jesus came to Jerusalem.
* In Matthew 21:12, what Jesus did that made the religious leaders mad.
* In Matthew 25:31-47, how Jesus said the nations would be judged.
* In Matthew 26:1-5, what the religious leaders planned during Holy Week.
* In Matthew 26:17-29, what happened during Jesus' last supper before His death
* In Matthew 27:15-31, why the authorities agreed to have the Roman soldiers kill Jesus.
* In Matthew 27:32-61, unusual things that happened when Jesus was put to death.

In John chapters 12-21, more events during Holy Week that Matthew did not mention.

*In 13:1-20, what Jesus did that surprised His disciples, and why He did it.

*In 18:25-19:16, what Pilate did to get the people to stop accusing Jesus, and why he failed.

*In 19:17-37, more things that happened when Jesus was put to death.

*In 19:28-42, more things that happened after Jesus was put to death.

*In 20:1-18, who saw Jesus first after He rose from the dead, and what He said.

*In 20:19-29, how Jesus removed Thomas' doubts.

*In 21:1-14, what Jesus did the third time He met with His disciples after He rose from the Dead.

*In 21:15-25, how Jesus let John know He had forgiven him for denying Him.

In 1 Corinthians 14, guidelines to worship in an orderly way.

In 1 Timothy 2, more guidelines to worship in an orderly way.

Shepherd the People of God (LEVEL 2)

FIND:

In Numbers chapters 1-4, duties of the Levites (ministers in the Old Testament).

*In Numbers 20:1-13, how Moses and Aaron misused their authority.

*In I Samuel 16:1-13, how David was chosen, as a leader of God's people

In 1 Tim. 3, qualifications for church leaders:
   a) prerequisites for elders shepherds, pastors or co-pastors) of a church.
   b) prerequisites for deacons (helpers, persons who take care of physical needs) of a church.

Plan Well Our Time Schedules (LEVEL 2)

FIND:

In Ecclesiastes, why we gain nothing if we only seek common pleasures.

In Eph. 5:15-17, guidelines to evaluate how we use the time God gives us.

Have Orderly Meetings for Church Business. (LEVEL 2)

FIND:

*In 1 Kings 12:1-24, what happened in a business meeting, that divided the people.

In Acts 15, examples of guidelines to lead a meeting to resolve a conflict.

Have Activities for Fellowship and Fun (LEVEL 2)

FIND:

In Leviticus chapters 23-27, the nature of the old festivals.

In Philippians 2:1-12, what is true humility, and what is the greatest example of it.

In Philippians, the kind of joy that we should have, and where it comes from.

Resolve Disputes and Divisions (LEVEL 2)

FIND:

IN Genesis 27-33, how the patriarchs caused, and solved, disputes.

In Numbers 11-21, cases of rebellion and how God dealt with them.

 *In 11:1-23 & 31-33, what God did for those who demanded meat to eat.

 *In 12:1-16, what God did to Miriam when she complained about Moses' black wife.

 *In 16:1-50, how God punished those who rebelled with Korah.

 *In 21:4-9, how God punished the complainers, and how He also healed them.

In Philemon 1, how Paul got two brothers in Christ to be reconciled.

Strengthen Family Life (LEVEL 2)

FIND:

In Genesis 1:27-28 and 2:18-25, the origin of the family and its purposes.

 a) guidelines for developing friendships,

 b) examples of good and bad leadership.

 *In 1:1-28, Ana's prayer and how God answered it.

 *In 3:1-20, how God called Samuel to serve Him.

 *In 17:1-58, how God used the boy David to save Israel from the Philistines.

 *In 18:1 through 19:17, why David had to flee from King Saul and how he got away.

 *In 24:1-22, how David spared Saul's life and how Saul responded.

In Ephesians 5:21 through 6:4, guidelines for keeping peace and order in the home.

Strengthen Each Others' Love (LEVEL 2)

FIND:

In 11 Samuel (the entire book), good and bad examples of leadership.

 *In 6:1 23, what happened when David took the Ark of the Covenant to Jerusalem.

 *In 7:1-29, what God promised King David.

 *In 9:1-13, what David did for Saul's lame son, and why.

 *In 11:1 through 12:23, David's two-fold sin and punishment.

In Romans 12, guidelines to cultivate love between brothers in Christ.

In Matthew 10:5-15, guidelines for visiting and evangelizing.

Apply Biblical Discipline to the Congregation (LEVEL 2)

In Numbers chapters 21-26, how God protected His people from idolatry.

 *In 4:1-24, what two women did to rescue Israel.

 *In chapters 6-7, how Gideon delivered Israel.

*In 1 Kings 18, how God used Elijah for remove idolatry from Israel.

In Hebrews 12, why we should appreciate the God's punishment.

Counsel Persons with Personal and Family problems (LEVEL 2)

*In 1 Kings 19, physical, emotional, social and spiritual causes of Elijah's discouragement

 (look for the things he did and said, that would have caused him to be depressed).

In Galatians, the kind of faith that keeps us firm in our liberty in Christ.

Train Counselors at a Basic Level (LEVEL 2)

In Job (the entire book), good and bad examples of how to counsel those who suffer.

In 1 and 2 Corinthians (both books), how Paul corrected grave errors.

Encourage and Pray for the Sick (LEVEL 2)

In Job chapters 1-3 and 42, the purpose and outcome, of Job's suffering.

*In chapters 1-2, 42:7-17, what God let Satan do to Job, and the outcome.

*In John 9, why the man was born blind, and why they expelled him from the synagogue.

In James 5:13-18, guidelines for dealing with the sick.

Bring Freedom to Any Who are Oppressed Demons (LEVEL 2)

FIND:

*In Mark 5:1-20 (compare Matthew 17:14-21), the authority of Jesus over demons.

Help the Needy (LEVEL 2)

*In Ruth (review the story), the results of the Boaz' kindness.

*In Acts 6:1-7 (compare Galatians 6:10), how we organize to deal with the needy.

Support Pastors and Christian Workers (LEVEL 2)

FIND:

In Malachi (the entire book), warnings of God, including against robbing Him, in 3:6-12.

In 2 Corinthians chapters 8-9, more guidelines for giving and supporting ministers.

Develop the Gifts and Ministries of the Believers (LEVEL 2)

FIND:

In Numbers 21-36, guidelines for leading the people of God.

In Ephesians 4, guidelines for using our spiritual gifts in an edifying way.

Use Teamwork in Ministry to Edify Others (LEVEL 2)

FIND:

In 1 Chronicles 11, how David's companions worked in loving harmony.

*In Acts 13:1-5 (compare Acts 10:23), how a church formed a missionary team.

Evangelize and Teach Children (LEVEL 2)

FIND:

In Deuteronomy 6 (compare 1 John 2:12-14), guidelines for instructing children.

The Young People Serve and Make Disciples (LEVEL 2)

FIND:

In Proverbs (the entire book), guidelines for young people for a holy life.

In Ephesians 6:1-3, more guidelines for young people for a holy life.

Fulfill our Christian Social Duties (LEVEL 2)

FIND:

Habakkuk (the entire book), duties and warnings of the leaders and people, for a just society.

Select and Train New Pastoral Level Students (LEVEL 2)

FIND:

*In Leviticus chapters 10 and 16, compared with Hebrews chapters 8-9,

    a) the seriousness of Christian ministry,

    b) ways in which Jesus' work is similar *and* different from Old Testament priests'.

*In 1 Kings (the entire book), good and bad examples of government. (Many of its chapters have stories that are good for children.)

In Micah, more examples of good and bad government, and warnings.

In 2 Timothy (the whole book), more guidelines for new ministers and workers.

Mobilize a Pastoral Students as Pastoral Trainers (LEVEL 2)

FIND:

*In 1 Sam. 16, the basis for choosing a future leader of the people of God.

*In 2 Kings, good and bad examples of leadership for the people of God. (Many of the chapters have stories that are good for children.)

In Titus (the entire book), guidelines for naming and mobilizing leaders in the churches.

Teach the Missionary Task, Focus on the World (LEVEL 2)

FIND:

*In Genesis 24, an example (illustration) of going far away to bring people to Christ.

*In Acts chapters 13-14, major events in Paul's first missionary trip. *(Select portions for the children.)*

Train Missionaries (LEVEL 2)

FIND:

*In Jonah (the entire book), how God prepared the primer missionary to go to a very pagan people group. (Select portions for the children.)

*In Acts chapters 15-28, the main events related to the apostolic team's missionary work. (Select portions for the children.)

BIBLE READINGS LEVEL 3

Pray with More Power (LEVEL 3)

FIND:

In Psalms 1-41, kinds of prayers (praise, complaint, confession, etc.)

*In Esther (select key portions from the entire book), what God did for his people because of the prayers of the faithful.

In Joel (select key portions from the entire book), prophecies of the coming of the Holy Spirit and of the coming judgment.

In Eph. 3:14-21 what a Christian leader asks for his people.

In 1 Tim. 2:1-5, what the people ask, for the authorities.

In Hebrews (select key portions from the entire book), how Jesus serves as our defense attorney and High Priest before God the Father.

Disciple People in New Areas and Cultures (LEVEL 3)

FIND:

*In Joshua 6, an example of faith and courage, for conquering new land for Jesus.

In Acts 1:8 (compare John 4:35), the different places where we are to witness for Jesus.

Coordinate the Multiplication of Churches (LEVEL 3)

FIND:

*In Exodus 18 (compare Titus 1:5), an example of how to coordinate many new ministries.

*In Acts 10 through 11:18, guidelines to help a new congregation to be born.

Keep Multiplying House Churches or Cell Groups (LEVEL 3)

FIND:

*In Acts 2:46-47 and 5:42 (compare Rom. 16:5), where they met for worship.

Strengthen Bible Study and Application (LEVEL 3)

FIND:

In James (select key portions from the entire book), examples of the *practice* of the Word.

Organize United Celebrations between Churches (LEVEL 3)
FIND:
*In 2 Chronicles 35:1-19 the benefits of gathering people from many places.

Strengthen the Ministry of Music (LEVEL 3)
FIND:
*In 1 Chronicles 5:12-14 (compare Psalm 150), the effect of sacred music, with God.
In Psalms 73-89, the style of the old hymns (Psalms were Hebrew hymns).
In Eph. 5:17-20, important purposes of music.

Improve the Preaching (LEVEL 3)
FIND:
In Ezekiel (select key portions from the entire book), examples of powerful messages (it is
   a book of messages).
In Revelation (compare Luke 21), prophecies of the final coming of Jesus.

Establish Discipling Networks among Leaders (LEVEL 3)
FIND:
*In 1 Kings 12, the cause of the division of the ancient kingdom.
*In Nehemiah (the entire book; compare with Matthew 20:20-28), guidelines for
   supervising leaders.
*In Acts 20:17-38, examples of how a supervisor relates with other leaders.

Develop Fellowship between Churches (LEVEL 3)
FIND:
In Hosea (the entire book; compare Psalm 133), how God expresses His desire for the
   unity of his people.
In John 17:20-23, what Jesus asked for His churches.

Strengthen the Fellowship between New and Old Believers (LEVEL 3)
FIND:
*In Matthew 20:1-16, the duty of the old members of the church with the new.

Develop a Ministry of Advanced of Counseling (LEVEL 3)
FIND:
In Psalms 90-106, expressions of healthy attitudes toward God and His works.
In Ephesians chapters 1-2, what a person is and has in Christ (make a list).
In Ephesians chapters 4-5, guidelines for forgiving and getting along with people and
   family.

Develop Fellowship Between Churches (LEVEL 3)
FIND:
In Hosea (the entire book; compare Psalm 133), how God wants his people to relate to
   each other
In John 17:20-23, what Jesus asked His Father to do for the people in His churches.

Cultivate Fellowship between Older and Newer Brothers (LEVEL 3)
FIND:
*In Matthew 20:1-16, the duty of older members of the church with newer ones.

Counsel Those with Very Difficult Problems (LEVEL 3)

FIND:

In Ephesians (review the entire book): What a person has and is in Christ, guidelines for getting along with each other and with family members, the duties of Christian husbands, wives, children and employees.

Evaluate, Reorganize and Extend Existing Ministries (LEVEL 3)

In Eph. 4:11-16, guidelines for harmonizing different ministries for edification of the body.

Form Discipling Chains to Train Leaders over a Wide Area   (LEVEL 3)

FIND:

*In 2 Chronicles 17:3-6 (compare 2 Tim. 2:2), an example of education by *extension*.

Strengthen Pastors and Elders of All the Churches (LEVEL 3)

FIND:

In 1 and 2 Timothy and Titus (review), guidelines for pastoral ministry (make a list).

Send Missionaries (LEVEL 3)

FIND:

In Psalm 67 (compare Matthew 28:18-20), the plan of God for the nations of the world.

*In Isaiah 6:1-8 (compare John 20:19-23 and 21:15-25), how the prophet responded to God's call.

In Acts chapters 13 through 28, *guidelines for missionary work.*